A PRACTICAL ILLUSTRATED GUIDE TO

ATTRACTING & FEEDING
GARDEN BIRDS

A PRACTICAL ILLUSTRATED GUIDE TO

ATTRACTING & FEEDING
GARDEN BIRDS

THE COMPLETE BOOK OF BIRD FEEDERS, BIRD TABLES BIRDBATHS, NEST BOXES AND BACKYARD BIRDWATCHING

25 step-by-step projects for birdhouses • Expert advice on feeding •
A directory of wild bird species • 760 photographs and illustrations

Contributing editor: JEN GREEN

HERMES
HOUSE

This edition is published by
Hermes House
an imprint of Anness Publishing Ltd
Hermes House
88–89 Blackfriars Road
London SE1 8HA
tel. 020 7401 2077
fax 020 7633 9499

www.hermeshouse.com
www.annesspublishing.com

If you like the images in this book
and would like to investigate using
them for publishing, promotions or
advertising, please visit our website
www.practicalpictures.com for
more information.

Publisher: Joanna Lorenz
Senior Editor: Dr Felicity Forster
Text: Dr Jen Green, David Alderton,
Christine and Michael Lavelle, Mary
Maguire, Deena Beverley, Andrew
Newton-Cox and Stephanie Donaldson
Photography: Peter Anderson, Michelle
Garrett, David Parmiter, Robert Pickett
and Peter Williams
Illustrations: Peter Barrett, Studio Galante,
Lucinda Ganderton, Stuart Jackson-Carter,
Martin Knowelden, Liz Pepperell and
Tim Thackeray
Maps: Anthony Duke
Jacket Design: Adelle Morris
Designer: Nigel Partridge
Production Controller: Steve Lang

ETHICAL TRADING POLICY
Because of our ongoing ecological
investment programme, you, as our
customer, can have the pleasure and
reassurance of knowing that a tree is
being cultivated on your behalf to naturally
replace the materials used to make
the book you are holding. For further
information about this scheme, go to
www.annesspublishing.com/trees.

A CIP catalogue record for this book
is available from the British Library.

PUBLISHER'S NOTE
Although the advice and information in this
book are believed to be accurate and true
at the time of going to press, neither the
authors nor the publisher can accept any
legal responsibility or liability for any errors
or omissions that may be made.

Front cover: Robin (*Erithacus rubecula*);
great tit (*Parus major*).
Page 1: Eurasian nuthatch (*Sitta europaea*).
Page 3: European goldfinch (*Carduelis
carduelis*); common blackbird (*Turdus
merula*); coal tit (*Parus ater*).

CONTENTS

INTRODUCTION

Birds have been a source of fascination and inspiration to people all over the world for many years. Attracting birds to your garden and observing the variety of species that visit can develop into an absorbing pastime – and one which offers an unparalleled insight into the natural world.

Birds have influenced human cultures across the world, featuring in customs, religious festivals and also in many common sayings. The familiar robin (*Erithacus rubecula*), for example, has become inextricably linked with the celebration of Christmas, while the return of the cuckoo (*Cuculus canorus*) from its wintering grounds is eagerly awaited as a sure sign of spring.

Whether your garden or backyard is in the countryside, a town or a city, it can play an important part in the conservation of wildlife, and especially birds. As farming becomes more intensive, and more and

Below: *Tits (Paridae) are among the most common visitors to British gardens. These small birds display their acrobatic abilities to full effect when balanced on bird feeders.*

more of the countryside is swallowed up by new housing and industrial developments, the natural habitats of many birds are being reduced or lost altogether. Gardens are now more essential for the survival of birds than ever. A little planning will ensure that your garden is a welcoming haven for birds.

HELPING BIRDS

The average garden is regularly visited by 15–20 species of birds, with occasional visits from 10 less common species. By simply erecting a bird table and nest box, you will not only be offering nature a helping hand, you will also provide yourself with hours of interest and entertainment. Your helpful garden friends will return the favour by controlling pests, such as aphids, slugs and snails, that threaten your flower-beds and vegetable patch.

ABOUT THIS BOOK

This book is a celebration of garden birds and sets out to reveal the diversity in both their form and lifestyles. The opening section describes the main features of birds and explores how they live. The second section offers detailed advice on how your garden can be planted or adapted to attract birds. It demonstrates how, with a little thought, you can greatly increase the number and variety of birds that visit your garden. It offers tips on what to feed birds and when, and how to plan your garden with birds in mind. There are planting suggestions to help you to achieve an ideal home for your feathered friends.

Birdhouses are a charming addition to any garden. They help to ornament and personalize it, and give an even greater satisfaction if you have made them yourself. The third section of this book offers a wide range of projects that will encourage birds. The projects given here range from simple decorated nest boxes to elaborate houses. There are creative ideas for feeders and birdbaths, with something to suit every garden and every level of practical expertise. There are also tips on maintaining birdhouses, where and when to site them and how to keep visiting birds safe from predators. All the projects in this book represent practical as well as attractive solutions for providing food, drink and shelter for birds. The fourth and final main section provides an extensive illustrated guide to the bird species that are likely to be seen in British gardens.

Creating a haven for birds is a thoroughly satisfying activity. It is pure joy when you see a bird starting to build its new home in a nest box that you have made. The whole experience is rewarding, from the pleasure you experience watching parent birds carrying food to the young in the nest, to the wait for fledglings to emerge and finally take wing.

Right: *Once you have discovered ways of attracting birds to your garden, you will be rewarded with sights such as this.*

HOW BIRDS LIVE

Birds display many diverse characteristics, but have several key features in common. The most obvious of these is the presence of feathers. The need for birds' bodies to be lightweight so that they can fly with minimum effort has led to evolutionary changes in their anatomy, and yet the basic skeletal structure of all birds is remarkably similar, irrespective of size. The other feature unique to birds is that all species reproduce by means of calcareous eggs. Actual breeding habits are very diverse, however. There is even greater diversity in the feeding habits of birds, as reflected by differences in bill structure and also in digestive tracts.

Left: *Many young birds look quite different from their parents. This is a juvenile great tit (*Parus major), *tentatively exploring its new surroundings.*

Above: *Thrushes such as this song thrush (*Turdus philomelos) *are welcome visitors to gardens because of their tuneful singing.*

Above: *House sparrows (*Passer domesticus) *are well adapted to life in both rural and urban gardens.*

Above: *Woodpeckers are among the largest and most dramatically coloured birds that sometimes visit gardens.*

PARTS OF A BIRD

The bird's skeleton has evolved to be light yet robust, both characteristics that help with flight. To this end, certain bones, particularly in the skull, have become fused, while others are absent, along with the teeth. The result is that birds' bodies are very light compared to those of other vertebrates.

In order to be able to fly, a bird needs a lightweight body so that it can become airborne with minimal difficulty. It is not just teeth that are missing from the bird's skull, but the associated heavy jaw muscles as well. These have been replaced by a light, horn-covered bill that is adapted in shape to the bird's feeding habits. Some of the limb bones, such as the humerus in the shoulder, are hollow, which also cuts down on weight. At the rear of the body, the bones in the vertebral column have become fused, which gives greater stability as well as support for the tail feathers.

AVIAN SKELETON

In birds, the greatest degree of specialization is evident in the limbs. The location of the legs is critical to enable a bird to maintain its balance. The legs are found close to the midline, set slightly back near the bird's centre of gravity. The limbs are powerful, helping to provide lift at take-off and absorb the impact of landing. Strong legs also allow most birds to hop over the ground with relative ease.

There are some differences in the skeleton between various groups of birds. For example, the neckbones of hornbills are slightly different to those of other birds.

FEET AND TOES

Birds' feet vary in length. The feet of wading birds are noticeably extended, which helps them to distribute their weight more evenly when moving over soft mud or floating vegetation. The four toes may be arranged either in a typical 3:1 perching grip, with three toes gripping the front of the perch and one behind, or in a 2:2 configuration, known as zygodactyl, which gives a surer grip. The zygodactyl grip is seen in a few groups of birds, notably woodpeckers and also parrots. Having two toes pointing in either direction gives the woodpecker a firm hold as it scales vertical tree trunks. The same arrangement helps some parrots to use their feet like hands for holding food.

Birds generally have claws at the ends of their toes, which have developed into sharp talons in the case of birds of prey, helping them to catch their quarry even in flight. Many birds also use their claws for preening, and they can provide balance for birds that run or climb.

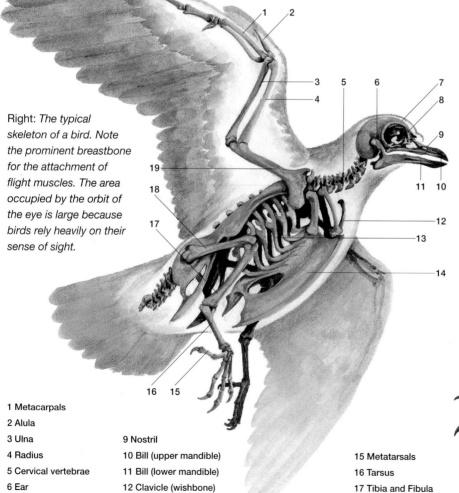

Right: *The typical skeleton of a bird. Note the prominent breastbone for the attachment of flight muscles. The area occupied by the orbit of the eye is large because birds rely heavily on their sense of sight.*

Parrot

Above: *Parrots use their feet for holding food, rather like human hands.*

Bird of prey

Above: *In birds of prey, the claws have become talons for grasping prey.*

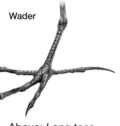

Wader

Above: *Long toes make it easier for waders to walk over muddy ground or water plants.*

Duck

Above: *The webbed feet of ducks provide propulsion in water.*

1 Metacarpals
2 Alula
3 Ulna
4 Radius
5 Cervical vertebrae
6 Ear
7 Cranium
8 Eye socket
9 Nostril
10 Bill (upper mandible)
11 Bill (lower mandible)
12 Clavicle (wishbone)
13 Ribs
14 Sternum (breastbone)
15 Metatarsals
16 Tarsus
17 Tibia and Fibula
18 Femur
19 Humerus

BILLS

The bills of birds vary quite widely in shape and size, and reflect their feeding habits. The design of the bill also has an impact on the amount of force that it can generate. The bills of finches such as chaffinches (*Fringillla coelebs*) are strong enough to crack seeds. A bird's bill has many purposes, being used not only for feeding but also for preening, nest-building and, where necessary, defence.

Above: *The narrow bill of waders such as this curlew* (Numenius arquata) *enables the bird to probe for food in sand or mud.*

Above: *Woodpeckers such as this great spotted have straight, sharp bills ideal for chiselling under bark in search of insects.*

Above: *The chaffinch* (Fringilla coelebs) *has a short, stout, cone-shaped beak suited to cracking seeds.*

WINGS

A bird's wing is built around just three digits, which correspond to human fingers. The three digits of birds provide a robust structure. The power of the wings is further enhanced by the fusion of the wrist bones and the carpals to create the single bone known as the carpometacarpus, which runs along the rear of the wing.

At the front of the chest, the clavicles are joined together to form what in

Above: *Birds of prey such as the sparrowhawk* (Accipiter nisus) *rely on a sharp bill with a hooked tip to tear their prey apart.*

Above: *The broad bill of the mallard* (Anas platyrhynchos) *allows it to filter plant food from the water.*

Above: *The treecreeper* (Certhia brachydactyla) *has a thin, curved bill suited to plucking insects from beneath bark.*

chickens is called the wishbone. The large, keel-shaped breastbone, or sternum, runs along the underside of the body. It is bound by the ribs to the backbone to provide stability, especially during flight. In addition, the major flight muscles are located in the lower body when the bird is airborne.

DARWIN'S FINCHES

In the 1830s, a voyage to the remote Galapagos Islands off South America helped the British naturalist Charles Darwin formulate his theory of evolution. The finches on the Galapagos Islands are all believed to be descended from a single ancestor, but have evolved in different ways. The changes are most obvious in their bill shapes. For example, some species have stout, crushing beaks for cracking seeds, while others have long, slender beaks to probe for insects. These adaptations have arisen to take full advantage of the range of edible items available on the islands, where food is generally scarce.

Below: *The finches of the Galapagos Islands helped to inspire Charles Darwin's theory of evolution. Some species have stout bills for crushing seeds, while those with pointed bills eat insects. Others have bills specialized for eating cactus, buds and fruit. The woodpecker finch* (Camarhynchus palidus) *(bottom) uses a cactus spine to winkle out grubs hiding in tree bark.*

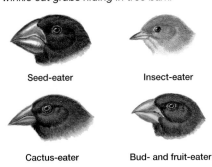

Seed-eater   Insect-eater

Cactus-eater   Bud- and fruit-eater

Grub-eater

FEATHERS

The presence of feathers is one of the main distinguishing characteristics that set birds apart from all other animals on the planet. The number of feathers on a bird's body varies considerably – a swan may have as many as 25,000 feathers, for instance, while a tiny hummingbird has just 1,000 in all.

Aside from the bill, legs and feet, the entire body of the bird is covered in feathers. The plumage does not grow randomly over the bird's body, but develops along lines of so-called feather tracts, or pterylae. These are separated by bald areas known as apteria. The apteria are not conspicuous under normal circumstances, because the contour feathers overlap to cover the entire surface of the body. Plumage may also sometimes extend down over the legs and feet as well, in the case of birds from cold climates, providing the extra insulation that is needed there.

Feathers are made of a tough protein called keratin, which is also found in our hair and nails. There are three main types of feathers on a bird's body: the body, or contour, feathers; the strong, elongated flight feathers on the wings; and the warm, wispy down feathers next to the bird's skin.

A diet deficient in sulphur-containing amino acids, which are the basic building blocks of protein, will result in poor feathering, creating 'nutritional barring' across the flight and tail feathers. Abnormal plumage coloration can also have nutritional causes in some cases. These changes are usually reversible if more favourable environmental conditions precede the next moult.

FUNCTION OF FEATHERS

Plumage has a number of functions, not just relating to flight. It provides a barrier that retains warm air close to the bird's body and helps to maintain body temperature, which is higher in birds than mammals – typically between 41 and 43.5°C (106 and 110°F). The down feathering that lies close to the skin and the overlying contour plumage are vital for maintaining body warmth. Most species of birds have a small volume relative to their surface area, which can leave them vulnerable to hypothermia.

A special oil produced by the preen gland, located at the base of the tail, waterproofs the plumage. This oil, which is spread over the feathers as the bird preens itself, prevents water penetrating the feathers, which would cause the bird to become so waterlogged that it could no longer fly.

Below: *The robin's plumage varies little between the sexes, with both males and females having the red breast.*

Left: *A bird's flight feathers are longer and more rigid than the contour feathers that cover the body, or the fluffy down feathers that lie next to the skin. The longest, or primary, flight feathers, which generate most thrust, are located along the outer rear wing edges. The tail feathers are often similar in shape to the flight feathers, with the longest in the centre.*

1 Primaries
2 Secondaries
3 Axillaries
4 Rump
5 Lateral tail feathers
6 Central tail feathers
7 Breast
8 Cere
9 Auricular region (ear)
10 Nape
11 Back
12 Greater under-wing coverts
13 Lesser under-wing coverts

Above: *Like other birds, tree sparrows* (Passer montanus) *spend time each day preening. This helps to keep feathers clean and tidy and also reduces parasites.*

The contour feathers that cover the body are also important for camouflage in many birds. Barring in particular breaks up the outline of the bird's body, helping to conceal it in its natural habitat.

The plumage has become modified in some cases, reflecting the individual lifestyle of the species concerned. Woodpeckers, for example, have tail feathers that are short and rather sharp at their tips, providing additional support for gripping on to the sides of trees. The woodpecker's stiff tail and feet with toes pointing forward and backward create a sturdy, tripod-like stance.

SOCIAL SIGNIFICANCE OF PLUMAGE

Plumage can also be important in social interactions between birds. Many species have differences in their feathering that separate males from females, and often juveniles can also be distinguished by their plumage. Although the rule does not apply in every case, cock birds are generally more brightly coloured, which helps them to attract their mates, while the female's dull colours help to conceal her while she incubates the eggs on the nest. The

difference between the sexes in terms of their plumage can be quite marked, for example in mallards (*Anas platyrhynchos*). Cock birds of a number of species have feathers forming crests as well as magnificent tail plumes, which are seen to greatest effect in peacocks (*Pavo cristatus*), whose display is one of the most remarkable sights in the avian world.

Recent studies have confirmed that birds that appear relatively dull in colour to our eyes, such as the starling (*Sturnus vulgaris*), with its blackish plumage, are seen literally in a different light by other birds. They can visualize the ultraviolet component of light, which is normally invisible to us, making these seemingly dull birds appear greener. Ultraviolet coloration may also be significant in helping birds to choose their mates.

MOULTING

Birds' feathering is maintained by preening, but it becomes frayed and worn over time. It is therefore replaced by new plumage during the process of moulting, when the old feathers are shed. Many birds moult their feathers according to a given pattern which varies according to species. In many cases the flight feathers are shed symmetrically, with the same number being lost from each wing at a time. This helps the bird to remain balanced when flying.

Moulting is most often an annual event. However, many young birds shed their nest feathers before they are a year old. Moulting may also be triggered by the onset of the breeding season. Some birds become more strikingly coloured at this time. Hormonal alterations in the body are important in triggering this process, with external factors such as changing day length also playing a part.

IRIDESCENCE

Some birds are not brightly coloured, but their plumage literally sparkles in the light, thanks to its structure, which creates an iridescent effect. One of the particular features of iridescence is that the colour of the plumage alters, depending on the angle at which it is viewed, often appearing quite dark or almost black from a side view. This phenomenon is particularly common in some groups of birds, notably members of the starling family (Sturnidae), which are described as having metallic feathers as a result.

In some cases, the iridescent feathering is localized, while in others it is widespread over most of the body. Green and blue iridescence is common, with reddish sheens being seen less often. Iridescence is especially seen in cock birds, helping them to attract their mates.

Below: *A starling (*Sturnus vulgaris*) displays its iridescent plumage.*

Right: *The feather shaft holds the feather in place in the skin. The barbs run off the shaft at regular intervals, rather like the branches of a tree, and divide into smaller branches called barbules. These have tiny hooks attached to them that reinforce the structure of the flight feather, making it more rigid.*

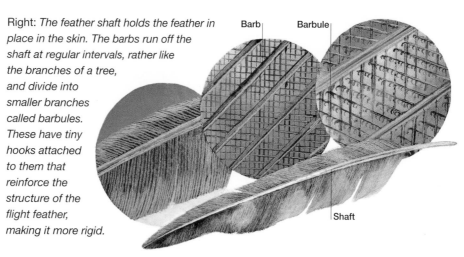

Barb

Barbule

Shaft

FLIGHT

Some birds seen in gardens spend much of their lives in the air, whereas others will only fly as a last resort if threatened. The mechanics of flight are similar in all birds, but flight patterns vary significantly, which can help you to identify the various groups in the air.

The structure of the bird's body has evolved to facilitate flight. It is important for a bird's body weight to be relatively light, because this lessens the muscular effort required to keep it airborne. The powerful flight muscles, which provide the necessary lift, can account for up to a third of the bird's total body weight. They are attached to the breastbone, or sternum, in the midline of the body, and run along the sides of the body from the clavicle along the breastbone to the top of the legs.

WEIGHT AND FLIGHT
There is an upper weight limit of just over 18kg (40lb), above which birds would not be able to take off successfully. Some larger birds, notably swans, need a run-up in order to gain sufficient momentum to lift off, particularly from water. Smaller birds can dart straight off a perch. Some of the heavier flying birds, such as pheasants, prefer to run rather than fly because of the effort involved in becoming airborne.

WING SHAPE AND BEAT
The shape of the wing is important for a bird's flying ability. Birds that remain airborne for much of their lives, such as swifts, have relatively long wings that allow them to glide with relatively little effort.

Above: *The barn owl's feathers have fringed edges. This allows it to fly without the slightest sound, and swoop down on its prey without being detected.*

The swift's narrow wings make it fast and also manoeuvrable. Some larger predatory birds, such as kites and falcons, use rising columns of air called thermals, caused by warm air rising from the ground, to provide uplift, and then circle around in them.

The number of wing beats varies dramatically between species. American hummingbirds are renowned for beating their wings more frequently than any other bird as they hover in front of flowers to harvest their nectar. Their wings move so fast – at over 200 beats per minute – that they produce a buzzing sound and appear

Above: *Predatory birds such as red kites use rising air currents to stay aloft. Such species may have difficulty flying early in the day when little warm air is rising.*

as a blur to the eyes. At the other extreme, heavy birds such as swans fly with slow, deliberate wing beats.

LIGHTENING THE LOAD
The lightness of a bird's skeleton helps it to fly. There have been evolutionary changes in body organs too, most noticeably in the urinary system. Unlike mammals, birds do not have a bladder that fills with urine. Instead, their urine is greatly concentrated, in the form of uric acid, and passes out of the body with their faeces, appearing as a creamy-white, semi-solid component.

Below: *These illustrations show a typical take-off sequence, in this case by a large bird of prey.*

1 When resting, a bird typically has a relatively upright stance.

2 As it leans forward for take-off, it raises its wings and starts to lift its legs.

3 Leaving its perch, the bird pushes off into the air, and opens its wings.

Above: *Waterfowl such as this mallard* (Anas platyrhynchos) *have few difficulties becoming airborne from water, as their plumage is designed to prevent waterlogging.*

FLIGHT PATTERNS

Different species of birds have various ways of flying, which can actually aid the birdwatcher in helping to identify them. For example, small birds such as tits (Paridae) and finches (Fringillidae) alternately flap their wings and fold them at their sides, adopting a streamlined shape, which helps to save energy. This produces a characteristic dipping flight which aids recognition. Large birds such as ducks and geese maintain a straighter course at an even height.

In some cases, it is not just the individual flying skills of a bird that help it to stay airborne, but those of its fellows nearby. Birds flying in formation create a slipstream, which makes flying less effort for all the birds behind the leader. This is why birds often fly in formation, especially when covering long distances on migration.

THE AEROFOIL PRINCIPLE

Once in flight, the shape of the wing is crucial in keeping the bird airborne. Viewed in cross-section from the side, a bird's wing resembles an aeroplane's wing, called an aerofoil, and in fact aeroplanes use the same technique as birds to fly.

The wing is curved across the top, so the movement of air is faster over this part of the wing compared with the lower surface. This produces reduced air pressure on top of the wing, which provides lift and makes it easier for the bird to stay in the air.

The long flight feathers at the rear edge of the wings help to provide the thrust and lift for flight. The tail feathers, too, can help the bird remain airborne. The kestrel (*Falco tinnunculus*), for example, having spotted prey on the ground, spreads its tail feathers to help it remain aloft while it hovers to target its prey.

A bird's wings move in a regular figure-of-eight movement while it is in flight. During the downstroke, the flight feathers join together to push powerfully against the air. The primary flight feathers bend backward, which propels the bird forward. As the wing moves upward, the longer primary flight feathers move apart, which reduces air resistance. The secondary feathers further along the wing provide some slight propulsion. After that the cycle repeats itself.

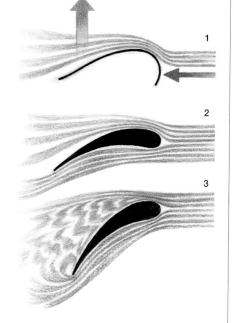

Above: *The way the air flows over a bird's wing varies according to the wing's position.*
1 When the wing is stretched out horizontally, an area of low pressure is created above the wing, causing lift.
2 As the wing is tilted downward, the flow of the air is disrupted, causing turbulence and loss of lift.
3 When the wing is angled downward, lift slows, which results in stalling. The bird's speed slows as a consequence. Splaying the tail feathers also increases drag and so slows the bird down, particularly prior to landing.

4 Powerful upward and downward sweeps of the wings propel the bird forward.

5 When coming in to land, a bird lowers its legs and slows its wing movements.

6 Braking is achieved by a vertical landing posture, with the tail feathers spread.

SENSES

The keen senses of birds are vital to their survival, in particular helping them to find food, escape from enemies and find mates in the breeding season. Sight is the primary sense for most birds, but some species rely heavily on other senses to thrive in particular habitats.

All birds' senses are adapted to their environment, and the shape of their bodies can help to reflect which senses are most significant to them.

SIGHT

Most birds rely on their sense of sight to avoid danger, hunt for food and locate familiar surroundings. The importance of

FIELD OF VISION

The positioning of a bird's eyes on its head affects its field of vision. The eyes of owls are positioned to face forward, producing an overlapping image of the area in front known as binocular vision. This allows the owl to pinpoint its prey exactly, so that it can strike. In contrast, the eyes of birds that are likely to be preyed upon, such as woodcocks, are positioned on the sides of the head. This eye position gives a greatly reduced area of binocular vision, but it does give these birds practically all-round vision, enabling them to spot danger from all sides.

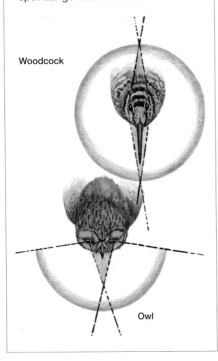

Woodcock

Owl

this sense is reflected by the size of their eyes, with those of starlings (*Sturnus vulgaris*), for example, making up 15 per cent of the total head weight. The enlargement of the eyeballs and associated structures, notably the eye sockets in the skull, has altered the shape of the brain. In addition, the optic lobes in the brain, which are concerned with vision, are also enlarged, whereas the olfactory counterparts, responsible for smell, are poorly developed.

The structure of the eye also reveals much about a bird's habits. Birds of prey have large eyes in proportion to their head, and have correspondingly keen eyesight. Species that regularly hunt for prey underwater, such as kingfishers, can see well in the water. Some aquatic birds have a muscle in each eye that reduces the diameter of the lens and increases its thickness on entering water, so that their eyes can adjust easily to seeing underwater. In addition, diving birds such as the common kingfisher (*Alcedo atthis*) have a lens that forms part of the nictitating membrane, or third eyelid, which is normally hidden from sight. Underwater, when this membrane covers the eye, its convex shape serves as a lens, helping the bird to see in these surroundings.

The positioning of the eyes on the head gives important clues to a bird's lifestyle. Most birds' eyes are set on the sides of their heads. Owls, however, have flattened faces and forward-facing eyes that are critical to their hunting abilities. These features allow owls to target their prey.

There is a disadvantage to this arrangement. Owls' eyes do not give a rounded view of the world, so they must turn their heads to see about them. It is not just the positioning of owls' eyes that is unusual. They are also able to hunt effectively in almost complete darkness. This is made possible in two ways. First, their pupils are large, which maximizes the amount of light passing through to the retina behind the lens, where the image is formed. Second, the cells here consist

Above: *Sight is the main sense for most birds, including this blackbird. Like humans, birds possess good colour vision.*

mainly of rods rather than cones. While cones give good colour vision, rods function to create images when background illumination is low.

The positioning of the eyes of game birds such as woodcocks (*Scolopax rusticola*) allows them to spot danger from almost any angle. It is even possible for them to see a predator sneaking up from behind. The only blind spot of these birds is just behind the head.

SMELL

The chemical senses (smell and taste) are relatively undeveloped in most birds, and garden birds are no exception. Very few birds have a keen sense of smell, with kiwis (Apterygidae) and vultures (forming part of the order Falciformes) providing notable exceptions. Birds' nostrils are normally located above the bill, opening directly into the skull, but kiwis' nostrils are positioned right at the end of the long bill. They probably help these birds to locate earthworms in the soil. Vultures have very keen eyesight, which helps them to spot dead animals on the ground from the air, but they also have a strong sense of smell, which helps them to home in on a carcass.

ECHOLOCATION

This technique helps Mascarene swiftlets (*Collocalia francica*) to navigate inside dark caves. These birds utter a stream of high-frequency clicks, which echo back off surrounding surfaces. The time lapse between clicks and echoes indicates the proximity of objects within range, which helps to prevent collisions.

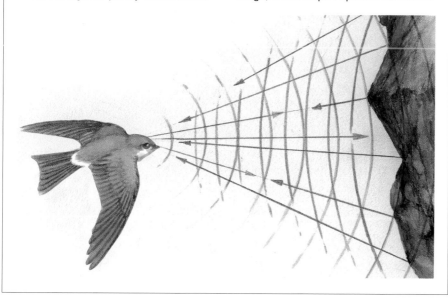

TASTE

The senses of smell and taste are linked, and most birds also have correspondingly few taste buds in their mouths. The number of taste buds varies, with differences between groups of birds. Blue tits may have as few as 24 taste buds. Pigeons possess around 50, while parrots have as many as 400. This compares to around 10,000 taste buds in our own mouths.

Below: *The common kingfisher (*Alcedo atthis*) is able to use sight to track prey such as fish underwater, thanks to a protective membrane that covers the eyes while the bird is submerged.*

Birds' taste buds are located all around the mouth, rather than just on the tongue, as in mammals. The close links between smell and taste can lead vultures, which feed only on fresh carcasses, to reject decomposing meat. They may start to eat it, but then spit it out once it is in their mouths, probably because of a combination of bad odour and taste.

HEARING

Birds generally do not have a highly developed sense of hearing. They lack any external ear flaps that would help to pinpoint sources of sound. The openings to their hearing system are located on the sides of the head, back from the eyes. These openings are usually hidden by the plumage, and so cannot be seen. Some owls have ear tufts, but these are usually unrelated to hearing.

Hearing is of particular significance for nocturnal species, such as owls, which find their food in darkness. These birds are highly attuned to the high-pitched squeaks and rustling noises made by rodents. The broad shape of their skull has the additional advantage of spacing the ear openings more widely, which helps them to localize the source of the sounds with greater accuracy. Hearing is also important to birds during the breeding season. They are able to pinpoint the calls of their own species within a chorus of birdsong, which helps to find mates. Later in the season, parent birds show particular sensitivity to sounds falling within the vocal range of their chicks, which helps them to locate their offspring easily in the critical early days after fledging.

TOUCH

The sense of touch is more developed in some birds than others. Those such as snipe (*Gallinago* species), which have long bills for seeking food, have sensitive nerve endings called corpuscles in their bills that pick up tiny vibrations caused by their prey. Vibrations that could suggest approaching danger can also register via other corpuscles located particularly in the legs, so that the bird has a sensory awareness even when it is resting on a branch.

INTELLIGENCE

Birds have considerable intelligence, with species such as tits noted for their problem-solving abilities. Some species are more intelligent than others. Field studies of wild birds suggest that corvids (members of the crow family, such as jays and magpies), have quite keen intellects. Jays are able to remember where they have cached food items such as acorns. Both corvids and parrots do well in laboratory tests, including tests involving recognition, tool-using and basic counting.

Below: *Owls such as this tawny owl (*Strix aluco*) have forward-facing eyes that are specialized to hunt in dim light. Keen hearing also helps this nocturnal hunter to track prey such as rodents.*

FINDING FOOD

The birds that visit your garden feed on a wide range of foods including seeds, berries, insects, slugs and worms. A few hunt larger prey, including other backyard birds. The shape of a bird's body and especially its bill is suited to finding and dealing with its particular diet.

As small flying creatures, birds have a high-energy lifestyle. Finding an adequate supply of food is vital to daily survival, and particularly essential in the breeding season. Birds' mating habits are timed so that abundant food is available during the period when parents must supply huge amounts of it to their hungry young.

Food not needed to fuel immediate activity is stored as fat, which is 'burned' or consumed when food is scarce. The aim of every feeding bird is to gain maximum nutrition with the minimum of effort. For this reason, many birds switch between various foods as they become abundant at particular times of year.

MEAT-EATERS

Animal foods such as insects, spiders, slugs and worms are high in energy and protein, but also take considerable energy to capture and swallow. Large insects such as bees and butterflies are high in nourishment but take more energy to tackle, while large quantities of tiny insects such as midges have to be eaten to provide a nourishing meal. Backyard birds that are insect-eaters aid gardeners in

Below: *House sparrows mainly feed on plant foods such as grain and seeds, but this individual has caught a worm.*

THE DIGESTIVE SYSTEM

Birds lack teeth, so their food must be small enough to be swallowed and digested easily. Birds have a storage organ known as the crop, located at the base of the neck. From here, food passes down into the proventriculus, where the digestive process starts, before entering the gizzard, which is equivalent to the mammalian stomach. Nutrients are then absorbed through the wall of the small intestine.

The digestive system of plant-eaters differs in various respects from that of predatory species. For example, plants are a less nourishing food than meat, so plant-eaters must possess longer digestive tracts than other birds, to process the large quantities of food they consume in order to obtain enough nourishment. In addition, digesting plant matter poses certain difficulties. The gizzards of seed-eating species such as finches have especially thick muscular walls, which serve to grind up the seeds. These birds often swallow small stones and grit, which remain in their gizzards and help to break down the seeds.

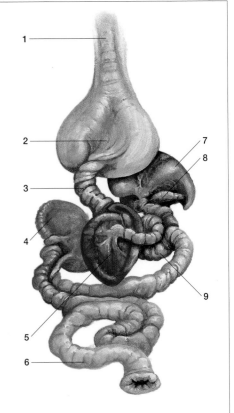

1 Oesophagus	6 Large intestine
2 Crop	7 Liver
3 Proventriculus	8 Spleen
4 Pancreas	9 Small intestine
5 Gizzard	

helping to control invertebrate pests. Species such as woodpeckers and treecreepers hunt for bugs beneath the bark of tree trunks. Other birds hunt among leaves or on the ground. Swifts, martins, flycatchers and nightjars hunt their food on the wing. Aerial hunters such as flycatchers prefer to feed on bluebottle-size insects, which provide good nutrition for little effort. Juicy worms satisfy most of the moisture requirements for species such as blackbirds and thrushes, so these birds rarely need to drink. The same birds can die if they consume slugs or snails containing conventional garden pesticides, so be careful to use environmentally-friendly pesticides if they frequent your garden.

PREDATORS AND SCAVENGERS

Some birds that visit backyards are active predators, seeking and killing prey including smaller birds. Sparrowhawks (*Accipiter nisus*) feed mainly on other birds and are named for their preference for hunting house sparrows (*Passer domesticus*). Another occasional backyard visitor, the peregrine falcon (*Falco peregrinus*) is among the most agile of hunting birds. Many predatory birds are opportunistic feeders, hunting when food is plentiful but scavenging when it becomes scarce.

Corvids (members of the crow family) such as magpies and jays are both scavengers and hunters. They are unpopular with bird-lovers because of their habit of stealing the

Above: *Pied wagtails (*Motacilla alba*) feed on a wide range of invertebrates, including flies, snails and this earthworm.*

eggs and nestlings of songbirds. The same species also alight on road kills and other casualties to find rich pickings to eat.

PLANT-EATERS

Many different types of birds are primarily plant-eaters, whether feeding on flowers, fruit, nuts, seeds or other plant matter. Plant-eaters have to eat a large volume of food compared to meat-eating species, because of the low nutritional value of plants compared to that of prey such as invertebrates. In the last century or so, many species have benefited from the

Below: *The goldfinch (*Carduelis carduelis*) can pluck seeds from pits in the seedhead of a teasel with its fine-tipped beak.*

spread of agriculture, which now provides them with large acreages of suitable crop plants to feed on. These birds' feeding habits bring them into conflict with farmers when they breed rapidly in response to a rapid expansion in their food supply.

FLOWER- AND FRUIT-EATERS

A number of birds rely on flowers as a source of food. Pollen is a valuable source of protein, while nectar provides sugars. Not surprisingly, flower-feeders tend to be confined to mainly tropical areas, where flowers are in bloom throughout the year.

Hummingbirds (Trochilidae) use their narrow bills to probe flowers for nectar. Some hummingbirds have developed especially curved or elongated bills, which allow them to feed on particular flowers. These birds help to pollinate the plants on which they feed by transferring pollen from flower to flower as they feed. Sunbirds (Nectariniidae) of Africa and Asia fill a similar evolutionary niche to hummingbirds, which they resemble in their small size and bright, often iridescent plumage.

Exclusively frugivorous (fruit-eating) birds such as fruit doves (*Ptilinopus* species) are found only in the tropics, where fruit is available throughout the year. Fruit- and berry-eaters help plants to reproduce. The seeds of the fruits they eat pass right through their digestive tracts unharmed, to be deposited far from the parent plant, which helps the plants to spread.

NUT- AND SEED-EATERS

Dry foods are a valuable resource to many different types of birds, ranging from parrots to finches. However, cracking nuts'

tough outer shells or husks can be a problem. Finches such as grosbeaks have evolved a particularly strong bill for this purpose. Hawfinches (*Coccothraustes coccothraustes*) are able to crack cherry stones to extract the kernel.

OMNIVORES

These are birds that eat both animal and plant foods. Most of these species are opportunists, switching between foods as they come into season. Many feed mainly on plant foods such as seeds or nuts in autumn and winter, and switch to insects to nourish themselves and their young in the breeding season.

ADAPTING TO THE SEASONS

Birds from temperate areas exist on a varied diet that is related to the seasons. Bullfinches (*Pyrrhula pyrrhula*), for example, eat buds in apple orchards in spring – when they can become a pest – while later in the year, they consume seeds and fruit. Their bills, like those of most other members of the finch family, are stout and relatively conical, which helps them to crack seeds effectively.

Some birds store plant food when it is plentiful, to sustain them through the winter. Nutcrackers (*Nucifraga* species) collect hazelnuts to feed on in winter. Acorn woodpeckers (*Melanerpes formicivorus*) drill holes in trees that they fill with acorns, creating an easily accessible larder for the winter, when snow may cover the ground.

Below: *Magpies are omnivores. Seeds, insects, carrion and other birds' eggs and nestlings all form part of their diet.*

SINGING, COURTSHIP AND PAIRING

Birdsong is a key element in courtship and pairing, serving to establish territory and attract mates. It is of particular interest to birdwatchers because it helps in species identification. Birds' breeding habits vary greatly. Some species pair up only fleetingly in the breeding season, while others pair for life.

In songbirds, the start of the breeding season generally coincides with the time of abundant food we know as spring. A number of factors trigger the onset of the breeding period. In temperate areas, as the days start to lengthen in spring, the increase in daylight is detected by the pineal gland in the bird's brain, which starts a complex series of hormonal changes in the body. Most birds form a bond with a single partner during the breeding season, which is often preceded by an elaborate display by the cock bird.

BIRDSONG

Many cock birds announce their presence by their song, which both attracts would-be mates and establishes a claim to a territory. Once pairing has occurred, the male may cease singing, but in some cases he starts to perform a duet with the hen, with each bird singing in turn.

Singing serves to keep members of the pair in touch with each other. In some species, the pair co-ordinate their songs so precisely that although the cock bird may

sing the first few notes, and then the hen, it sounds as if the song is being sung by just one bird. Other birds may sing in unison. In a few species, it may even be possible for experts to tell the length of time that the pair have been together by the degree of harmony in their particular songs.

Above: *Feral pigeons, also known as rock doves* (Columba livia) *are sociable birds that often gather to feed in flocks. This pair of pigeons is exhibiting a type of courtship behaviour known as kissing, which is linked to ritualized feeding.*

Studies have revealed that young male birds start warbling quite quietly, and then sing more loudly as they mature. Young songbirds know just the basics of their species' song by instinct. As they mature, they refine their singing by copying the songs of the adults around them. Finally, when their song pattern becomes fixed, it remains constant throughout the bird's life.

It is obviously possible to identify different species by differences in their song patterns. However, there are sometimes marked variations between the songs of individuals of the same species that live in different places. Local dialects have been identified in various parts of a species' distribution, as in the case of chiffchaffs (*Phylloscopus collybita*) from neighbouring valleys separated by hills or mountains. In addition, as far as some songbirds are concerned, recent studies have shown that over the course of several generations, the pattern of songs produced by individuals can alter markedly.

Below: *The song thrush* (Turdus philomelos) *sings its melodious song in spring to establish a breeding territory.*

Below: *Reed buntings* (Emberiza schoeniclus) *identify their mates by song and also by the different colours of the male and female.*

Above: *Ritualized feeding plays an important role in the courtship behaviour of European robins (*Erithacus rubecula*). During courtship the male offers the female food items such as earthworms to prove he is a suitable partner. He then feeds the hen during nest-building and while she incubates the eggs on the nest.*

SONG PRODUCTION

Birds produce their sounds – even those species capable of mimicking human speech – without the benefit of a larynx and vocal cords like humans. The song is created in a voice organ called the syrinx, which is located in the bird's throat, at the bottom of the windpipe, or trachea.

The structure of the syrinx is very variable, being at its most highly developed in the case of songbirds, which possess as many as nine pairs of separate muscles to control the vocal output. As in the human larynx, it is the movement of air through the syrinx that enables the membranes here to vibrate, creating sound as the bird exhales. The pitch of notes is controlled by rings of cartilage that tighten or loosen to vary the sounds produced.

An organ called the interclavicular air sac also plays an important role in sound production, and birds cannot sing without it. The distance over which bird calls can travel is remarkable – up to 5km (3 miles) in the case of species such as the bittern (*Botaurus stellaris*), which has a particularly deep, penetrating song. High, shrill notes can also carry long distances. Diminutive wrens produce a very loud song relative to their small size.

Song complexity also varies greatly among types of garden birds. Species such as the cuckoo seem content to repeat a single phrase with very little variation that human ears can detect. In contrast, species such as thrushes and robins have several hundred different phrases in their repertoire. These are combined in myriad different ways to produce a song which is constantly changing.

COURTSHIP DISPLAYS

Many birds rely on their breeding finery to attract their mates. The bright or bold colours of male birds are designed to warn off rival males and attract the females. Thus it is usually the female that selects her mate. She bases her choice not only on her potential mate's appearance but also on his singing talents, and in some cases, on his ability to demonstrate nest-building or food-providing skills. Male kingfishers present their mates with fish to vouchsafe their ability to provide food for their young, while male robins may proffer worms.

Some types of birds, though not generally garden birds, assemble in communal display areas known as leks, where hens witness the males' displays and select a mate. A number of different species, including some game birds and also hummingbirds, establish leks. In a few species, such as the bowerbirds of Australia, the male constructs elaborate bowers of grass that he decorates with items of a particular colour, such as blue, varying from flowers to pieces of glass.

PAIR BONDING

Many male and female birds form no lasting relationship, although the pair bond may be strong during the nesting period. It is usually only in potentially long-lived species, for example, storks and waterfowl such as swans, that a lifelong pair bond is formed.

Pair bonding in long-lived species has certain advantages. The young of such birds are usually slow to mature, and are therefore often unlikely to nest themselves for five years or even more. By remaining for a period in a family group, the adults can improve the long-term survival prospects of their young.

Below: *Studies of the song patterns of chiffchaffs in neighbouring valleys show slight regional variations.*

NESTING AND EGG-LAYING

Birds vary in their nesting habits, some constructing very simple nests and others making elaborate ones. All birds reproduce by laying eggs, which are covered with a hard, calcareous shell. The number of eggs laid at a time – known as the clutch size – varies between species, as does egg coloration.

Most birds construct their nests from vegetation, depending on which materials are locally available. In coastal areas, some seabirds use pieces of seaweed to build theirs. Artificial materials such as plastic wrappers or polystyrene may be used by some birds.

Different types of birds build nests of various shapes and sizes, which are characteristic of their species. Groups such as finches build nests in the form of an open cup, often concealed in vegetation. Most pigeons and doves construct a loose platform of twigs. Swallows are among the birds that use mud to construct their nests. They scoop muddy water up from the surface of a pond or puddle, mould it into shape on a suitable wall, and then allow it to dry and harden like cement.

The simplest nests are composed of little more than a pad of material, resting in the fork of a tree or on a building. The effort entailed in nest construction may reflect how often the birds are likely to nest. The platforms of pigeons and doves can disintegrate quite easily, resulting in the loss

Above: *House martins (*Delichon urbita*) are so-named for their habit of forming their mud nests under the protective eaves of houses. This largely aerial bird touches down only when breeding. It raises up to three broods between April and September.*

of eggs or chicks. However, if disaster does befall the nest, the pair will often breed again within a few weeks.

Cup-shaped nests are more elaborate than platform nests, being usually made by weaving grasses and twigs together. The inside is often lined with soft feathers. The raised sides of the cup nest lessen the likelihood of losing eggs and chicks, and also offer greater security to the adults during incubation. The hollow in the nest's centre is created by the birds compressing the material here before egg-laying begins.

Suspended nests enclosed by a domed roof offer even greater security. They are less accessible to predators because of their design and also their position, often hanging from slender branches.

NEST SITES

Many birds use tree holes for nesting. Woodpeckers (Picidae) are particularly well equipped to create nesting chambers,

Above: *Birds' nests are often located in secluded spots. If detected, they should always be left undisturbed and untouched.*

using their powerful bills to enlarge holes in dead trees. The diameter of the entry hole thus created is just wide enough to allow the birds to enter easily, which helps to prevent the nest being robbed.

Some birds rely on the safety of numbers to deter would-be predators, building communal nests that are occupied by successive generations and added to regularly. Rooks are highly social corvids. Their communal sites, known as rookeries, may contain several hundred nests.

Other birds, such as the common cuckoo (*Cuculus canorus*) and the cowbirds (*Molothrus*) of North America, simply lay and abandon their eggs in the nests of other species. The foster parents-to-be do not seem able to detect the difference between their own eggs and that of the intruder, so they do not reject the

Above: *Robins build domed nests of moss or leaves lined with hair. Nests may be sited in a bank, dense shrub or crook of a tree.*

cuckoo or cowbird egg. They incubate it along with their own brood, and feed the foster chick when it hatches out.

Birds that nest on the ground are especially vulnerable to predators and rely heavily on their fairly drab plumage as camouflage. Skylarks (*Alauda arvensis*) have another means of protecting the nest – they hold one wing down and pretend to be injured to draw a predator away.

Some birds return to the same nest site each year, but many birds simply abandon their old nest and build another. This may seem a waste of effort, but it actually helps to protect the birds from parasites such as blood-sucking mites, which can otherwise multiply in the confines of the nest.

MATING

For most birds, mating is a brief process. The male usually mounts the female, twisting his rump so that the cloacas, or body openings, of the two birds touch for a second. Spermatozoa swim up the hen's reproductive tract, and fertilize the ova at an early stage in the process. Generally, only one mating is required to fertilize a clutch of eggs. Hens can also lay unfertilized eggs if no male is around, but these eggs will not hatch however long they are incubated. The period between mating and egg-laying varies according to species. In small birds, the interval may be as little as ten days, while in larger species such as owls, it may be several months.

THE REPRODUCTIVE SYSTEMS

The cock bird has two testes located within his body. Spermatozoa pass down the vas deferens, into the cloaca and then out of the body. Insemination occurs when the vent areas of the male and female bird are in direct contact during mating. Cock birds do not have a penis for penetration, although certain groups, such as waterfowl, may have a primitive organ that is used to assist in the transference of semen in a similar way.

Normally only the left ovary and oviduct of the hen bird are functional. Eggs pass down through the reproductive tract from the ovary.

1 Testes
2 Kidneys
3 Vas deferens
4 Cloaca
5 Ova
6 Infundibulum
7 Magnum
8 Isthmus
9 Egg with shell contained in the hen's reproductive tract
10 Cloaca

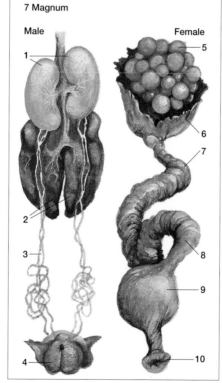

EGG SIZE AND COLOUR

The size of eggs produced by different species of birds varies dramatically. An ostrich's egg is thousands of times heavier than the eggs laid by wrens or hummingbirds. The coloration and markings of a bird's eggs are directly

linked to the nesting site. Birds that usually breed in hollow trees produce white eggs, because these are normally hidden from predators and so do not need to be camouflaged. The pale coloration may also help the adult birds to locate the eggs as they return to the nest, thus lessening the chances of damaging them. Birds that build open, cup-shaped nests tend to lay coloured and often mottled eggs that are camouflaged and so less obvious to potential nest thieves.

CLUTCH SIZES

The number of eggs laid at one time varies according to species, as does the number of clutches produced in a year. Birds such as blue tits (*Parus caeruleus*) lay just one clutch of 10–12 eggs in spring. In contrast, female blackbirds (*Turdus merula*) can produce three clutches of up to four eggs in a single season. Birds' breeding habits are often related to the food that will be fed to the nestlings. For example, blue tit nestlings are fed on caterpillars, which are most abundant in springtime. Blackbird nestlings are reared on earthworms, which may be found throughout the year.

Below: *Ostriches lay the largest eggs in the world, which can weigh up to 1.5kg (3.3lb). In comparison, a chicken's egg, shown in front of the ostrich egg, looks tiny. The egg nearest to the viewer is a hummingbird egg. These tiny birds lay the smallest eggs in the avian world, weighing only about 0.35g (0.01oz).*

HATCHING AND REARING CHICKS

Birds are vulnerable to predators when breeding, especially when they have young in the nest. The chicks must be fed frequently, necessitating regular trips to and from the nest, which makes it conspicuous. The calls of nestlings represent a further danger, so the breeding period is often short.

Most birds incubate their eggs to keep them sufficiently warm for the chicks to develop inside. Larger eggs are less prone to chilling during incubation than small eggs, because of their bigger volume. In the early stages of the incubation period, when the nest may be left uncovered while the adult birds are foraging for food, eggs can withstand a lower temperature. Temperature differences also account for the fact that, at similar altitudes, incubation periods tend to be slightly longer in temperate areas than in tropical regions.

The eggshell may appear to be a solid barrier but in fact contains many pores, which are vital to the chick's wellbeing. These tiny holes allow water vapour and carbon dioxide to escape from the egg, and oxygen to enter it to reach the embryo.

INCUBATION TIMINGS
The incubation period often does not start until more than one egg has been laid, and sometimes not until the entire clutch has been completed. The interval between the laying of one egg and the next varies – finches lay every day, whereas birds such as gannets may lay only one egg every six

days. If incubation does not start until egg-laying has finished, the chicks will all be of a similar size when they hatch, which increases their overall chances of survival. Among species such as owls, incubation generally starts after the first egg is laid. This results in one chick that is larger than its fellows. This large individual frequently bullies its nest mates.

The cock and hen may share incubation duties, as in the case of most pigeons and

Above: *Spring sees the onset of the nesting season, when parent birds work hard to gather food such as insects for their chicks.*

doves, or just one member of the pair may incubate. Among garden birds, this is usually the hen, but there are exceptions in the wider bird world. For example, in ostriches (*Struthio camelus*) and most other large flightless birds, it is the male who incubates the eggs and cares for the

Below: *A fertile chicken's egg, showing the development of the embryo through to hatching. 1. The fertilized egg cell divides to form a ball of cells that gradually develops into an embryo. 2. The embryo develops, nourished by the yolk sac. 3. The air space at the rounded end of the egg enlarges as water evaporates. 4. The chick is almost fully developed and ready to hatch. 5. The chick cuts its way out, and its feathers quickly dry off.*

1

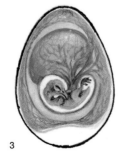
2

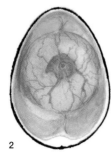
3

4

5

NEST PARASITISM

This is common in many species of cuckoo, such as the European cuckoo (*Cuculus canorus*). The males do not establish breeding territories, but mate with females at random. The females lay a single egg in the nests of host species such as reed warblers (*Acrocephalus scirpaceus*). The rapid development of the cuckoo's egg is vital so that the chick hatches first, and can then throw the other eggs or chicks out of the nest. In this way, it monopolizes the food supply brought by its foster parents. Any other chicks that do survive this initial stage die later, as they lose out in competition for food with their gigantic nest mate.

Below: *Foster parents such as this reed warbler continue to feed the young cuckoo even when the imposter dwarfs them in size.*

resulting chicks. Anis (*Crotophaga*) breed communally, and all members of the group share the task of incubation. Incubation periods vary among species, ranging from as few as 11 days in the case of American cowbirds (*Molothrus*), to over 80 days in some albatrosses (Diomedeidae).

HATCHING

When hatching, the chick uses the egg tooth on the tip of its upper bill to cut through the inner membrane into the air space at the blunt end of the shell, which forms as water evaporates from the egg. The chick starts to breathe atmospheric air for the first time. About 48 hours later, it breaks through the shell to emerge from the egg.

Chicks hatch out at various stages of development, and are accordingly able to leave the nest sooner or later. Species that remain in the nest for some time after hatching, including finches (Fringillidae), hatch in a blind and helpless state and are entirely dependent on their parents at first. Birds in this group are known as nidicolous. If not closely brooded, they are likely to become fatally chilled. In contrast, species that leave the nest soon after hatching, known as nidifugous, emerge from the egg and are able to move around on their own at this stage. They can also see and feed themselves almost immediately. The offspring of many game birds such as pheasants as well as waterfowl and waders are nidifugous, which gives them a better chance of survival, as they can run to escape from predators. Young waterfowl cannot take safely to the water at first, however, because they lack the oil from the preen gland above the base of the tail to waterproof their feathers.

REARING AND FLEDGING

Many adult birds offer food to their offspring, even some nidifugous species. This can be a particularly demanding period, especially for small birds that have relatively large broods. Great tits (*Parus major*), for example, must supply their offspring with huge quantities of insects. They typically feed their chicks up to 60 times an hour, as well as keeping the nest clean by removing faeces.

Young birds usually leave the nest from about 12 to 30 days after hatching. However, some species develop much more slowly. Among birds generally, albatross chicks are particularly slow developers, spending up to eight and a half months in the nest.

Above: *The broad and often colourful gape of chicks allows parent birds to feed their offspring quickly and efficiently. Weak chicks that are unable to raise their heads and gape at the approach of a parent will quickly die from starvation.*

When they first leave the nest, many young birds are unable to fly, simply because their flight feathers are not fully functional. If these feathers are not completely unfurled from the protective sheaths in which they emerged, they cannot function effectively. The strength of the wing muscles also needs to be built up, so it is not uncommon for young birds to rest on the sides of the nest, flapping their wings occasionally, before finally taking to the air for the first time. Chicks that are unable to fly immediately on fledging remain reliant on the adults, especially the cock, for food until they become fully independent. It is a common sight to see immature songbirds following a parent around the garden, begging for food.

Below: *Blue tits (*Parus caeruleus*) are typical of many birds that leave the nest before they are able to fly effectively. The young remain hidden in vegetation and are fed by their parents in the critical early days after leaving the nest.*

BIRD BEHAVIOUR

The field of bird behaviour, or avian ethology as it is known, is very broad. Some patterns of behaviour are common to all birds, whereas other actions are very specific, just to a single species or even to an individual population. Interpreting behaviour is a fine art, and of special interest to keen birdwatchers.

All bird behaviour essentially relates to various aspects of survival, such as avoiding predators, obtaining food, finding a mate and breeding successfully. Some behaviour patterns are instinctive, while others develop in certain populations of birds in response to particular conditions. Thus the way in which birds behave is partly influenced by their environment as well as being largely instinctual.

AGGRESSION
Birds can be surprisingly aggressive toward each other, even to the point of sometimes inflicting fatal injuries. Usually, however, only a few feathers are shed before the weaker individual backs away, without sustaining serious injury. Conflicts of this type can break out over feeding sites or territorial disputes. The risk of aggressive outbreaks is greatest at the start of the breeding season, when the territorial instincts of cock birds are most aroused. Size is no indicator of the potential level of aggression, since some of the smallest birds, such as wrens and hummingbirds (Trochilidae) can be extremely ferocious.

Below: *A dispute breaks out between a pair of great tits (*Parus major*) over food. Birds often fight with wings outstretched as they seek to batter their opponent into submission.*

Above: *Blue tits are opportunistic feeders, able to learn new forms of behaviour to reach rich food sources, as their habit of pecking the tops of milk bottles shows.*

Age, too, plays a part in determining behaviour, since young birds often behave in a very different way to the adults. Some forms of bird behaviour are relatively easy to interpret, while others are a great deal more difficult to explain.

ADAPTING BEHAVIOUR
One of the first studies documenting birds' ability to adapt their behaviour in response to changes in their environment involved blue tits (*Parus caeruleus*) in Britain. The study showed that certain individuals learned to use their bills to tap through the shiny metallic foil covers on milk bottles to reach the milk inside. Other blue tits followed their example, and in certain areas householders with milk deliveries had to protect their bottles from the birds. In addition, the tits concerned demonstrated the ability to distinguish bottles containing creamy milk from ones holding skimmed milk from the colours of their tops. The study showed that the birds directed the overwhelming majority of their raids at bottles containing the creamier milk.

The way in which birds have learned to use various types of garden feeders also

Above: *In birds such as starlings (*Sturnus vulgaris*), preening may serve to reinforce bonds between individuals, as well as keeping the feathers clean.*

demonstrates their ability to modify their existing behaviour in response to new conditions when it benefits them. A number of new feeders on the market designed to thwart squirrels from stealing the food exploit birds' ability to adapt in this way. The birds have to squeeze through a small gap to reach the food, just as they might to enter the nest. Once one bird has been bold enough to enter in this fashion, others observe and soon follow suit.

PREENING
Although preening serves a variety of functions, the most important aspect is keeping the feathers in good condition. It helps to dislodge parasites and removes loose feathers, particularly during moulting. It also ensures that the plumage is kept waterproof by spreading oil from the preen gland at the base of the tail.

Preening can be a social activity too. It may be carried out by pairs of males and females during the breeding season, or among a family group. This behaviour is seen in a variety of birds, including members of the finch family. In some cases preening may be a prelude to mating.

BATHING

Preening is not the only way in which birds keep their plumage in good condition. Birds often bathe to remove dirt and debris from their plumage. Small birds wet their feathers by lying on a damp leaf during a shower of rain, in an activity known as leaf-bathing. Other birds immerse themselves in a pool of water, splashing around and ruffling their feathers.

Some birds, especially those found in drier areas of the world, prefer to dust-bathe, lying down in a dusty hollow known as a scrape and using fine earth thrown up by their wings to absorb excess oil from their plumage. They then shake themselves thoroughly and preen their feathers to remove the excess oil.

SUNBATHING

This may be important in allowing birds to synthesize vitamin D3 from the ultraviolet rays in sunlight, which is vital for a healthy skeleton. This process can be achieved only by light falling on the bird's skin, which explains why birds ruffle their plumage at this time. Some birds habitually stretch out while sunbathing, while others, such as many pigeons, prefer to rest with one wing raised, leaning over at a strange angle on the perch.

MAINTAINING HEALTH

Some people believe that when birds are ill, they eat particular plants that have medicinal properties, but this theory is very

Below: *A wren sunbathing. Many birds tend to sunbathe with their wings outstretched and often an open beak.*

difficult to prove. One form of behaviour that does confer health benefits has been documented, however: it involves the use of ants. Instead of eating these insects, some birds occasionally rub them in among their feathers. This causes the ants to release formic acid, which acts as a potent insecticide, killing off lurking parasites such as mites and lice. Jays (*Garrulus glandarius*) and also starlings (Sturnidae) and Eurasian blackbirds (*Turdus merula*) are among the species that have been observed using insects in this way.

Members of the crow family have also been seen perching on smoking chimney pots or above bonfires, ruffling their feathers and allowing the smoke to penetrate their plumage. The smoke is thought to kill off parasites in a process that confers the same benefits as anting.

Above: *When bathing, birds frequently dip down and use their wings and tail to splash the water. This ensures their whole body receives a wetting.*

DISPLAYS

Birds often signal their intentions to one another using displays, or ritualized gestures. Such actions are used in courtship, to co-ordinate flock behaviour, and also reinforce territorial claims and resolve disputes. A songbird wishing to warn another off a food source will fluff itself up and spread its wings to look as big as possible. Its rival may indicate submission by crouching low to minimize its size.

Below: *A greenfinch dive-bombs another. Birds show aggression with feathers fluffed. If this does not work, a bird may attack.*

MIGRATION

Some birds live in a particular place all year round, but many are only temporary visitors. Typically, species fly north into temperate latitudes in spring, and return south at the end of summer. They have a wide distribution, but are seen only in specific parts of their range at certain times of the year.

Many species of birds take long seasonal journeys. The birds that regularly undertake such seasonal movements on specific routes are known as migrants, and the journeys themselves are known as migrations. Migrations are different from so-called irruptions, when flocks of certain types of birds suddenly move to an area where conditions are more favourable.

Birds migrate to seek shelter from the elements, to find safe areas to rear their young and, in particular, to seek places where food is plentiful. Birds such as waxwings (Bombycillidae) irrupt to a new location to find food when supplies become scarce in their habitat, but such journeys are less frequent and are irregular.

The instinct to migrate dates back millions of years, to a period when the seasons were often much more extreme, which meant that it was difficult to obtain food in a locality throughout the year. This forced birds to move in search of food. Even today, the majority of migratory species live within the world's temperate

Below: *Many birds, including this barn swallow* (Hirundo rustica), *set out on migration after moulting. Damaged plumage can make the task of flying harder.*

Above: *Many British chiffchaffs travel to the Mediterranean or south of the Sahara for winter. Some remain in Britain, in the south.*

zones, particularly in the Northern Hemisphere, where seasonal changes remain pronounced.

ROUTES AND ALTITUDES
The routes that the birds follow on their journeys are often well defined. Land birds try to avoid flying over large stretches of water, preferring instead to follow coastal routes and crossing the sea at the shortest point. For instance, many birds migrating from Europe to Africa prefer to fly over the Straits of Gibraltar. Frequently birds fly at much greater altitudes when migrating. Cranes (Gruidae) have been recorded flying at 5,000m (16,400ft) when crossing the mountainous areas in France, and geese (Anatidae) have been observed crossing the Himalayas at altitudes of more than 9,000m (29,500ft). Even if the migratory routes are known, it is often difficult to spot migrating birds because they fly so high.

SPEED AND DISTANCE
Migrating birds also fly at greater speeds than usual, which helps to make their journey time as short as possible. The difference can be significant – migrating swallows (*Hirundo rustica*) travel at speeds between 3 and 14kmh (1.8–8.7mph) faster than usual, and are helped no doubt by the greater altitude, where the air is thinner and resistance is less.

Some birds travel huge distances on migration. Arctic terns (*Sterna paradisea*) are renowned for covering distances of more than 15,000km (9,300 miles) in total, as they shuttle between the Arctic and Antarctic. They fly an average distance of 160km (100 miles) every day. Among garden birds, British barn swallows travel all the way to South Africa to overwinter. Experienced birds may complete the return journey in around five weeks, covering about 300km (185 miles) a day. However studies suggest that as few as 25 per cent of young swallows manage to complete the round trip and return to their birthplace.

Size does not preclude some birds from migrating long distances. The tiny ruby-throated hummingbird (*Archilochus colubris*) flies over the Gulf of Mexico from the eastern USA every year, a distance of more than 800km (500 miles).

PREPARING FOR MIGRATION
The migratory habits of birds have long been the subject of scientific curiosity. As late as the 1800s, it was thought that

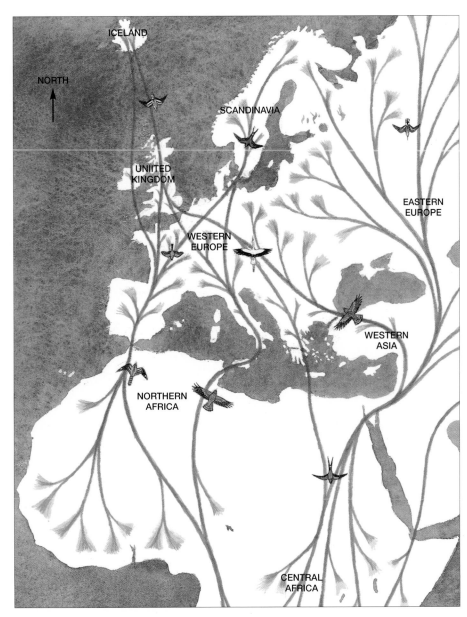

Above: *The routes taken by birds migrating back and forth to Africa from parts of Europe and western Asia are shown here. Crossings are not always made by the most direct route, if this would entail a long and possibly dangerous sea journey.*

swallows hibernated in the bottom of ponds because they were seen skimming over the pond surface in groups before disappearing until the following spring. Now we know that they were probably feeding on insects to build up energy supplies for their long journey ahead.

Even today, the precise mechanisms involved in migratory behaviour are not fully understood. We do know that birds feed up before setting out on migration, and that various hormonal changes enable them to store more fat in their bodies to sustain them on their journey. Feeding opportunities are likely to be more limited than usual when birds are migrating, while their energy requirements are, of course, higher. In addition, birds usually moult just before migrating, so that their plumage is in the best condition to withstand the inevitable buffeting that lies ahead.

NAVIGATION

Birds use both learned and visual cues to orientate themselves when migrating. Young birds of many species, such as swans, learn the route by flying in the company of their elders. However, young birds such as European cuckoos set out on their own and reach their destinations successfully without the benefit of experienced companions, navigating by instinct alone. Birds such as swifts (Apopidae) fly mainly during daytime, whereas others, including ducks (Anatidae), migrate at night. Many birds fly direct to their destination, but some may detour and break their journey to obtain food and water before setting out again.

Experiments have shown that birds orientate themselves using the position of the sun and stars, as well as by following familiar landmarks. They use the Earth's magnetic field to find their position, and thus do not get lost in cloudy or foggy weather, when the sky is obscured. The way in which these factors come together has, however, yet to be fully understood.

BANDING BIRDS

Much of what we know about migration and the lifespan of birds comes from banding studies carried out by ornithologists. Bands placed on birds' legs allow experts to track their movements when the ringed birds are recovered again. The rings are made of lightweight aluminium, and have details of the banding organization and when banding was carried out. Unfortunately, only a very small proportion of ringed birds are ever recovered, so the data gathered is incomplete. However, now other methods of tracking, such as radar, are also used to follow the routes taken by flocks of birds, which supplement the information from banding studies.

Below: *A swan has been fitted with a tracking device attached to its leg. The coloured bands can help to identify individual birds from some distance away.*

SURVIVAL

The numbers of a particular species of bird can vary significantly over time, affected by factors such as the availability of food, climate, disease and hunting. When the reproductive rate of a species falls below its annual mortality rate, it is in decline, but this does not mean it will inevitably become extinct.

For many birds, life is short and hazardous. Quite apart from the risk of predation, birds can face a whole range of other dangers, from starvation and disease through to either deliberate or inadvertent human persecution. The reproductive rate is higher and age of maturity is lower in species that have particularly hazardous lifestyles, such as blue tits (*Parus caeruleus*). Such species often breed twice or more each year in rapid succession.

RISING AND FALLING NUMBERS
Some birds have a reproductive cycle that is geared to allow them to increase their numbers rapidly under favourable conditions. In parts of the world where rainfall is erratic, for example, seed-eating birds multiply quickly when the rains come. Rainfall not only ensures the rapid germination of the grasses that form the basis of their diet, but also replenishes rivers, lakes and other water sources. During periods of drought when food and

Below: *As grain-eaters, pigeons in rural areas worldwide have benefited from the spread of agriculture, while in cities, food scraps are available in refuse. These opportunists have also adapted to other changes in their environment, for example, the chance to roost on power lines.*

water become harder to find, the same bird populations may well plummet, but they can grow again rapidly when conditions become more favourable.

Regular fall-offs in populations can occur on a cyclical basis in the case of predatory birds such as owls, that feed mainly on one type of food, such as rodents. In years where conditions favour rodents, the parent birds are able to rear more chicks. When rodent numbers decline, the owls' breeding success plummets, only to recover when the rodent population rises again.

Above: *Predatory birds such as barn owls (Tyto alba) do well in years when conditions favour prey such as rodents, allowing them to multiply. In years when rodent populations are lower, there is less food for barn owl adults and their young.*

GROUP LIVING
Living within a group offers several major advantages to birds such as starlings (Sturnidae) and pigeons (Columbidae). Flocks of birds are able to exploit large supplies of food as they become available. Birds that live in flocks also find their mates more easily than other birds. Another advantage is the safety of numbers. An aerial predator such as a hawk will find it harder to recognize and target individuals in a flying mass of birds, although stragglers are still likely to be picked off.

Coloration can increase the safety of birds in flocks. In Florida, USA, there used to be feral budgerigar flocks made up of multicoloured individuals. The different colours reflected the diversity of colour varieties that were developed through domestication. Today, however, green is by far the predominant colour in such flocks, as it is in genuine wild flocks, simply because predators found it much easier to pick off individuals of other colours. Greater

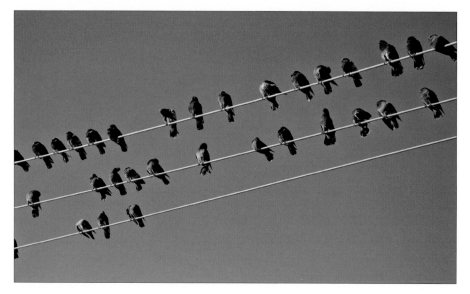

CRYPTIC COLORATION

Camouflage, also known as cryptic coloration, enables a bird to hide in its natural surroundings. It offers distinct survival benefits in concealing the bird from would-be predators. Cryptic coloration has the effect of breaking up the bird's outline, allowing it to blend in with the background in its habitat. Posture and, in particular, keeping still can also aid concealment, as movement often attracts the attention of potential predators.

Below: *Camouflage allows birds such as this pheasant to forage while remaining undetected by enemies. However, cryptic coloration is also useful to predators such as owls.*

urban areas, road systems, mines, farms and other developments worldwide has greatly reduced the amount of wild habitat that is available to birds. In Britain, the modernization of farming has meant the eradiction of hedgerows and also increased use of chemicals, both of which have had serious consequences for many species of native birds.

However, the expansion of agriculture has not always had a negative effect on bird populations. In countries such as Australia, it has resulted in the greater availability of water in what was formerly arid countryside, which has enabled birds such as galahs (*Eolophus roseicapillus*), a type of cockatoo, to spread.

Other birds have benefited more directly from human intervention, as is the case with the common starling (*Sturnus vulgaris*). These birds have spread across North America, following their introduction from Europe in the late 1800s.

Similarly, the common pheasant (*Phasianus colchicus*) is now native across most of Europe, thanks to human interest in these game birds, which are bred in large numbers for sport shooting. Many more survive than would otherwise be the case, thanks to the attention of gamekeepers who not only provide food, but also help to curb possible predators in areas where the birds are released.

ENVIRONMENTAL CHANGE

In the last decade or so, scientists believe that global warming has started to affect habitats worldwide, producing generally warmer conditions and in some regions, making extreme weather events such as

Above: *The rasping call of the corncrake was once a common sound in the British countryside, but intensive farming practices have produced a rapid decline.*

droughts more common. Research shows that this has started to affect birds' breeding habits and migration patterns. Some species appear to be benefiting from environmental changes. However birds that reproduce slowly are likely to be highly vulnerable to any changes in their surroundings, whether caused by climate change or other factors, such as habitat loss, hunting or disease.

Below: *Group living provides safety in numbers for birds such as starlings (*Sturnus vulgaris*). These birds spend much of the year together in a flock.*

numbers of the green budgies survived to breed and pass on their genes to their descendants, and so green became the dominant colour in the feral flocks.

Group living also means that when the flock is feeding and at its most vulnerable, there are extra eyes to watch out for predators and other threats. Within some flocks, individual birds take it in turns to act as sentinels, and screech loudly at any hint of danger.

EFFECTS OF HUMANS

It is generally assumed that human interference in the landscape is likely to have harmful effects on avian populations. In the last century or so, the expansion of

BIRDS IN TOWNS AND CITIES

Some birds display a remarkable ability to adapt to modern life, settling in the heart of towns and cities. They use buildings for nesting and, in the case of predatory birds, as vantage points for hunting, like they would trees or rocky crags in the wild. All this means that cities can be great places to watch birds.

Cities tend to be slightly warmer than the surrounding countryside, and this warm microclimate offers a number of advantages for birds. Drinking water is less likely to freeze in cold weather, and in spring, insects are more abundant at an earlier time, as plants bud and grow more quickly because of the warmth.

RESIDENTS AND VISITORS
Some birds live permanently in cities, taking advantage of parks, whereas others are less regular visitors, flying in to roost at night from outlying areas, or pausing here on migration. Deserted buildings offer a snug and relatively safe retreat for birds that roost in flocks, whereas birds of prey

Above: *Songbirds such as robins (*Erithacus rubecula*) do well in urban gardens and parks. This one is perched on railings bordering a square in a busy city.*

Below: *City parks offer the best chance of spotting a wide range of species in urban environments, particularly if a pond or lake offers a habitat for species such as ducks.*

Above: *Out of all birds, the feral pigeon (*Columba livia*) has adapted best to urban life, to the extent that it is now a common sight in cities around the world, including in the British Isles.*

seek the inaccessible ledges of high-rise buildings. The abundance of feral pigeons (*Columba livia*) in built-up areas attracts peregrine falcons (*Falco peregrinus*), proving that these predators are just as adaptable as their prey. The falcons may keep pigeon populations in check but, if not, their numbers can also be curbed by feeding them with corn, which acts as a contraceptive.

Migrating birds still pass through cities on occasions, notably huge flocks of common starlings (*Sturnus vulgaris*). These congregate not just in city parks, but also roost on buildings and tree-lined streets when breaking their journey, creating a noisy chatter and plenty of mess.

BENEFITS AND DANGERS
A life above the bustle of city streets generally offers predatory species a fairly safe existence, compared with more rural areas where they risk being shot illegally. There are still dangers lurking on the city streets, however. Homes or high-rise office blocks with large expanses of glass can lure birds to a fatal collision.

Right: *Many bird species thrive in towns and cities. There are plenty of places for perching, nesting and rearing young. However, the spread of cities also causes many avian populations to decline, by altering neighbouring habitats. When new development encroaches on surrounding land, it becomes hard for many birds to find food.*

TIPS FOR OBSERVING BIRDS IN TOWNS AND CITIES
• Early morning is a good time to spot birds at close quarters in cities, before many people are out and about to disturb avian residents.
• Join the local ornithological society to gain insight into the more unusual species that have been observed in local towns and cities.
• If you venture outside your garden to spot birds, don't forget about the dangers of traffic in your enthusiasm.

Typical sightings in towns and cities, depending partly on location:
• Pigeons and doves
• Sparrows
• Magpies
• Owls
• Gulls

1 House sparrows
2 Starlings
3 Peregrine falcon
4 Feral pigeons
5 Common crows
6 Mallards
7 Moorhen
8 Black-headed gulls

BIRDS IN COUNTRY GARDENS

A wide variety of birds are likely to be seen in country gardens. As well as the species that naturally visit in search of food among the trees and shrubs, the addition of feeding stations will help to draw birds to rural garden settings. As many as 40 species have been observed regularly visiting bird tables in the UK.

Tidy, immaculately manicured gardens generally support less bird life than well-established gardens with plenty of mature shrubs that can be used for roosting and nesting. If there are stands of trees nearby, or even just lining the road outside, the range of birds visiting the garden will increase, and larger species will become more common. Artificial nesting sites, such as nest boxes of various types and sizes, can also help to increase the variety and numbers of birds that visit your garden on a regular basis.

Birds face a major danger in gardens in the guise of the domestic cat. Huge numbers of individuals fall victim to these

Above: *Bird feeders help to attract birds into gardens by providing them with additional food sources. The extra food is especially valuable during the months of cold weather.*

Above: *Fieldfares arrive from their northerly breeding grounds to winter in European gardens and farmland, where they are likely to feed on fallen fruit. These birds can be identified by their harsh calls.*

pets annually. The majority of the casualties are young fledglings, which lack the awareness and caution of adult birds. In areas where the cat population is especially high, there may be local declines in bird numbers. However, studies suggest that bird populations do not seem to be adversely affected by cats overall.

HELPERS AND PESTS
Birds are often regarded as gardeners' friends because they help to control the number of invertebrate pests in gardens. For example, tits (Paridae) eat aphids on rose bushes, and thrushes (Turdidae) hunt snails. At certain times of year, however, some birds can themselves become pests. Pigeons (Columbidae), in particular, often dig up newly planted seeds and eat them before they can germinate, unless the seeds are protected in some way. Later in the year, some species eat ripening berries.

RESIDENTS AND VISITORS
Birds such as robins, blackbirds and tits are resident in garden settings throughout the year. Others are temporary visitors, migrating to warmer climes for the winter period. For example, swallows and many

warblers frequent British gardens in spring and summer only, and then head south for the winter. Meanwhile, winter migrants from farther north may appear in gardens at about the same time, as in the case of the fieldfare (*Turdus pilaris*). Yet other species, such as waxwings, appear infrequently when food becomes scarce in wild habitats. Studies provide clear evidence that actual shifts in the behaviour and distribution of birds are currently occurring because of the availability of garden habitat and the provision of food there. For example, the Eurasian blackbird (*Turdus merula*), traditionally a woodland bird, is now a common sight in gardens.

Right: *In many respects, rural gardens offer an ideal habitat for birds. Food is readily available in these surroundings, as well as trees and shrubs, which provide good opportunities for roosting and nesting. Unfortunately, gardens can often be dangerous places for birds to visit, thanks to the popularity of cats as pets. Nor are cats the only danger. Predatory birds, notably magpies (Pica pica) and jays (Garrulus glandarius) will raid the nests of smaller birds, taking both eggs and chicks.*

TIPS FOR OBSERVING BIRDS IN COUNTRY GARDENS
• Positioning a bird table near a window will allow you to watch birds from inside the house, but take care to site it well away from cover where cats could lurk and ambush birds.
• Keep a pair of binoculars handy indoors so you can get a good view of the bird table and any unexpected visitors to it, plus a notepad to record any unusual birds you see.
• You can encourage invertebrate-eating birds to visit your garden by creating a wild area or by establishing a compost heap where invertebrates can multiply.
• Try to avoid using insecticides on your garden, as these reduce the food that will be available for birds.
• Ordinary slug pellets will poison slug-eaters such as thrushes feeding in your garden. Use pellets that are described as safe for birds instead.

Typical sightings in rural gardens, depending on location:
• Tits
• Thrushes
• Starlings
• Finches

1 Rooks
2 Spotted flycatchers
3 Collared dove
4 Robin
5 Chaffinch
6 Mistle thrush
7 Blue tit
8 Wren
9 Dunnock
10 Blackbirds

WOODLAND BIRDS

If your home lies near a woodland habitat, be it a forest plantation, countryside copse or even a tree-lined avenue in a city centre, your garden will be visited by woodland birds. However many of these species are quite shy and secretive by nature, which can make them difficult to observe.

Bird life is more prolific and varied in and near deciduous, broad-leaved woodlands than in coniferous forests, largely because of greater feeding opportunities in the former setting. Nonetheless some species manage to thrive in coniferous forests.

DECIDUOUS WOODLANDS

A wide variety of food types exists for birds in deciduous forests. The species here may eat all sorts of foods, ranging from seeds to berries and invertebrates, depending on the time of year. Deciduous woodlands are more open than coniferous ones, particularly in winter when trees lose their leaves. This means that there is a significant understorey of vegetation and insects are more plentiful. Migratory birds feed in these woods in summer. Ground birds of various types, including pheasants (*Phasianus colchicus*), may be found here. During the breeding season woodland birds

gather in clearings to display and mate. However in winter these leafless woods provide little shelter and food for birds, so at this time these birds may visit gardens.

CONIFEROUS WOODLANDS

Birds such as crossbills thrive in coniferous woodlands in Europe. Their curving bills allow these specialized members of the finch family to extract the seeds from pine cones effectively. Woodpeckers and corvids such as jays prepare for the cold winter weather by burying stores of nuts or hiding them in trees. Owls are frequently found in coniferous forests, preying on the rodents that can be quite plentiful there. However, they may be forced to hunt elsewhere if their prey numbers plummet following a shortage of pine cones.

Evergreen coniferous woodlands provide shelter all year round for birds, but here too food supplies are far from guaranteed.

Below: *Some predatory birds have adapted to life in temperate forests, especially owls such as this European eagle owl (Bubo bubo). These hunters depend largely on rodents for food.*

Below: *Trees provide safe nesting sites, especially for birds such as woodpeckers that can create their own nest holes. Here a great spotted woodpecker (Dendrocopos major) chisels into bark.*

TIPS FOR OBSERVING WOODLAND BIRDS
• Spring is a good time to spot woodland species, before the trees are covered in foliage, providing concealment for birds.
• In summer, woodland trees teem with invertebrates, which attract insectivorous birds in search of prey.
• Stand quietly in wooded areas and listen. Hidden among foliage, woodland birds use song to announce their presence to others. Such species are as frequently detected by sound as by sight.

Typical sightings in gardens with or near wooded areas, depending on location:
• Woodpeckers
• Finches
• Owls
• Warblers

There are barren years when the trees do not produce as many cones as usual, forcing the birds to abandon their regular haunts and seek food elsewhere, including in gardens. These unpredictable movements, known as irruptions, occur when birds such as waxwings suddenly appear in large numbers outside their normal range, searching for alternative sources of food. They later disappear just as suddenly as they arrived, and may not return again for many years.

Right: *Deciduous woodlands offer an ideal habitat for birds during the warm months of the year, providing a variety of food, excellent cover and a variety of nesting sites. Selective planting can help to recreate these conditions in your garden to attract woodland species. During the winter months, life here can become much harsher. Once the leaves have fallen, the birds will be much more conspicuous, and food is likely to be scarce.*

1 Wood warbler
2 Hobby
3 Redstart
4 Treecreeper
5 Tawny owl
6 Blackcap
7 Jay
8 Great spotted
  woodpecker
9 Pheasant
10 Song thrush

AQUATIC BIRDS

Some birds are drawn to gardens with or near ponds and streams because of feeding opportunities, while others seek sanctuary from would-be predators in these surroundings. Aquatic species can be attracted to your garden by the presence of even a small water feature, such as a pond or bog.

A wide variety of birds haunt streams, ponds and lakes, but not all are easy to observe because of their camouflage. The dense plant growth often found by water also provides concealment.

FINDING FOOD
Many predatory birds hunt in wetland habitats including garden ponds, swooping low over the water to seize fish by day or even at night. Some fish-eating birds, notably kingfishers (Alcedinidae), dive to seize their prey, which they may feed to their young in nest sites built into the banks of streams. Other hunters rely on different strategies to catch food. Herons (Ardeidae) lurk by the water's edge and seize fish that swim in range of their sharp, powerful bills. Rails (Rallidae) often forage by slow-flowing or still water with well-established reed beds, but these birds are shy by nature. Their mottled plumage and slim body shape make them hard to spot.

NESTING
Some birds are drawn to ponds, bogs or streams in gardens not so much by food but by the nesting opportunities there.

Below: *Moorhens (Gallinula chloropus) are more commonly seen by the water's edge than in open water. Long toes spread their weight as they walk across boggy ground.*

Above: *Kingfishers (Alcedo atthis) may venture into gardens with ponds in search of fish and other prey. Despite their bright colours, they are difficult to spot.*

Swallows (*Hirundo rustica*) collect damp mud from the water's edge to make their nests, and may also catch midges flying above the water surface. Many birds that actually nest by ponds and streams, such as ducks and moorhens, seek seclusion when breeding. They hide their nest away, or make it hard to reach by choosing a spot surrounded by water.

Swans and geese have been known to nest by large ponds in gardens. Mute swans (*Cygnus olor*) construct large nests, which restricts their choice of sites. Both sexes defend the nest ferociously. These largish birds are capable of inflicting painful blows with their wings on intruders, so be careful not to venture too close.

Above: *Lapwings (Vanellus vanellus) are sometimes seen in gardens near marshland. These birds are also known as peewits because of the sound of their calls.*

Right: *Reed beds or dense plant growth by the edge of ponds and streams in parks and gardens provide cover for aquatic birds. The slender shape of some freshwater birds allows them to move easily through thick vegetation, avoiding detection. Fortunately, birds swimming into open water will be much easier to spot.*

TIPS FOR OBSERVING AQUATIC BIRDS
• Patience is essential when watching aquatic birds, as many are shy and easily frightened away.
• Plant cover can make birdwatching difficult, but can also provide concealment for birdwatchers.
• Great care must always be taken near water. If you have a water feature in your garden, you may need to install steps to ensure children will not be in danger if they are drawn to the water's edge.

Typical sightings in gardens with or near ponds, lakes or streams, depending on location:
• Coots and moorhens
• Kingfishers
• Herons
• Ducks
• Geese and swans

1 Jackdaws
2 Starlings
3 Magpie
4 Pigeons
5 Black-headed gulls
6 Coots
7 Mallards
8 Tufted ducks
9 Mute swan
10 Wigeons
11 Pintails
12 Wood duck
13 Goldeneyes
14 House sparrow

WATCHING BIRDS

Thanks to their widespread distribution, birds can be seen in virtually any locality, even in the centre of cities. You don't need any special equipment to watch birds, but a pair of binoculars will help you to gain a better insight into avian behaviour, by allowing you to study birds at close range.

Observing the birds that visit your garden can give hours of pleasure. It will also allow you to build up a detailed picture of the species that frequent your area. You may be surprised at the variety of visitors. Some species visit on a daily basis, others only at certain times of year. As you become an experienced birdwatcher, you will become attuned to seasonal changes that occur through the year, as birds moult, court a mate, nest and raise their families, and as migrants depart for warmer climes in autumn and return again in spring.

Birds may be observed at any time of day, with the early morning being a prime time of feeding activity. You may be able to observe bird behaviour from behind the cover of tall vegetation in the garden, or from the house, particularly if you position a bird table or feeder nearby. Alternatively you could construct your own hide.

GETTING A GOOD VIEW
Binoculars can be purchased from bird reserves, camera shops and similar outlets, but it is important to test them before

Above: *Binoculars provide a close-up view of birds, allowing you to observe details of anatomy, plumage and also behaviour that cannot be seen with the naked eye. They will also help you spot shy species.*

deciding which model to buy, particularly as they vary significantly in price. When buying binoculars, you need to consider not only the power of magnification, but also how closely they can be focused, especially as you are going to use them at home, where the bird table is likely to be relatively close. Of course, you can also take them on birdwatching ventures farther afield, to local parks, woods or wetlands for example. There you will be able to observe different birds and probably a greater variety of species than can be seen at home.

FIELDSCOPES
As well as binoculars, dedicated bird-watchers often use birding telescopes, called fieldscopes. These are ideal for use indoors or in hides as they can be mounted in various ways, using either a clamp fitting or a tripod. Fieldscopes are equipped with lenses similar to those in binoculars, but are more suited to long-term use, when you are watching a nest or the bird table for example, as you do not have to keep

---

DRAWING BIRDS FOR REFERENCE

1 Sketching birds is relatively straight-forward if you follow this procedure. Start by drawing an egg shape for the body, with a smaller egg above, which will become the head, and another to form the rump. A centre line through the head circle will form the basis for the bill. Now add circles and lines to indicate the position of the wings and tail. Add lines for the legs and then sketch in the feet and claws.

3 Coloured pencils will allow you to add more detail after you have rubbed out any unwanted pencil markings.

2 Use an indelible fine-line felt-tip pen to ink in the shape of the bird that you have drawn previously in pencil, avoiding the unwanted construction lines.

4 If you take a number of prepared head shapes with you into the field, you can fill in the detail quickly and easily, enabling you to identify birds later.

holding the scope while waiting for birds to appear. Instead, set up the scope so it is trained on the nest or feeder, then simply be patient until the birds appear.

MAKING NOTES

When observing birds either in the garden or farther afield, it is always useful to have a notebook handy to write down details and make sketches. When sketching, proceed from a few quick pencil lines to a more finished portrait as time allows. Water-soluble pencils are helpful for colouring sketches, as the colours can be spread using water and a small paintbrush.

If you spot a bird you cannot identify, jot down the details quickly in your notebook. Note any sound the bird makes, and also its colours and markings. Notice the length of neck and legs, and the shape of the bill. Assess the bird's size in relation to familiar species, and try to decide which family you think it belongs to. Your notes can then be compared with a field guide or another source of information to identify the bird.

Above: *Taking notes will enable you to build a comprehensive picture of all the birds that visit your garden at different times of year. Note the date and time, and the species and gender of birds if you know them.*

Above: *To get a really close-up view, you can buy a special camera for installing inside a nest box. This provides a wonderful opportunity to observe behaviour without disturbing either the chicks or their parents.*

MAKING A TEMPORARY HIDE

1 Making a hide doesn't need specialized equipment – just a large cardboard box, paints, stakes and a little creativity.

2 Open out the cardboard box and paint it. The pattern or colour is not important; your body shape will be hidden behind it.

3 Preparing the hide can be great fun and is something that the whole family or friends and neighbours can join in with.

4 To support the cardboard, drive a few stakes into the ground until they are firm enough to support the weight of the hide.

5 Hides are traditionally made of dull-coloured material, some with military-style camouflage. In the case of a garden hide, the colour is rarely important. Gardens are often full of extreme contrast, and so why not design a colourful hide that children will love to make?

ATTRACTING BIRDS TO YOUR GARDEN

Birds are a delight in the garden at all times of year. In spring and summer their singing provides pleasure, while in winter their colourful plumage helps to brighten dull days. Urban and suburban gardens can be havens for wild birds, especially if you put out food and water. Birds will soon come to know it as a food source and it will become a regular stopping-off point. If nest boxes are provided, birds may well set up home too. There is immense pleasure to be had from knowing that you are helping wild bird populations to thrive and from watching the species which come to feed.

Left: *In spring, the provision of foods and also nesting materials may help many types of birds to rear their young successfully.*

Above: *Feeders containing different foods placed at varying heights in the garden will help to attract a greater variety of birds.*

Above: *House sparrows are among the bird species that benefit from the provision of seeds and nuts in feeders.*

Above: *Planting shrubs such as holly will attract berry-eating birds in winter when they are most vulnerable to the elements.*

BIRDS IN DOMESTIC GARDENS

Birds have always lived around people. As human settlements developed, birds were happy to move into buildings which provided cosy roosts and also food scraps. The art of domesticating wild birds has a long history, though in the early days this was generally because birds were seen as a source of food.

Pigeons were probably the first birds to be domesticated, because they were good to eat, their food requirements were simple and they were prolific breeders. Both the Egyptians and the Romans built towers for pigeons on their rooftops, fitted with internal ledges on which the birds could roost and nest.

The Native Americans had a different reason for inviting wild birds to share their homes. They used bottle-shaped gourds to make nest boxes for purple martins, whose massed presence helped to deter vultures from raiding the meat left out to

Below: Birds will make use of even the smallest urban spaces. This compact courtyard area contains a small tree, a mixture of flowers, herbs, vegetables and climbers, and an open-fronted nest box postitioned in a sheltered place on the wall.

dry in the sun. Nest boxes made from gourds are still used in North America today, and east of the Rocky Mountains the entire purple martin population lives in sites provided by humans.

HISTORY OF BEFRIENDING BIRDS
It was not until fairly recently that people began to encourage birds into their gardens purely for the joy of watching them. Gilbert White noted in his diary for June of 1782 that his brother Thomas had nailed up scallop shells under the eaves of his house, with the hollow side facing upward against the wall, for house martins to nest in. This strategy proved very successful, as the martins began to move in almost immediately.

In the early 19th century the pioneering naturalist Charles Waterton, who turned his estate in Yorkshire, England, into a nature

Above: *Barn swallows are among the species that establish their own homes on buildings, forming mud nests under eaves.*

reserve, developed stone nest boxes for barn owls and built a tower for jackdaws, similar to a garden dovecote.

Baron von Berlepsch was an early popularizer of nest boxes in Britain. During the late 19th century he spent much time experimenting, eventually originating a design that replicated a natural woodpecker's nest, consisting of a section of tree trunk that had been hollowed out at one end, an entry hole that went into this chamber from the front, and a wooden lid with an attachment for fixing at the back. This simple rustic design was effective, and similar nest boxes are still used today.

Since then, designs for nest boxes and birdhouses have burgeoned, ranging from purely functional structures to ornate miniature versions of their owners' homes.

PLANNING A GARDEN FOR BIRDS
If you wish to make your garden a haven for wild birds, it's important to take the birds' needs into account throughout the planning and planting process. A long-established garden or backyard, with mature trees, flowering plants and a diverse selection of shrubs, surrounded by a thick

Above: Pyracantha, also known as firethorn, shelters birds from the elements. In autumn the scarlet berries provide food.

Above: Sunflowers provide blazing colour in gardens, and many types of birds feed on the oil-rich seeds.

hedge, is ideal, and if your house is old it probably has lots of nooks and crannies in its walls which are good for roosting.

Not everyone is lucky enough to have such perfect conditions, but if you are considering making some changes, it is often not difficult to improve on what you already have. An urban garden may not get as great a variety of visitors as a rural one, but it has some advantages. The city air is warmer so there is less threat of frost. Town birds are also used to co-existing with people, so will tolerate close observation.

CHOOSING PLANTS FOR BIRDS

You need varied vegetation that will attract insects, which will be needed once the birds are nesting. The best plants are ones that will produce plenty of nuts, berries and seeds. Birds need cover for protection, so hedges are perfect. Shrubs such as hawthorn and pyracantha are a good choice, as they provide shelter from wind and rain, and for nesting. In the autumn their berries make fine pickings. If possible, keep one part of your garden wild. If you can find room for a tree, plant a native

species that the birds are adapted to. Shrubs such as elder produce luscious berries which are enjoyed by dozens of species. A fruit tree such as apple or pear will benefit both you and the birds.

Many border plants attract bees, butterflies and moths, which the birds feed on in the summer, as well as providing seeds in the autumn. Good choices include

cornflowers, Michaelmas daisies, evening primroses, poppies, snapdragons and, best of all, sunflowers, whose seeds are irresistible to nuthatches and finches.

A lawn is ideal for observation. Water the grass regularly in dry weather to bring the worms to the surface. Let the grass grow long around trees – the weeds will provide seed for finches.

Right: This garden is ideal for attracting birds. It contains shrubs and hedges for protection, a variety of flowering plants for seeds and insects, and a lawn where you can sit and observe your feathered friends.

STRUCTURES TO ATTRACT BIRDS

By providing a range of feeding, nesting and watering structures and distributing them around the garden, you can attract a wide range of bird species. Tables, feeders, nest boxes, birdhouses, roosts and birdbaths are also beautiful structures in their own right, and will enhance any garden.

Seeing birds regularly visiting your garden is enormously rewarding, and the inclusion of a few simple structures will ensure that your garden is attractive to birds.

BIRD TABLES

A bird table is the most obvious and effortless way to attract birds into your garden, and winter is the best time to set one up, when the natural food supply is scarce and the ground too hard for the birds to penetrate with their beaks.

Your bird table may be supported on a post or brackets or it may hang from a branch. It needs a roof to keep the rain off and a rim to prevent the food from being blown away. Other additions, such as a scrap basket, seed tube or water port, may be incorporated into the design.

FEEDERS

Pet and garden suppliers stock a huge range of feeders for different types of nuts or seeds. These are useful, as seeds are otherwise easily scattered and blown away. Some of the designs that are readily available are squirrel-proof. Mesh feeders are designed to dispense nuts, while feeders made of plastic tubing are designed for seeds.

There are also feeders that are designed to be stuck on to a window. Provided you don't mind the birds making a mess of your window and walls, these will enable you to study your avian visitors at close proximity. As an alternative to buying feeders, you could try making your own, using the ideas for constructing inexpensive versions given later in this book.

NEST BOXES

Simple nest boxes are generally designed to hang from a tree or wall. Ready-crafted boxes may be made of plain wood, preserved with creosote, or rustic-looking hollowed-out logs fitted with roofs. It is often best to choose a box that is designed with a specific type of bird in mind. The all-important factor is the size of the entry hole to admit nesting birds.

If you are building your own nest box, wood is probably the best material to use, though if it is thinner than 15mm (⅝ in) it may warp and won't offer much insulation. Old floorboards are a good source of timber if you can get them, as they are well seasoned. Although softwood is easier to work with, hardwoods such as oak are longer lasting. Exterior or marine plywood can be used in any situation.

Wherever possible, use the wood with the grain running vertically. This will help the rain to drain off. Glue all joints before screwing them together, or use galvanized nails, which are better for damp conditions as they will not rust easily.

The most important thing is that the box should be warm and dry, but not so airtight that condensation becomes a problem. Some birdhouse-builders drill small holes high on the sides of the box to create ventilation and so lessen condensation. There is still plenty of room for improvement with traditional designs and materials, so feel free to experiment.

BIRDHOUSES

These are ornamental versions of nest boxes. They have a dual purpose, providing a safe nesting site for birds while also satisfying your aesthetic need to decorate the garden. Designs ranging from plain to highly ornamental are available from bird reserves, garden and pet shops, and are usually post-mounted. The important thing to check when buying a birdhouse is that

Left: Many types of roofed bird tables can be purchased quite cheaply. Better still, you can construct your own.

Above: *A post-mounted dovecote provides a sheltering place for pigeons, and also makes an attractive addition to the garden. Choose a site that is protected from prevailing winds, rain and too much sun.*

it will fulfil the requirements of the type of birds you want to attract. Each of the projects featured here indicates the typical inhabitants that it is designed for, although you also need to consider local breeds.

ROOSTS

Most birds sleep at night, with their beaks hidden under one shoulder, their heads tucked in and their feathers puffed up to keep them warm. They need regular roosting places that are protected from the elements and from predators. Birds will often use nest boxes for this purpose, so don't despair if your house or box has not been selected for a nest site – it is still probably being used as a roost or shelter, so it will be doing an important job, and possibly saving birds' lives in severe weather conditions, including icy temperatures and storms.

BIRDBATHS

Birds get most of the water that they require from their food, but they still need supplies to supplement this. Seed-eaters, for example, need plenty of drinking water

Right: *These cosy woven roosts provide a place for birds to sleep or shelter from inclement weather. They are inexpensive and look the part tucked between the branches of a tree.*

to compensate for the lack of moisture in their diet. Most birds drink by dipping their beaks into the water, then tilting their heads back, though pigeons are able to suck water up through their bills. Because birds don't sweat, they need another way to keep cool: they lose moisture by opening their mouths and panting.

The main purpose of providing water for birds is not for drinking but for bathing. They need to keep their feathers in good condition for both flight and insulation, and baths are just as important in winter as they are in summer. If their plumage is not

Above: *Birds need regular bathing to keep their feathers in good condition. During winter, break any ice regularly and never put antifreeze into the water.*

properly maintained they will not survive the cold winter nights. So in frosty weather, it is vital to check daily that your birdbath has not frozen over.

You will find that a design for a birdbath with an ingenious anti-freezing device has been included in this book. It is important never to put antifreeze or salt into the water, as this can kill birds.

FEEDING TIMES AND BOX LOCATIONS

When providing tables, feeders and nest boxes in your garden, it helps to understand birds' daily rituals and preferred feeding times and food types so that you can get the best results. It is also important to choose appropriate sites for your nest boxes, to maximize their safe use and minimize aggression.

In the United Kingdom, common feathered visitors include the blackbird, house sparrow, blue tit, robin, chaffinch, greenfinch, magpie, tree sparrow, collared dove, wren and dunnock, while in mainland Europe, colourful species such as bluethroats, bee-eaters and rollers may also pay regular visits to gardens.

Migration makes for interesting changes. At the end of winter some of your regulars will return to the countryside or migrate to more suitable breeding grounds. You may suddenly notice the odd bird that has never visited your garden before: it may be looking for food to fuel its long journey, or it may have been swept off course. In the winter there will be many visitors looking for food, but during spring the battle for territory will begin, limiting the number of birds in your garden.

DAILY RITUALS

Birds wake up just before dawn, when they sing with great gusto. This dawn chorus involves many different species and lasts about half an hour, heralding the daylight.

Breakfast is the best time to observe birds' behaviour, as they often quarrel over food. You will soon start to notice their

Below: *Tits enjoy eating from bird tables, and their bold, perky behaviour is always entertaining to watch. The black chest stripe shows that this is a great tit.*

pecking order. The first birds to visit the garden may be blackbirds and thrushes, who come to scan the lawn in search of worms and soft grubs. They hunt quietly and carefully, pausing between hops and watching for their prey. Starlings, who arrive later, appear to stab here and there at the ground until they find a tasty morsel.

Birds have two important daily activities. The first is to find and eat food, which is done throughout the day; the second is to take care of their feathers. These must be kept in perfect condition for both flight and insulation. After bathing comes preening. Birds collect fatty oil from

Above: *Though wonderful to watch, fledglings must learn to survive, so any human intervention is not a good idea.*

the preen gland at their rump and smear it over the feathers before stroking them back into place.

WHAT TO FEED WHEN

Birds will quickly come to depend on your support, so once you have enticed them into the garden, you need to make sure that they continue to thrive. It is important to maintain supplies of food and water through the winter. Birds will appreciate fresh food on the table early in the morning, or at least at a regular time. If you go away, fill your feeder and leave fat balls to sustain the birds until your return.

Birds need food with a high fat and carbohydrate content, as they may lose up to 10 per cent of their body weight overnight in bad weather, so suet, cheese, bacon rinds and dripping will help them build up their energy reserves. Crows, starlings, tits and woodpeckers are particularly attracted to bacon rind, fat and cheese.

The shape of a bird's beak roughly indicates its diet. Finches have hard, thick beaks which are designed to crack and crush. They feed mostly on grain and seed.

Above: *Take care that nest boxes are mounted high enough on trees so that there is no danger of animals, such as cats, reaching the box, especially when there is a ledge attached to the outside.*

Above: *Feeders containing either seeds or peanuts can be used to attract house sparrows (*Passer domesticus*) and goldfinches (*Carduelis carduelis*) to your garden. Both have considerable agility.*

Robins and wrens, with their slender, soft beaks, eat caterpillars, grubs and other insects. Gulls, starlings and blackbirds have general-purpose bills, which allow them to eat a bit of everything. Whatever the species, they all enjoy culinary variety, and kitchen scraps are always welcome.

Bread is the food most commonly put out for birds, but it is not particularly good for them. If you do give it, soak it first in water or, even better, fat. In fact any dried foods – especially fruits – should be soaked. Never give birds desiccated coconut or uncooked rice. These swell up in their stomachs and can kill. Kitchen leftovers such as baked potatoes and spaghetti are good: they are soft enough for birds to eat but difficult for them to pick up whole to fly away with. Keep some of your windfall apples and pears in storage until winter, when they will be most welcome on the bird table. Don't worry if birds don't visit your feeder immediately – it may take up to two weeks for a bird table to be accepted by the neighbourhood bird population.

SITING AND MAINTAINING BOXES

When choosing sites for your birdhouse and other accessories, there are several points to bear in mind. Will birds be left in peace there? It's not a good idea to erect a table, nest box or birdbath where children play or where the pet cat tends to prowl. Birds must have shelter nearby to which they can flee if danger threatens.

Place nest boxes so that they are protected from the prevailing wind, rain and strong sunlight. If you put a box on a tree, notice which side of the trunk has more algae growing. This will be the wet side, so place the box on the opposite side. If you angle the box slightly forward it will give more shelter to the occupants.

Be careful not to damage the tree by banging nails into it; special securing devices are available for this purpose. Boxes don't have to be rigidly mounted, as long as they are secure. Boxes that hang from a wire or string work well and may offer better protection from predators such as cats and squirrels.

The best time of year to put up nest boxes is in the autumn. They can then act as roosts during the winter and be ready for early spring when the birds start choosing their breeding sites. During the winter you can insulate them with cotton, straw or wood shavings for roosting birds, but remember to remove this padding before nesting begins in the spring. Cleaning out birdhouses and nest boxes after the breeding season is very important. Wash the boxes out with mild disinfectant diluted with plenty of water. Always wear rubber gloves to protect yourself from any parasites that may be lurking inside.

If birds do nest in your boxes, don't be tempted to sneak a look – the shock may cause the mother to abandon her brood or the young chicks to leave their nest prematurely. The best help you can give nesting birds is to leave them undisturbed.

AVOIDING AGGRESSION

To discourage fighting, don't overdo the number of boxes you set up in your garden. Robins and tits can be very territorial and aggressive with other members of their own species. A bird's territory is a fixed area that it will defend for either feeding or breeding or both. If a bird does not manage to establish its territory it will be unable to nest or breed, and may even die of hunger. The gestures birds make to communicate with each other are known as displays.

To show aggression, a bird will puff up its feathers, raise its wings and point its beak at its rival to look menacing. To show submission, a bird will crouch down and sleek its feathers in. Fights most commonly occur when a newcomer arrives in the territory of an established group, and the stranger's status needs to be evaluated. Occasionally, birds will fight to the death.

Below: *Water can be provided for birds in small gardens by hanging up bowls or attaching containers or troughs to a wall.*

GARDEN MENACES

In the last hundred years or so, birds generally have been threatened by changes to or loss of the wild habitats where they feed and breed. In gardens and parks, feeding and nesting birds may be at constant risk from menaces such as cats, squirrels and predatory birds from hawks to magpies.

Most of the songbirds that visit your garden die young through either predation or natural causes, such as cold. The average life expectancy for an adult songbird is less than two years. This compares to a potential lifespan of nine years for tits, a dozen years for robins and sparrows, and up to 20 years in the case of larger species such as blackbirds and starlings.

It is not only winters that are perilous; summers claim as many lives, and breeding time is as dangerous as migration. If you encourage birds to visit your garden, it is also your duty to protect them, especially from 'unnatural' predators such as cats.

PREDATORY BIRDS

Birds of prey such as sparrowhawks and to a lesser extent, kestrels, can be a danger to garden birds. Sparrowhawks approach fast and low, appearing as if out of nowhere to seize small birds in their talons. Kestrels hover in the air and then drop like a stone to capture their prey. However the latter

Below: The jay (Garrulus glandarius), a shy woodland bird, is among the members of the crow family known to raid the nests of songbirds to take eggs and chicks.

species is less of a danger since kestrels usually hunt in open country, and nowadays over motorways. In the 1950s and 1960s, populations of sparrowhawks and other predatory birds declined due to use of the powerful pesticide DDT, but they have risen again since DDT has been banned in most countries. Scientists estimate that a breeding pair of sparrowhawks needs to kill 2,000 small birds to raise their family.

Members of the crow family, known as corvids, are a danger to nesting birds worldwide. Crows, rooks, jays, jackdaws and especially magpies raid songbirds' nests to steal eggs and nestlings. Magpies in particular conduct systematic raids, returning to raided nests after a suitable interval to take replacement clutches. These habits make magpies and their kin unpopular with songbird-lovers. However, there is no hard scientific evidence that predation by corvids has any long-term effect on populations of songbirds.

Providing thick cover for nesting birds, such as dense shrubs and hedges, increases their chance of survival. You could also put wire mesh over the nest entrance to exclude corvids while allowing small nesting birds to enter. This is best done once the eggs are laid and the birds

Above: Sparrowhawks (Accipiter nisus) are bold enough to hunt in gardens. Their broad wings and long tail make these predators speedy and also agile.

start incubating, otherwise there may be a real danger that the parent birds could abandon the nest.

Woodpeckers (Picidae) have been known to drill into nest boxes with their long, sharp bills, or simply reach inside to steal the nestlings. Enclosed nest boxes for birds such as tits can be protected by backing the nest hole with a metal plate drilled with a similar-sized hole.

RATS, MICE AND SQUIRRELS

Food left on the ground encourages rats and mice, which will take every opportunity to steal and eat birds' eggs. The rodents are attracted to surplus food, so don't put out too much at any one time. If you store bird food outdoors do so in a strong, sealed container. This will also help to prevent the food from being spoiled by moisture.

The grey squirrel is a menace to songbirds both in North America and now in parts of Europe, where it was introduced in the 1800s. With their keen intelligence, acrobatic skills and sharp teeth and claws, these rodents are a menace on bird feeders

Above: *A grey squirrel displays the acrobatic skills that make it a menace at bird tables. Feeders that are enclosed by a stout wire cage can help thwart such raids.*

and tables. Mounting tables on smooth, slippery posts, which can be made from plastic drainpipes, will prevent squirrels and also cats and rats from clambering up to steal food. A number of squirrel-resistant feeders can also be purchased nowadays. These usually consist of a feeder enclosed by a strong wire cage designed to admit small birds but exclude squirrels. However, these rodents are very destructive, and have been known to bear away the whole feeder, so they can attack it at their leisure! Some bird-lovers resort to providing the squirrels with their own supply of nuts in the hope they will leave bird feeders alone.

Grey squirrels not only steal birds' food but also raid nest boxes to steal eggs and young birds. A metal plate around the entrance hole will help to prevent squirrels from enlarging the hole by gnawing. Tree-mounted boxes can be fitted with smooth protective collars of plastic projecting from the entrance hole, or be mounted on a slippery backplate. Some people take the precaution of building an internal ledge underneath the entrance hole of the box, so that the nestlings have somewhere to hide should a predator trespass.

CATS
The biggest threat to garden birds is not wild mammals but the much-loved domestic cat. In the UK the cat population exceeds 7 million, of which at least 2 million are feral cats living in the wild and hunting for survival. Scientists estimate that between 30 million and a staggering 75 million birds are killed by cats each year in the UK alone. Since the higher figure only represents each cat killing a bird every month or so, it is certainly credible. Unlike magpies and squirrels, domestic cats kill adult birds, which is more likely to have an impact on bird populations.

If you have a cat, put a bell on its collar to alert the birds to its presence, or keep it inside while the birds are at their morning feed. Alternatively, a pet dog let out at the same time will help to deter visiting cats. To prevent cats from killing in your garden, position feeders and bird tables out in the open, where felines cannot use the cover of shrubs to stalk their prey. Make sure nest boxes are sited in places cats cannot reach. You can also put chicken wire or nylon mesh around a box, as long as there is room for the birds to get in and out.

PROTECTION FOR WILD BIRDS
In every part of the world there are organizations that are involved with the protection and conservation of wild birds, and all are happy to answer queries. Contact local groups for information about the birds in your area.

In many areas including Britain, other European Union countries and North America, it is against the law to kill, injure or capture wild birds, or remove or destroy their eggs. Contact your local police or a

Above: *Mice and even rats can be surprisingly acrobatic, raiding food sources high above the ground with the help of a nearby shrub or tree.*

conservation organization, such as the RSPB in Britain, if you see or suspect someone is killing or trapping wild birds or stealing eggs. We can all play a part in helping to ensure that these remarkable little creatures survive in all their variety, despite losses to their natural habitats.

Below: *The domestic cat's natural agility and hunting instincts make it a formidable predator. Fitting a bell will alert birds to the cat's presence before harm is done.*

FEEDING BIRDS

The simplest way to attract birds to your garden, or even window box, is to put out food for them, particularly during the months of winter when natural foods become much scarcer. However, you may provide appropriate food for garden birds throughout the year if you wish.

Whatever feeding method you decide upon, be consistent. A wasted journey to an empty bird table uses a bird's precious energy supply, especially as winter progresses and food becomes more difficult to find. Ideally, feed birds twice a day in winter: once in the early morning and again in the early afternoon.

In spring and summer, feeding can still be helpful, but do follow rules for safety and hygiene. Do not use peanuts unless they are in a mesh container; this will prevent the larger pieces, which can choke baby birds, from being removed. In summer, avoid fat cakes; the fat will melt and become very messy, and can also glue birds' beaks together.

Below: *Roofed bird tables will keep birds – and the food provided – dry in wet weather. This one was made from pieces of fallen wood collected from the forest floor.*

Above: *Lard cakes studded with seeds appeal to many varieties of bird, including this starling (Sturnus vulgaris).*

Above: *Ground feeders provide food for birds that forage for seeds at ground level, such as dunnocks, finches and thrushes.*

BIRD TABLES

Ideally, a bird table should be placed approximately 2–3m (6½–10ft) from a bush or tree, which can provide safety for birds in case of danger, and at least 5m (16½ft) from the house. Many birds are nervous of open sites, but equally they can have accidents flying into house windows, and may be scared away by the movement of people inside the house. Window stickers featuring birds of prey are available which, when stuck to the window panes, indicate the presence of an otherwise invisible surface and will deter smaller birds from flying too close to the house.

A bird table gives you a clear view of feeding birds, and offers the birds some protection against predators and the elements. Use wood that has not been treated with wood preservative if you are making your own table. A roof will keep the food and the birds dry. If you don't make a roof, drill a few holes in the floor of the table for drainage. A small lip around the edge of the food table can prevent lighter food items from being blown away by wind. The bird table must be cleaned from time to

Above: *A wire mesh around the food source prevents the birds from extracting whole peanuts. This is important during the nesting season because young nestlings and fledglings can choke on whole nuts.*

time and any food that is past its best should be removed. An adequate supply of water should be provided all year round, but this can be as simple as a bowl of water placed on the surface of the table, or a separate facility.

GROUND STATIONS

Some birds, such as dunnocks and song thrushes, are habitual ground feeders. Pheasants, finches, buntings and turtle doves may also be attracted to ground feeding stations – a wooden or plastic hopper secured to a strong base. Place a ground feeder away from the bird table, so that the food is not contaminated by droppings from the birds above.

HANGING FEEDERS

Some species, such as tits, that are adapted to feeding in trees will benefit from a more challenging feeder. Blue and great tits can cling upside-down from various types of hanging feeders, and may be joined by siskins and nuthatches. Many types of feeder are available, or you can make or adapt your own, using the projects

Above: *Seed balls and strings of nuts are a welcome supplement to the meagre diet which is available to many birds in winter. Remember to keep a supply of fresh water on hand, as dried food does not contain enough natural moisture.*

shown later in this book. Some foods are also suitable for hanging without a feeder, for example, peanuts in their shells, half coconuts, popcorn garlands and also fat cakes on strings.

Right: *Hanging feeders offer an easy challenge to species with natural acrobatic abilities, such as tits (Paridae). In this way, suspended feeders can provide an added spectacle at the bird table.*

WHAT TO FEED BIRDS

As warm-blooded or endothermic animals, birds have to expend considerable energy maintaining an even body temperature. This process is particularly costly in terms of energy in cold weather, so when temperatures drop toward freezing point, providing food for birds is especially important.

Birds, like many wild creatures, enjoy a range of foods, many of which are easy to obtain. Leftovers are a valuable but variable commodity, so don't rely on them. Seed is useful and can be supplemented with such items as pinhead oatmeal or porridge oats, sultanas, shredded suet and toasted breadcrumbs. Other popular items for the bird table include canned sweetcorn and fresh fruit, broken into pieces.

The more different food types can be left in different positions and types of feeder, the better. Whatever you decide to place out for the birds, make sure that you stick to natural foods, rather than chemically altered or processed items, such as margarine. Keep food fresh – only leave out enough for a day or two – and never allow food or feeding debris to accumulate because it can rapidly spread disease.

FAT PRODUCTS
The best types of base for fat cakes are lamb and beef fats, either in natural form or as processed suet. Because these are

Below: *A live feeder can help a variety of birds, including robins, that rely on prey to feed their young.*

Above: *Half a coconut filled with seeds and melted fat is a good way of providing supplementary food for small, clinging birds.*

hard, they do not melt too readily in warm weather, which can potentially glue birds' beaks together. Specialist manufacturers add enticements to their fat cakes but you can easily make your own at home with a mixture of seeds, fruits and nuts following the recipes on the next pages.

LIVE FOOD
Some birds, robins in particular, can benefit from supplements of live food, such as waxworms and mealworms, particularly during the late winter period when food is scarce and their breeding cycle begins. The worms can easily be purchased from pet shops or by mail order, and can be placed on tables or in specialist feeders.

SEEDS AND GRAINS
Use best-quality seeds from a reliable source, not sweepings or waste seeds as these are neither of interest nor of nutritional value to the birds. Black sunflower seeds rather than the striped variety are the favoured food of many

species. The skins of this type are the thinnest of all sunflower varieties, making them easy for the birds to open. All types of sunflower seeds are safe for young birds to eat, so they may be offered all year round. Canary seeds, melon seeds, hemp seeds, small wheat, kibbled and flaked maize, corn kernels and oatmeal are all good sources of nutrition. The exact mixture of seeds you put out can be fine-tuned to attract particular species of birds to your garden. You could consult a specialist catalogue for more details.

UNSALTED PEANUTS
Buy only high-quality 'safe nuts', marked as such by the Bird Food Standards Association or other reputable body, to ensure that the nuts are free from lethal toxins. Whole peanuts are best avoided during the nesting season because of the danger they pose to nestlings. They should be chopped, if left on a table, or placed in a mesh peanut feeder from which adult birds can take only small fragments.

Below: *A string of peanuts provides nutrition and can also look attractive if hung in a well-chosen site such as this.*

COMMON BIRD FOODS

The variety of seed and other food supplements that are commonly available in the shops for birds has increased vastly in the last few years. All have their own merits and will be preferred by different types of birds. Trial and error will show what goes down best with the feathered population in your local area, but here are some ideas.

Mixed seed
Consists of various seed types for a wide range of birds, but can be of variable quality.

Black sunflower seed
More commonly known as the 'oil sunflower', this seed – as its name suggests – is rich in oil and ideal for winter-feeding a range of garden birds.

Striped sunflower seed
This type of seed has a lower oil content than the black variety, and is useful in the spring when natural foods become more abundant.

Niger
Sometimes called thistle seed, this tiny black birdseed, cultivated in Asia and Africa, is high in calories and oil content, and is quickly devoured, especially by finches of various types.

Grain
Consists of any commercially grown crops in the grass family, including wheat, millet, maize and oats.

Bread
This is eaten by many species. Brown bread is best, but whatever type you offer, make sure that it has been thoroughly soaked to avoid the danger of it swelling in birds' stomachs.

Dried and fresh fruit
Always popular, dried fruit should be soaked as for bread. Fresh fruits, especially pears and apples, are enjoyed by blackcaps and thrushes. These fruits are particularly useful in winter.

Half-coconut
Hanging on a string, a half-coconut offers good value for money and provides delightful entertainment when acrobatic tits come to feed. Once the flesh has been stripped, the shell can be filled with wholesome bird pudding, a mixture of nuts, seeds and melted fat.

Fat ball
A ball of suet into which other dried foodstuffs have been incorporated. It is usually hung in nets or special feeders.

Suet cake
The block type of suet food contains a mixture of seeds that provides a balanced diet for many species. It is ideal for feeding birds when you are away, although the fat content can sometimes attract scavenging mammals, such as rats, to a table.

Fruit suet treats
Mainly for bird tables or feeders, this suet-based cake is best made with moist, dried fruit and peanut granules, and is popular with larger birds.

Dried mealworms
These freeze-dried grubs are an excellent source of protein for carnivorous birds.

Peanuts
In their shells, peanuts can be strung on thread or wire, but don't use multistranded thread as birds may get their feet caught in this. Do ensure the nuts are fresh – mouldy ones produce a toxin which kills many garden birds.

Hazelnuts
Wedged into tree bark, hazelnuts will appeal to nuthatches, which will enjoy hammering them open.

Cheese
Grated cheese is a popular food, especially with robins.

Leftovers
Household foods such as hard-boiled eggs, jacket potatoes, uncooked pastry and stale cake and biscuits are all widely available choices that birds will enjoy. Feel free to experiment, taking care not to offer dehydrated, spicy or very salty foods, as these can be dangerous.

Grit for digestion
Although not actually foodstuffs, grit, sand and gravel aid digestion, particularly for seed-eaters.

Mixed seed

Black sunflower seeds

Niger

Dried fruit

Fresh fruit

Fat ball

Suet cake

Fruit suet treats

Dried mealworms

Peanuts

Cheese

Leftovers

SWEET TREAT

This prettily shaped pudding will look lovely in the garden and make feeding the birds much more fun, especially if you want to interest your children in birdwatching. You can also mould fat puddings in empty yogurt pots, but remember to let the mixture cool before filling.

YOU WILL NEED
75g/3oz lard
pan
shelled nuts
seeds
berries
wooden spoon
string
heart-shaped mould
raisins
dried cranberries
garden wire
wire cutters
bowl of water
ribbon

TYPICAL FEEDERS
starlings
tits
nuthatches
waxwings

Above: *Starlings love sweet foods, and may drive away competing visitors to this treat.*

1 Place 75g/3oz lard in a pan and slowly melt it over a gentle heat. When the lard has completely melted, stir in a generous mixture of shelled nuts, seeds and also berries.

2 Lay a doubled piece of string in the bottom of a mould and spoon in the nut and seed mixture, embedding the string within. Smooth the top of the pudding and leave it to cool completely.

3 Thread raisins and cranberries alternately on to a piece of garden wire long enough to surround the heart pudding. Twist the ends together and soak the wreath in water to plump up the fruit.

4 When the pudding is set, turn it out of the mould and tie the string to the twisted ends of the wire so that the heart is suspended in the middle of the wreath. Tie a ribbon over the join to hide it.

OTHER SWEET TREATS
These simple recipes are designed to bring birds flocking to your garden and ensure a happy and satisfied bird population. For both, you will need a filling made with nuts, seeds and dried fruit, and either museli or cooked rice.

Orange sunrise pudding
Prepare a mixture of muesli, fruit, nuts and seeds for the filling. All these ingredients should be fully soaked to rehydrate before mixing. Cut an orange in half, and remove the flesh to create a hollow. Fill with the mixture.

Bejewelled apple
An apple stuffed with colourful, nutritious goodies is a visual as well as a nourishing feast. Hollow out an apple that is past its best. Fill it with a mixture of cooked rice, seeds, rehydrated dried fruit and berries. Make sure the fruit has been thoroughly rehydrated before adding.

FAT TREAT

When the weather gets colder, garden birds keep warm by eating high-energy foods such as this hanging fat, fruit, seed and peanut snack. The design will suit acrobatic birds such as tits. You could make several and crumble one on to the bird table too, for less agile species.

YOU WILL NEED
packet of suet
pan
wooden spoon
bird seed
raisins
fresh peanuts
aluminium foil
scissors
garden string
yogurt pot or plastic plant pot

TYPICAL FEEDERS
tits
sparrows
finches
starlings
woodpeckers

Below: *When hung from a tree, this tasty fat treat makes a very pretty garden decoration in its own right.*

1 Melt half a packet of suet in the pan. Keep it on the heat until the suet is melted, and stir until the fat goes clear.

2 Take the pan off the heat. Add mixed bird seed, broken-up peanuts and a few raisins. Stir the mixture, then allow it to cool.

3 If you are using a plant pot, cut out a circle of aluminium foil to fit inside the base of the pot to cover the drainage holes.

4 Twist a length of garden string to make a thick cord. Tie a knot at one end. This will prevent the snack falling off when hanging.

5 Hold the knot at the bottom of the pot with the string upright. Now spoon the fat, seed, peanut and raisin mixture into the pot. When the pot is full, firm the mixture down with the back of the spoon. If you have more mix, repeat with another pot.

6 Stand the pot outside to allow the mixture to cool and set. When it has set and is quite hard, remove the snack from the pot by squeezing the pot sides carefully. Peel off the foil base. Now hang the treat from a branch using the loop of string.

FESTIVE TREATS

These treats will bring colour to your garden on dark days of the year, and provide birds with the sustenance they need most in cold weather. The ideas described here will make good presents for friends who are already birdlovers, or they could be the start of an engrossing hobby.

CRANBERRY WREATH

To make this wreath you will need glazed sliced cranberries, a length of wire, garden string and a pretty ribbon. Thread the cranberries on to the wire to form a ring. Twist the ends together and tie a loop of string at the top to hang the wreath. Now add the ribbon tied into a bow at the top.

CRANBERRY TERRINE

This delectable treat is very easy to make. Melt down some lard or white fat in a pan. Place a layer of rehydrated cranberries into the base of an individual oval tin. Slowly pour over just enough melted fat to secure the berries in place. Leave it to cool and set. When set, add more melted fat to form another layer. Allow this to cool and set before adding the final layer of berries, secured with a little more melted fat. Leave it to set, and remove by inverting the pan. Run a little warm water over it to aid release.

NUT AND BERRY LOAF

A festive loaf will delight the birds in midwinter. Soak brown breadcrumbs in water until soft. Mix in rehydrated berries,

seeds and nuts. Grease an individual loaf tin, and add the mixture, pressing down well. Bake in a moderate oven for approximately 15 minutes or until the top is golden-brown and the loaf leaves the sides of the tin. Leave to cool slightly, remove from the tin and cool on a wire rack.

GIFT BASKET

A basket of bird food makes a lovely gift. You will need several different types of food as pictured. Roll plastic pots diagonally in squares of brown paper to form bouquet-like cones. Put a different type of bird food in each. Recipes for additional bird treats could also be included, or a decorative container to hold water.

Above: *A wreath of glazed, sliced cranberries will be appreciated by the feathered community.*

Left: *Bags containing different varieties of bird food make a great gift, packed into an attractive wooden basket.*

A BIRD BORDER

Winter is the period of the year when birds most need our help. A border planted with birds in mind can be a real lifeline at this time, providing a diverse array of foods, including seeds, berries and even the odd overwintering insect among the vegetation. The border will also provide colour throughout the year.

A bird border doesn't have to be wild or overgrown, but can look attractive all year round. There are few absolute rights or wrongs when you plan one, but growing a wide variety of plants to attract wildlife in general will offer garden birds food and shelter, helping them both survive winter and feed their hungry fledglings the following spring. Think of your bird border as a roadside café, a place where birds can feed and rest before moving on.

CHOOSING A SITE

Some species of birds are much more sensitive to disturbance than others, particularly during the nesting season. For this reason it is usually best to set aside a quiet area for a bird border. The ideal backdrop might be a hedge or line of berry-bearing shrubs. If you are planting against a fence or wall, clothing it with climbing plants and shrubs can turn it into a 'living boundary' which may well provide cover and nesting sites. Bird borders can be made on any scale with even a small one proving useful, although the more space and diversity you can devote to such a feature, the more birds will benefit.

Below: The song thrush is an example of a bird species that is carnivorous in the summer but switches to berries and seed during the dormant winter months.

CHOOSING THE RIGHT SPECIES

Depending on where you live, it is often best to include a range of native plants in your border, and you should try to include as many different kinds as possible. In the example shown opposite, a formal backdrop has been created by using a hedge made of yew (*Taxus baccata*), although beech (*Fagus sylvatica*), holly

*Below: Evening primrose (*Oenothera biennis*) flowers attract insects, providing food for birds. Finches also eat the seeds.*

Above: Barberry is an ideal plant to include in a bird border, offering nestlings protection from predators in spring, as well as a rich crop of autumn berries.

(*Ilex aquifolium*) and hornbeam (*Carpinus betulus*) are equally effective, all providing good shelter for birds. If space permits, try a less formal hedge of native shrubs, pruned on only one side in alternate years to provide an excellent source of food and nectar, as well as nesting and shelter.

Trees are also extremely useful, although large forest species – such as oak (*Quercus*) – are often too large for most gardens. If choosing trees for a town garden, make sure you use smaller examples like the ones shown in this design. Mountain ash (*Sorbus aucuparia*), holly (*Ilex aquifolium*) and the crab apple (*Malus* 'Red Sentinel') will provide perches and shelter, and are an excellent food source when in fruit.

A range of shrubs will provide cover from predators and the worst of the weather. Native species might come top of the list, but it is equally important to consider a range of evergreen and deciduous types to give variety and hiding places in winter. The barberry (*Berberis*

thunbergii atropurpurea) is an attractive semi-evergreen whose thorny branches offer protection to smaller birds from the likes of cats. Firethorn (*Pyracantha coccinea*) offers similar protective cover for larger birds, and both have berries that can be eaten over winter. The Oregon grape (*Mahonia aquifolium*) is a slightly shorter, evergreen, prickly leaved shrub with berries that ripen in summer, while both elder (*Sambucus nigra*) and blackcurrant (*Ribes nigrum*) are deciduous species that attract many insects and bear summer berries.

Ideally, in addition to these woody plants, you should aim to plant a range of annual and herbaceous plants. Natives are very useful but, if you want a more ornamental look, choose a range of showier species that will attract insects in spring and summer, and later produce good seed heads to help feed small birds.

Lastly, you might want to leave some space in your border for a birdbath and feeders, providing food supplies when natural sources run low.

Above: *The shy jay is an occasional visitor to the urban garden. It will take a range of foods, including insects, seed and fruits.*

Above: *The greater spotted woodpecker usually feeds on wood grubs and other insects, but occasionally eats fruit in winter.*

BIRD BORDER

A good bird border needs to provide a range of food throughout the seasons. The plants featured here are chosen to either attract insects or bear fruit in the summer, or to be rich in seeds and/or fruit in the winter months. It also includes a range of trees, shrubs and smaller herbaceous plants.

1 *Polygonum bistorta* – Common bistort
2 *Artemisia vulgaris* – Mugwort
3 *Helianthus annuus* – Sunflower
4 *Sorbus aucuparia* – Rowan
5 *Berberis thunbergii atropurpurea* – Barberry
6 *Achillea millefolium* – Common yarrow
7 *Oenothera biennis* – Evening primrose

8 *Lavandula angustifolia* – English lavender
9 *Ribes nigrum* – Blackcurrant
10 *Sambucus nigra* – Elderberry
11 *Pyracantha coccinea* – Firethorn
12 *Ilex aquifolium* – Holly
13 *Angelica sylvestris* – Wild angelica
14 *Amaranthus caudatus* – Love-lies-bleeding

15 *Myosotis arvensis* – Field forget-me-not
16 *Mahonia aquifolium* – Oregon grape
17 *Malus* 'Red Sentinel' – Crab apple
18 *Taxus baccata* – Yew
19 *Dipsacus fullonum* – Teasel
20 *Solidago virgaurea* – Golden rod
21 *Lunaria annua* – Honesty
22 *Viburnum opulus* – Guelder rose
23 *Tanacetum vulgare* – Tansy
24 *Melissa officinalis* – Lemon balm
25 *Ribes uva-crispa* – Gooseberry
26 *Cotoneaster horizontalis* – Herringbone cotoneaster
27 *Fragaria vesca* – Wild strawberry

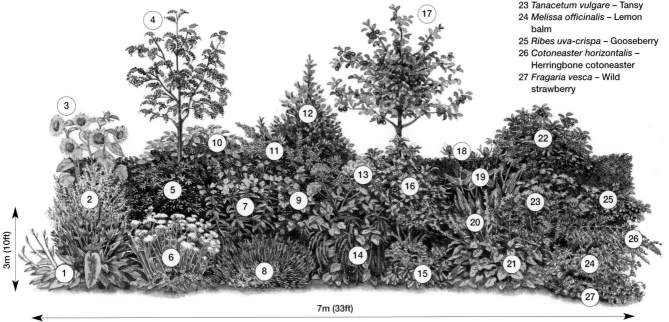

3m (10ft)

7m (33ft)

A WILD GARDEN FOR BIRDS

Wild gardens offer the closest substitute to a natural habitat for birds and, if designed properly, can also be very attractive. However, a wild garden should not be thought of as a low-maintenance option and allowed to become completely chaotic. Regular maintenance will still be required.

Wild gardens differ from other styles of wildlife garden primarily because they use only native plants. It is precisely because of this that more traditional gardeners sometimes deride them, regarding them as little more than weed patches. But many native plants are not only supremely beautiful, they are also well adapted to the site and soil conditions of the area. In addition, many provide cover for birds, and foods such as seeds and berries.

Thankfully, recent years have seen a reversal of the traditional form of gardening, with native plants now being commonly seen in an ornamental setting. With a little imagination they can form an immensely attractive display. Avoid plants that are known to be invasive – there are always less troublesome, attractive alternatives. Native plants also offer certainty that they are excellent choices for local birds in terms of their food value.

Below: *Wildflower areas are more accessible if paths are mown through. Several species of butterfly will lay their eggs alongside the mown paths, producing caterpillars that feed birds such as tits.*

Above: *Seed-eaters such as sparrows, jackdaws and this dunnock find a wealth of food in wild gardens.*

MAINTENANCE
Always choose a range of plants that will flower and also provide foods such as seeds and berries over as long a period as possible. When it comes to maintenance, most native plant species are no different from other garden plants. However, here

Above: *In dappled shade areas, a mass of spring bulbs such as wild garlic offers a welcome early supply of nectar for insects.*

the general effect can be somewhat untidy. Fallen plant debris harbours many overwintering insects which are eaten by birds. Those dead flowers in the borders are often a rich source of seed for birds in winter. The real difference in making a wild garden is that you will have created a refuge for birds and a host of other creatures using a rich diversity of native plants, many of which are becoming increasingly rare in the wild.

Below: *Many different butterflies are attracted to wild gardens, where they feed on nectar from flowers. Their caterpillars provide food for birds.*

WILD GARDEN

A design for a wild garden has to be as well thought out as a formal design. Care should be taken to include as many different habitats as possible, especially wildflower meadows and deciduous trees which support myriad insects to feed birds. Short-cut grass areas are kept to a minimum. Deadwood is allowed to remain to harbour more insect food for birds.

Large deciduous trees provide cover and nest sites

Nectar-rich border attracts insects to feed birds

Lacewing hotel attracts predators of aphids

Hedging links all areas of the garden

Bird table ideally sited close to the house as kitchen scraps are put out daily

Ground feeder to attract birds

Shrubs offer cover and nesting areas for birds

Bird box on shady side of tree

Pond surrounded by vegetation provides cover for aquatic birds

Bog gardens provide cover for aquatic birds and other wildlife

Large log piles offer homes for invertebrates that are eaten by birds

Compost heaps offer homes to reptiles and many insects

Wildflower meadows are fantastic for insects and the birds that feed on them

Standing deadwood offers a habitat for many invertebrates that feed birds

Mown paths are essential for access around the garden

Various different types of bird feeders will encourage more species to feed

Bird hide to observe the wildlife visiting the feeders

Above: *Water lilies provide walkways for moorhens and a landing pad for damselflies, dragonflies and frogs.*

Right: *Allowing short grass to regenerate can result in areas rich in cow parsley, whose seeds feed birds in autumn.*

LAWNS FOR BIRDS

In many gardens, grassy areas all too often consist of manicured lawns, which are of only limited benefit to birds and other wild creatures. With just a few changes to the way we maintain our lawns, however, we can transform them into superb wildlife habitats.

The commonest use of grass in the domestic garden is in a lawn. These often carefully tended features mimic grassland in certain respects but, in many ways, the traditional lawn is quite different from its wild counterpart. In its close-cropped, well-tended state, a lawn might look good to humans but as a habitat for birds it doesn't offer much. Changing a lawn from what is effectively a green desert into a thriving habitat often involves little more than reducing the amount of mowing you do, and outlawing the use of fertilizers, pesticides and weedkillers. This will have an almost immediate benefit for birds and other wildlife, but it may take some years before the full effects appear. And the time saved maintaining the lawn can be spent more usefully elsewhere in the garden.

Above: *Spring and summer are the most spectacular time for meadows. Flowering reaches its peak at this time and the sight is truly stunning.*

THE IMPORTANCE OF LONG-GRASS AREAS

There is a simple truth where grass in your garden is concerned. If a lawn is less frequently mown and not walked on wherever possible, it soon becomes richer in invertebrates that are eaten by birds. Indeed, long-grass habitats are some of the most useful undisturbed areas in the garden and are very simple to provide. Where space is limited they may be restricted to strips of uncut grass alongside a hedge, or around the base of a tree. However, if space allows they can form more extensive areas. Whatever the size of a long-grass area, they are an important, sheltered habitat and may provide cover for birds and a range of other creatures. Insects such as bumblebees or other wild bees often like to nest in longer grass, while grasshoppers or the caterpillars of moths will feed on the grass leaves and small creatures such as spiders and beetles move in to eat them. All these species provide food for invertebrate-eating birds, while seed-eaters such as finches, pigeons, dunnocks and sparrows may also search the area for food.

WILDFLOWER MEADOWS

Lawns that are converted into a wildflower meadow can be an important refuge for declining wildflowers, and are an excellent habitat for many insects and spiders that are eaten by birds. Lawns facing the sun are especially useful, attracting solitary bees and butterflies, and plants such as clover (*Trifolium*), knapweed (*Centaurea*), trefoil (*Lotus*) and vetches (*Anthyllis, Coronilla* and *Hippocrepis*) are excellent food plants that provide nectar.

TYPES OF GRASS

In nature, grassland is a rich and varied habitat that is moulded by the effects of geography, climate, soil and, in many cases, human intervention. Choosing the right type of grassland for your needs will depend on all these factors. Where you live will automatically decide the first three, but the last factor is mostly your choice, and depends on what you want in the garden. Short grass or downland turf is most commonly seen in temperate regions. It is

Below: *Pigeons and doves are seed-eaters that may find rich pickings in long grass. Other birds feast on insects that lurk there.*

Below: *Field poppies are still a fairly common sight in pastureland. Sparrows and dunnocks feed on the seeds.*

Above: *Lawns provide good hunting grounds for birds that feed on invertebrates such as snails and earthworms, including this blackbird (*Turdus merula*).*

usually the result of grazing sheep, and the consequent short-cropped turf contains a multitude of flower species. It is the closest model to the modern garden lawn, and can be maintained by regular (if infrequent) cutting by a mower on a high setting.

Hay meadows are a traditional way of managing grassland for the hay that is cut in the summer months and stored for animal fodder. The long grass frequently harbours many species of wildflower during spring and early summer, creating an extremely pretty artificial habitat. Wildflower seeds are eaten by birds such as finches. Traditional forms of management often resulted in poor soil that reduced the vigour

Below: *Wildflowers and some insects provide life and colour to gardens, as well as food for birds.*

Above: *Traditionally, garden lawns were kept short by mowing and although this keeps the grass healthy, it results in a poor wildlife habitat.*

of the grasses and favoured the growth of wildflowers. Sadly, modern intensive agriculture has seen a severe decline in these habitats and consequently in many wildflower species which benefit birds.

Wet meadows or flood meadows are largely similar to hay meadows, except that they are subject to seasonal flooding, usually in winter, and consequently harbour different species of birds. All types of meadow can be established in gardens to

benefit birds, but note that they need to be situated carefully and cut during the summer months, when they are not that attractive. Also note that they can be hard to establish on lawns that have been previously well fertilized.

Prairie is a term used to describe the vast areas of flower-rich grassland that once clothed North America, and is similar to the European steppe. The soils in these wild habitats are often richer than those found in artificial meadows, and they are often full of flowering plants which yield seed for birds. Many are now familiar plants in British gardens. The effect is relatively easy to establish in most gardens because it depends on rich soil, with similar mowing regimes to those used in meadows.

Marginal grassland is a term used to describe remnants of grassland plant communities that survive on field margins, roadsides or waste ground. These areas are often a last, vital refuge for grassland birds and also native flower species and their dependent wildlife that were formerly common in the area. The same effect can be created in your garden by leaving a wild grassy area at the base of a hedge. In terms of maintenance, all you need to do is cut the grass back every year or two, preferably in late winter.

Below: *Even when you intend to let the grass grow, short cut paths allow access and create vegetation of different heights that benefits insects. Some insects lay their eggs by paths, providing food for birds.*

PLANTING A WILDFLOWER MEADOW

Any area of long grass is a valuable habitat, providing cover for birds, insects and other wildlife. Wildflower meadows and flowery lawns are actually easier to make than you might think. You can add wildflowers by re-seeding an area or by planting pot-grown plants into existing grass.

The first step in transforming an existing lawn is to think about what you want it for, and how much you want to change. If it is important to keep the same amount of lawn, the simplest approach may be to change to wildlife-friendly maintenance. Alternatively, reduce the area of short cut lawn to a minimum, with wildflowers.

CHANGING AN EXISTING GARDEN LAWN

Assuming that you intend to keep some lawn, the simplest change is to let flowering plants colonize it. Reduce the frequency of cutting, and stop fertilizing, using pesticides and weedkillers, and watering it. The initial effect may be hard to see, but low-growing, broad-leaved plants will soon begin to get a foothold. Even allowing areas on a clover-rich lawn to have a flowering break for a week or two will help the bees.

MAKING A WILDFLOWER LAWN

Most grassland wildflowers grow best in full sun and open spaces with minimal root competition from trees, so choose your site accordingly. New lawns are best grown

Right: *Insect-eating birds and seed-eaters such as this sparrow will benefit from a wildflower meadow, which will also enhance the diversity of your garden.*

PREPARING THE GROUND AND SOWING WILDFLOWER MEADOWS

1 Start the project by marking out the area you intend to convert to a wildflower meadow. It is best to use a rope or hose to establish flowing lines and curves.

2 Once you have finalized where the edge of the meadow is to be, cut the line in the existing turf using a half-moon edging iron, following the line made by the rope.

3 Lift the existing turf, digging deep enough to remove all grass plants. Plants growing in wildflower meadows prefer nutrient-poor substrate and little topsoil.

4 Once the turf has been lifted and removed, lightly cultivate the whole area with a fork, before raking it to produce a light, crumbly seed bed ready for sowing.

5 Mix the wildflower seed into the grass seed prior to sowing. This will make it easier to distribute evenly. Lightly sow the mix at a rate of 15g/m^2 (½oz per sq yd).

6 The grass and wildlflower seedlings will soon emerge, and the light sowing rate ensures that the grass does not swamp the less vigorous wildflowers as they develop.

from seed that can either be bought ready mixed or you can mix your own. Ideally, the mix will produce about 60–80 per cent grass coverage, with the remainder being wildflower. The seed mix is sown sparingly – to avoid the grasses out-competing the wildflowers – at a rate of about 15g/m^2 (½oz per sq yd), or less.

You can make an existing lawn richer in flowering plants that will benefit birds by over-seeding in autumn with a mix of wildflower seed. To over-seed an area, you should cut the grass as low as possible and rake away the debris, leaving bare patches of soil. The seed is mixed with some fine, dry sand, thinly sown over the bare patches and then raked in lightly.

The results from over-seeding can be quite variable, and many gardeners prefer to plant out pot-grown wildflowers directly into an existing lawn. Mow the lawn early in the season and scrape or use bare patches for planting into. Arrange the young plants in groups of three to nine for the best effect and maximum chances of success. Once planted, the lawn can be mown on a high setting every two to three weeks in the first year to reduce the competition from grasses. The following year, the lawn can be mown less.

MOWING LONG GRASS

The amount of time and effort a bird-friendly lawn needs will vary. Shorter lawns need little change to their maintenance because the basic method of mowing remains the same, albeit less frequent.

Long grass is trickier, not least because it can be a fire hazard during dry weather. Always site an area of long grass at least 6m (20ft) away from buildings or other

---

TOP PLANTS FOR A WILDFLOWER MEADOW

Choosing flowers for a wildflower lawn will depend on which species are native to, or will succeed best in, your area. Below are some suggestions for plants that will benefit birds by providing seed and supporting insects, depending on location.

SHORTER GRASS

Cowslip (*Primula veris*) An ideal plant for areas of grass that are cut somewhat infrequently. Suited for hedge bottoms, it produces copious nectar that attracts insects and insect-eating birds in late spring.

Harebell (*Campanula rotundifolia*) The diminutive harebell is widespread in the wild, being found across much of the northern hemisphere. It is ideal for dry sites where its flowers attract bees and insect-eating birds.

Red clover (*Trifolium pratense*) A pea family member with round, red flower-heads that produce copious nectar for bees. Often included in agricultural mixes of grass seed because of its ability to fix nitrogen in the soil and enhance grass growth.

LONG GRASS

Field scabious (*Knautia arvensis*) A nectar-rich meadow flower with pretty blue-mauve pincushions on branching stems throughout summer and well into autumn, when its seed is often eaten by birds.

Ox-eye daisy (*Leucanthemum vulgare*) This pretty perennial produces an abundance of yellow-centred, white daisy flowers in summer, and later seeds for birds. Many daisy flowers – including coneflowers (*Echinacea*) and asters – are suited to long grass.

Wild carrot (*Daucus carota*) This wild ancestor of the cultivated carrot has a delicate filigree head of dainty flowers in summer – an excellent source of food for hoverflies, butterflies and other insects that feed birds.

Cowslip

Red clover

Field scabious

Wild carrot

---

combustible items. A buffer zone of conventional lawn can be made more attractive by cutting the first strip of lawn next to the tall grass on the highest mower setting, and reducing this by one setting on each consecutive strip so that the longer grass blends in gradually.

Mowing a margin between long grass and features such as flower-beds means that the grass will not collapse on to them following rain or storms. If you have a large lawn, mow a path through it so you can watch ground-feeding birds and other wildlife without having to trample on the tall grass. Frequently mow areas you want to keep as paths to keep the grass low.

Hay and water meadows are usually best cut after they have stopped flowering, although if space allows you can try leaving some areas of long grass uncut until late winter to provide shelter for birds and hibernation sites for insects. When you do cut the grass, remove all the clippings, usually after letting them lie for a day or two to let any wildlife escape.

PLANTING WILDFLOWERS INTO EXISTING GRASS

1 Set out small wildflower plants grown in pots, and, once positioned, cut out and remove a plug of turf before planting.

2 The wildflower plants, once planted into the turf, have a head start and are able to compete with the surrounding grass plants.

HEDGEROWS FOR BIRDS

Widely used as boundaries and dividing features in landscapes for centuries, hedges are important habitats for birds and many other creatures. Properly managed, they provide shelter and food for birds and other wildlife, and are home to many once common and often beautiful wildflower species.

A hedge can be defined as a boundary of closely planted woody shrubs or trees. The earliest known use of the word dates back to Anglo-Saxon times. The Anglo-Saxons used hedges as a way of defining ownership of land, but their hedges were not the same as those we know today, being more like a rough fence, and often containing as much deadwood as living material. They used many species that benefit birds, such as hawthorn (*Crataegus monogyna*) – haw also means hedge in Old Saxon – and briar roses.

In centuries past, people exerted less pressure on wildlife and hedges were just another place for birds and other animals to shelter and forage. With increased land clearance, intensified agriculture and a growing population, however, habitats have dwindled and hedges have become an important refuge for many native species. In this way ancient agricultural hedges are a tangible link with the wildlife that once inhabited the woodland edge and open spaces, containing a rich variety of birds and other animal life and a multitude of plant species, both woody and herbaceous. Hedges are often a prime habitat in their own right.

Below: *Hedgerows are often rich in seed- and berry-producing shrubs that provide an ideal food source for overwintering birds.*

THREATS TO TRADITIONAL HEDGEROWS

The intensification of agriculture in recent decades, coupled with the introduction of large machinery, has meant that many areas that were traditionally managed using hedgerows as part of the rural landscape have been transformed beyond recognition.

Machines work more efficiently in large fields, and hedges were seen as taking up valuable land that could produce crops. In addition, hedges in the United States contained a lot of barberry (*Berberis*), and this was identified as the alternative host species of the wheat rust *Puccinia graminis*, which is a serious fungal disease of commerically grown wheat.

The net effect of this was that farmers on both sides of the Atlantic were encouraged to remove hedges and in doing so this rich and vital habitat was removed from the andscape. In the case of European hedges, the rich legacy of over a thousand years was lost in some cases, and it left birds and other wildlife in a precarious position. Gardens became one of the few places where hedges remained common, and as such they are an invaluable resource for birds.

Above: *Even where a more formal effect is required, you can choose a species that benefits birds, such as this hornbeam.*

GARDEN HEDGES AND WILDLIFE

The modern approach to hedges, especially in garden settings, has been to cultivate a tight-cropped and controlled shape with many closely planted

Below: *Hedgerow species such as this hawthorn have abundant spring blossom that attracts insects and in turn birds.*

specimens of the same species. But while highly decorative, these have limited appeal to wildlife. Some birds are able to find shelter in the dense growth, but the range of species is limited, as is the likelihood of finding much food.

The answer often lies in planting a mixed, native hedge. Remember that a mosaic of plant species will favour a wider range of wildlife. Choose plants that provide food in the form of nectar-rich flowers and berries for overwintering birds. Hawthorn (*Crataegus*), wild roses (*Rosa*), holly (*Ilex*), hazel (*Corylus*) and elder (*Sambucus*) are good all-round choices.

TYPES OF HEDGE
Hedges are quite diverse, partly as a result of their function but also because of how they are maintained.

Mixed hedges Quite simply, a mixed hedge is one where the intention is to grow a range of species and provide a habitat that has the maximum species diversity. This type of hedge is most like a natural woodland edge.

Single-species hedges These hedges are common, especially in gardens, where their intention is to provide a consistent backdrop or feature. They can be useful for birds provided that a suitable species is chosen.

Formal hedges Found in highly manicured gardens and cut with a smooth face, the high frequency of their cutting and general absence of flowers or fruits mean that formal hedges are less useful for birds.

Informal hedges As the name suggests, these are hedges where the cutting regime does not entail frequent cuts or a smooth face or finish. They can be planted as single- or mixed-species hedges.

Dead hedges These barriers consist of dead branches and twigs that are firmly staked in place. Climbers are allowed to ramble through them and provide excellent shelter for birds.

You could also try barberry, cotoneaster and pyracantha, which produce lots of berries for the birds.

Resident birds may also appreciate hedges for shelter and also breeding, which is why wildlife hedges can't be trimmed in the nesting season, from early spring to late summer. Human impact can be further lessened by cutting back (not too tightly) only one side of the hedge on alternate years. Ideally, hedges should be pruned in late winter so that birds can take advantage of the insects, fruits and buds during the cold months, and again in summer and autumn.

Hedgerows are especially important habitats because they share key characteristics with two other habitats –

Above: *Informal mixed hedges are the kind most likely to attract birds such as chiffchaffs, which may build their nests near the base of the hedge.*

woodlands and open fields – providing corridors for wildlife, and allowing species to disperse and move from one habitat to another. Always allow the hedge bottom – the portion where the base of the hedge adjoins another habitat such as grassland – to become overgrown with grasses and flowers. The bottom is characteristically the dampest and most fertile area, and often proves to be the part richest in wildlife. Plants also find it difficult to spread across open fields, and 'travelling' along the base of a hedge is their only realistic option.

Below: *The bases of hedgerows often provide a refuge for woodland flowers. This area is also rich in birds and other wildlife that find refuge there.*

Below: *Honeysuckle is a good example of a hedgerow climber that is both useful for birds and also moths, and is also ideal as an ornamental plant.*

PLANTING A WILDLIFE HEDGE

Wildlife hedges are a real boost to a bird-friendly garden. The best usually consist of mixed plant species that provide nesting sites and year-round cover for birds. They may also produce flowers and berries. Single-species hedges provide less variety, but may still be useful if managed properly.

When deciding what sort of hedge will most benefit birds and other wildlife, you must also consider your own needs. If the hedge is also to provide security or a barrier, or if you need a certain height, then check the plants' possible dimensions. Also note that a wildlife hedge will not be frequently pruned, and can grow both tall and wide in a single season.

The most bird-friendly hedge includes a range of four or five species in varying numbers. The exact species will vary considerably according to the conditions, but any plants chosen should always be compatible in their maintenance requirements when grown as a hedge.

CHOOSING HEDGE PLANTS

Start by walking around your neighbourhood, looking at the hedges and seeing what plants are growing well. Try to choose at least half of your plants from locally indigenous species because they'll often be most valuable to native birds. If possible, when looking at other hedges growing locally, make notes about the

Above: *Birds, such as this linnet, find cover and a food supply in a well-managed wildlife hedge that is not cut too frequently.*

range and types of wildlife they attract. A single-species hedge can be very useful, if only because all the plants will have similar maintenance requirements. For plants that flower and set fruit, you could try fuchsia, escallonia or barberry, all of which attract birds. Traditional agricultural hedges mainly consist of up to 80 per cent of one species, such as hawthorn, but will usually also contain other trees and shrubs. This creates a variety of blossom, berries and scent with a range of niches that make such a hedge the best choice for birds. If you have a large garden, this type of hedge may be appropriate, but for a typical suburban semi-detached or terraced house, a single-species hedge may be more aesthetically pleasing.

PREPARATION AND PLANTING

When planting a wildlife hedge, prepare the soil properly beforehand. Dig a trench at least 50cm (20in) wide, and mix plenty of organic compost and a general fertilizer such as blood, fish and bone at around 50g per m² (2oz per sq yd). Refill the trench and allow it to settle for a couple of weeks before planting. Hedges are usually planted as either single rows of plants, about 30cm

SETTING OUT AND PLANTING A HEDGE

1 Start by levelling your previously prepared ground, using a rake to ensure that there are no rises and dips on the row.

2 Consolidate the ground to make sure there are no void spaces by lightly treading the area with a flat foot rather than a heel.

3 Rake the ground level, either with a rake or using the back of a fork. It is always best to start planting into level ground.

4 Using a spade to make a planting pit, slide the roots down into the hole, ensuring all are covered.

5 Using the heel of your boot, make sure the plant is firmly planted, with no air spaces around the stem.

6 Use guards to protect the stems from rabbits. These also shelter the young plants from the wind.

CUTTING A HEDGE

1 Once the hedge begins to outgrow its setting, it must be cut. This should be done before or after nesting time.

2 Set out a line of canes every couple of metres (7ft) or so to mark the line you want to cut, thereby producing a good face.

3 Before cutting the top, set out a string line to mark the desired height and ensure that a straight line is maintained.

4 Even for neat wildlife hedges, the finished cut should not be too tight as it will still preserve a somewhat informal look.

(1ft) apart, or as staggered, double rows with the same distance between the plants and rows. When planting, peg out a line of string to keep the hedge straight. Species such as beech and hawthorn (*Crataegus*) are best planted at a 45-degree angle to encourage thick growth at the base.

To stimulate dense, twiggy growth, trim off one-half to two-thirds of the total height of the hedge and then, for the first two or three years, remove at least half of the new growth during the winter period. Mulch the base of the rows annually, and apply an organic feed just before you do this.

MAINTAINING YOUR HEDGE

Once established, trim your hedge every second or third year, but avoid doing so when birds are nesting. The ideal time is in late winter, making nuts and berries available to birds for the longest possible period. Try cutting opposite faces of the hedge in alternate years where space is restricted, or if a slightly more formal shape is desired, because this will produce some flowers and fruit each year.

The best shape for a wildlife hedge is an 'A' shape because the sloping sides allow light and rain to reach the bottom of the hedge. An established hedge, say four to five years old, can be enhanced by planting climbers that benefit birds, such as honeysuckle (*Lonicera*), roses (*Rosa*) and clematis. Take care, though, because planting climbers before the hedge is well established can result in the hedge being overwhelmed and strangled. You can also plant hedgerow wildflowers at the base to provide extra cover for birds.

TOP HEDGE PLANTS FOR BIRDS

Any hedge has potential as a wildlife habitat, but the species described here are among the most useful to the widest range of birds.

Alder buckthorn (*Rhamnus frangula*) A thornless tree with five-petalled, green-white flowers, this is visited by many insects that are hunted by birds. It will grow in damp soil and sites that were once marshes. The flowers are followed by pendulous red berries that turn black in autumn and are eaten by birds.

Blackthorn (*Prunus spinosa*) Also known as sloe, the flowers of this thorny plant attract early bees and butterflies, while the leaves support caterpillars that feed nestlings. The whole plant supports over 150 species of wildlife. It doesn't like heavy shade but withstands strong winds, making it a good plant for coastal areas.

Hazel (*Corylus avellana*) This well-known plant is also called hazelnut or cobnut. It supports woodpeckers and at least 70 insect species in addition to squirrels and small rodents that are attracted to the nuts which ripen in late summer and early autumn. It is best left untrimmed for at least two seasons if you want to get any nuts.

Sweet briar (*Rosa rubiginosa*) Also known as the eglantine rose, the leaves and stems of this European species have a brownish-red tint. It forms a dense mass. The bright pink flowers that appear from late spring to early summer give way to bright red hips that are enjoyed by birds. The leaves of this species have a fruity scent when rubbed because of the sticky, brownish glands on the underside.

Wayfaring tree (*Viburnum lantana*) This small, attractive shrub is naturally found on chalk and limestone soils. It sports bright red berries in autumn that sustain birds. These are preceded by clusters of scented white flowers in late spring and early summer. White, silky hairs coat the undersides of the leaves and young stems.

Alder buckthorn

Blackthorn

Hazel

Sweet briar

WOODLAND AREAS FOR BIRDS

Wooded areas provide a rich and varied habitat for birds and other wildlife species. Woodland varies greatly, depending on location and the tree species within it. In many cases, it is also a product of the way in which it has been managed. A wooded area in your garden can benefit many kinds of birds.

Vast areas of the Earth's surface are still covered with trees. Natural, undisturbed woodlands are one of the most diverse habitats found anywhere on the planet. There are many different types of woodlands. Each type harbours a different community of birds and other wildlife,

Below: *Trees are tall, long-lived plants that form a dense shady habitat. Ground-cover plants only grow in spring before the trees form their leaves.*

which is important if you wish to create a wooded areas in your garden.

Almost all woodlands can be divided vertically into a series of layers called storeys, which contain different plant species. The tallest and most dominant trees form the topmost layer, called the canopy. The canopy can either be closed, in the case of dense woodland, or more open, with sunlight penetrating between the trees. Beneath the canopy is a layer of less dominant tree species, called the

Above: *Nuthatches feed on a variety of woodland foods, including berries and acorns. They supply insects to their young.*

understorey, and beneath that is a layer of smaller, woody plants and immature trees called the shrub layer. The ground layer, sometimes called the forest floor, is covered to a greater or lesser extent with a layer of herbs. The soil is continuously enriched by the decomposing leaves, shed from the trees either throughout the year, in the case of evergreens, or in autumn in the case of deciduous trees.

Below: *Fallen leaves and seed coats often naturally form dense layers on woodland floors. These slowly break down to release nutrients for trees and other plants.*

Above: *Taking a long time to die, trees often become full of deadwood, which in turn provides a habitat for invertebrates.*

Above: *Clearings in woodlands, such as this one alongside a path, often attract birds and other wildlife.*

and results in a habitat that repeatedly transforms from a clearing into a woodland habitat. Many familiar woodland birds, such as jays and woodpeckers, are well adapted to coppiced woodlands. Pollarding is a similar system but involves cutting the branches from a tree stem 2m (6ft) or so above ground level. Pollarding was mostly practised in wood-pastures and grazing areas where cutting above head height protected the new shoots from being damaged by browsing animals.

TYPES OF WOODLAND

Broad-leaved woodlands contain a greater variety of birds than any other wooded area found outside the tropics. They are dominated by trees with wide, flat leaves. There is considerable variation between broad-leaved woodlands in different locations in respect of the birds and other wildlife they contain. The trees here mostly lose their leaves in autumn in order to survive harsh winter weather.

Coniferous woodlands grow naturally in northern parts of North America, Europe and Asia. The trees here are mostly adapted to a cold, harsh climate and a short growing season. Coniferous woodlands are less productive in terms of birds than deciduous woodlands, but nonetheless support species such as woodpeckers, owls and crossbills.

Temperate rainforests grow in areas with warm summers and cool winters, and can vary enormously in the kinds of plant life they contain. In some, conifers dominate, while others are characterized by broad-leaved evergreens. These are mostly restricted to coastal areas in the north-west Pacific, south-western South America, New Zealand and Tasmania. However, small, isolated pockets of temperate rainforest grow in Ireland and Scotland. Despite their relative rarity, these are amazingly diverse natural habitats and home to some of the world's most massive trees.

TRADITIONAL MANAGEMENT

In many areas where woodland once formed extensive cover, much has now been removed and the vast majority that remains has long been managed by people. Despite the loss of ancient 'wildwoods', the remaining managed woodlands prove to be excellent habitats for birds, whose exact nature depends on the system of management employed.

Coppicing is a traditional method of woodland management, by which young tree stems are cut down to 30cm (1ft) or less from ground level to encourage the production of new shoots. This is done repeatedly through the life of the tree

THE BEST WOODLAND FOR BIRDS

The ability of woodland to support birds and other wildlife varies considerably. The age of a woodland and the variety of plant species it contains have their part to play, as does the way in which it has been managed. Generally, open woodland, especially when deciduous, is more accessible than closed woodland to species that browse and graze, and tends to be richer in ground-level plants.

The woodland floor is often rich in species that feed on decaying plant matter. Deadwood is also important for many insect species that live in rotting wood and feed many types of birds. Where the greatest concentrations of wildlife occur will vary greatly according to the type of woodland, but the richest areas always tend to be those that border other habitats, for example at woodland margins. The latter is the easiest to recreate in a garden.

Below: *Chaffinches frequent parks and gardens, but are mainly woodland birds. Their diet includes caterpillars, shoots, seeds and berries.*

PLANTING TREES AND SHRUBS

Trees and shrubs form the essential framework of any garden, providing cover for a variety of birds, as well as nesting sites that are well above the ground and safe from ground-dwelling predators. The secret to success in planting lies in careful ground preparation, stock selection and planting.

When selecting plants, always choose trees and shrubs that are vigorous, healthy and suitable for the site conditions or intended usage. They should always be free from any obvious signs of damage, pests or disease. If you are buying bare-rooted stock, make sure that the roots never dry out before planting, and keep them covered at all times – even a couple of minutes left exposed to cold or drying winds can cause a lot of damage. You should plant them as soon as possible; if the soil is frozen or waterlogged, plant them in a temporary bed of compost, at a 45-degree angle (this is called heeling in), and keep them moist until you are in a position to be able to plant them out.

PREPARING THE GROUND
Despite what is written in many books and guides, organic additives such as compost can be a mixed blessing if they are incorporated into soil at planting time. An enhanced soil mix does improve the soil

Right: *Greenfinches nest in small colonies in thick shrubs, creepers or conifer trees. About half a dozen pairs may nest together.*

PLANTING AND STAKING TREES

1 Container-grown trees should be thoroughly watered an hour before you plant them. Soak really dry ones overnight.

2 Clear any weeds and cut any suckers coming from the roots as these may slow the tree's top and root growth.

3 Once you remove the pot, tease out any encircling roots to encourage root spread in the soil and to prevent root-balling.

4 Dig the planting pit and ensure that it is deep enough for the root-ball. Check by lying a spade or fork on its side.

5 Backfill the pit, firming the soil with a heel every 8cm (3in) to make sure it is well planted and contains no large air pockets.

6 Drive the stake in at an angle to avoid damaging the roots. Face the stake into the prevailing wind for stronger root growth.

7 Secure the stem of the tree using a tie, nailed on to prevent movement. Choose one with a spacer to stop the stem chafing.

8 The tree should remain staked for about a year, during which time the tie must be checked and loosened.

MULCHING A TREE

1 Young trees growing in grass are often slow to establish due to competition from the surrounding plants.

2 Remove the turf around the tree. Create a cleared circle around the stem of the tree that is 1m (3ft) in diameter.

3 Thoroughly water the ground and then apply an even layer of mulch to a depth of about 5cm (2in) on the cleared circle.

4 The tree must be kept clear of weeds and vegetation for around 4 or 5 years. Water thoroughly in dry conditions.

but also causes the plants to become 'lazy'. Quite simply, the roots like compost better than the surrounding soil and circle round as if in a pot, resulting in an unstable 'corkscrew' growth pattern known as girdling. Avoid this by applying organic matter across the surface after planting. This creates more natural conditions and encourages insects including beetles. Apply fertilizers only if really needed, after planting but before mulching.

WHEN TO PLANT

Plant deciduous species during early winter, when they are dormant. Evergreens, on the other hand, tend to do well if planted either in early autumn or late spring. Trees and shrubs growing in containers can be planted throughout most of the year, provided that the ground is kept sufficiently moist, although they too will generally establish best in the cooler months. Never plant when the soil is frozen, excessively dry or waterlogged, as this may damage the roots and lower stem. Make planting holes big enough, allowing a quarter to a third of the diameter again of the root spread. Check that the plant is at the same depth as it was before.

STAKING AND PROTECTION

Large shrubs and trees require staking to prevent them blowing over in their first season. Smaller, more vulnerable stock is protected by putting it in a tree or shrub shelter that helps stems thicken, promotes rapid upward growth and protects plants from rodents and sometimes deer attack.

TOP TREES FOR BIRDS

If you have the space, trees are a valuable feature for birds, and by choosing the species carefully, you can greatly enhance the wildlife potential of a garden.

Apples and crab apples (*Malus sylvestris*) These are a familiar fixture in many gardens. The older varieties are best, supporting diverse insects on the leaves and stems. The buds are eaten by some birds, as is the fruit. The tree is of most use to birds if left largely unpruned.

Oak (*Quercus robur*) While this long-lived tree has outstanding value for birds, it is too large to grow in most gardens. There are over 600 species, enjoying different climates, and some are the richest habitat trees available for insects and birds.

Pine (*Pinus sylvestris*) Pines are among the best conifers for birds, offering a source of seeds that are taken by many species. The dense crowns are used by nesting birds such as owls. These trees are an excellent choice for dry soils, although they eventually grow quite tall.

Red mulberry (*Morus rubra*) The mulberry produces berries throughout the summer that are eaten by at least 40 different bird species. It makes an ideal tree for moist, fertile soils. Keep it clear of paths and patios as the fruit can be messy.

Rowan (*Sorbus aucuparia*) A medium-sized tree that is well suited for the smaller garden, with numerous closely related species and cultivars. Birds visit rowan trees but rarely make them a permanent habitat. Insects love the flowers, while birds, especially thrushes, often feed on the attractive, bright red berries.

Southern beech (*Nothofagus alpina*) A fast-growing and, eventually, quite large forest tree, only worth growing in a big garden. In many places it supports a variety of species that feed on the nuts and live in the tree, especially in the gnarled bark of older specimens.

Crab apple

Oak

Pine

Southern beech

CREATING WOODLAND EDGES

Woodland edges are found where forests and woodlands give way to more open areas. These are potentially highly productive habitats for birds, offering a wide range of foods, shelter and also breeding sites for species that are usually restricted to wooded areas.

Woodland is most diverse at its edges, either in the treetops of the upper canopy, where there is plenty of light, or adjoining another habitat. Here, species from both areas meet and share the space. The exact nature of the edge is largely dependent on the adjoining habitat. Often this is grassland or cultivated land but, equally, it could be marsh or open water. Either way, the woodland produces an abundance of growth each year during the growing season. This leads to a rich organic layer deposited over the soil that produces very fertile ground, both within and just beyond its limits. Most gardens, even relatively large ones, do not have room for an area of naturalized woodland, but you might be able to accommodate a group of several small or medium-sized trees, which will support many insect species and provide food and perches for birds.

SITING A WOODLAND EDGE

A woodland edge is easier to recreate than you might think. Even if space is limited, shrub borders fulfil some of the role of a woodland edge, and, if managed correctly,

Above: *Woodland edges are home to a great abundance of flowers, such as this blackberry, which thrive in dappled shade areas. Birds feed on the fruits.*

Left: *Where trees and shrubs give way to grassland, the mosaic of different habitats is naturally rich in plants and birds.*

REMOVING A TREE STAKE

1 Start by removing any nails that were used to secure the tie to the stake, then unbuckle the tie. Do this carefully and avoid pulling at it as this could potentially damage the bark of the tree.

2 Gently loosen the tie by feeding the belt back through the spacer block that was used to prevent the tree's stem from chafing on the stake. Check the stem for any sign of damage.

3 Remove the stake by gently rocking it back and forth until it can be pulled upward. If it is too firmly in the ground you might have to cut it off with a saw, taking great care to avoid the stem.

Above: *Greater spotted woodpeckers regularly visit gardens near woods, and may appear often if you plant a woodland edge.*

hedges can also attract woodland-edge species. Choose a strip along an edge of the garden facing the sunniest direction. This means you'll minimize shade on the rest of the garden while the woodland-edge border gets the benefit of sunshine, which will widen its appeal to a greater range of species. Alternatively, make it face the afternoon sun. This will, of course, cast shade on your garden in the morning, but this need not be a problem. The plants often benefit most from the afternoon sun, especially in the cooler seasons. When

Below: *Planting a mixture of trees and flowering shrubs in narrow strips mimics the edge of a woodland. You should remove tree stakes after one year.*

TOP WOODLAND EDGE PLANTS FOR BIRDS

Woodland edges are naturally rich in flowering and fruit-bearing species, many of which provide a vital food resource for a rich variety of visiting birds.

CANOPY PLANTS

Apples and crab apples (*Malus*) Deciduous, small, shrubby, spring-flowering tree with abundant round, fleshy, apple-like fruits that follow large, cup-shaped, white, pink-flushed flowers that attract bees. A food source for many insects and birds.

Rowan (*Sorbus*) This group includes the familiar rowan tree or mountain ash *Sorbus aucuparia*, which becomes heavily laden with bright red berries that are enjoyed by birds in late summer and early autumn. A versatile genus with many species and cultivars.

Box elder (*Acer negundo*) A small, usually fast-growing and fairly short-lived maple whose winged seeds are sometimes eaten by birds and other animals. Its sugary sap is sometimes eaten by squirrels and songbirds.

SHRUB LAYER

Rose (*Rosa*) Roses can be extremely attractive shrubs. If possible, plant a wild species and choose single flowers over double types as these are best for visiting insects. The hips that follow the flowers are often eaten by birds.

Rubus An important group of bird-friendly shrubs that includes the common blackberry (*R. fruticosus*). Care should be taken when choosing this as it can quite easily become very invasive. Many other species and cultivars are good garden specimens.

Viburnum An extremely varied group of plants that includes a wide range of species and hybrids, with good wildlife value and an attractive appearance. Choose varieties with berries, such as the guelder rose (*V. opulus*) to provide food for birds.

Crab apples   Rowan   Rose   Viburnum

choosing a site for your border, don't forget to discuss your plans with neighbours, whose gardens may be affected by shade. A wall or a fence is the ideal back boundary for your woodland edge because it can provide support for some of the climbing plants that benefit birds.

PLANTING AND MAINTAINING A WOODLAND EDGE

Plant a woodland edge so that there is a general increase in height from the front to the back of the area or border, thereby allowing light to reach all the plants. The tall plants at the back are called the 'canopy edge' plants. In a narrow border, you will need around one canopy tree for about every 5m (17ft). Choose smallish, sun-loving woodland trees, particularly those that bear berries to feed birds. The plants in front of this are the shrub layer, with the

herbaceous layer forming the smallest layer at the front. Growing under the canopy trees, these layers can include both sun-loving and shade-tolerant plants because the canopy trees cast very little shade on the border. There is always room for variety, though, and many smaller, more shade-loving plants, such as early perennials and bulbs, can easily be planted among the taller woody plant species.

Rather surprisingly, managing an area of your garden like a woodland edge takes far less time and work than you might imagine. Once planted, you just need to keep the area well watered until everything is established. You should also keep an eye on the border for the next few years, making sure that no one plant is dominating and smothering the others. Eventually, though, the area should need little or no maintenance.

PONDS FOR BIRDS

A wildlife garden would not be complete without a pond, which provides a bathing and drinking site for birds and a habitat for many other creatures. With its aesthetic appeal, a pond makes a worthy addition to any design, but where space is limited, even the smallest patch of water can be useful.

The term pond is surprisingly vague, there being no clear distinction between a large pond and a small lake. The average garden pond is relatively small, but a well-designed pond can attract a greater variety of wildlife than any other single feature in the garden.

WILDLIFE VALUE

A pond provides not only a drinking and bathing site for birds, but also a breeding site for amphibians and for a whole host of insects, such as dragonflies, that spend part of their life here. In addition, it is the sole habitat for a range of other creatures, from water snails that spend their life beneath the water to pond skaters that spend most of their life on the water surface.

Below: *Even a relatively small area of water can be an attractive garden feature, which results in a surprisingly diverse habitat for birds and other creatures.*

Above: *Aquatic birds such as coots and moorhens may take refuge in gardens near wetlands or with water features.*

Right: *Ponds are full of interest, often revealing curiosities such as this empty dragonfly larva case in the summer.*

PLANTS FOR WETLANDS

Natural wetlands contain both open water and wet ground, with different plant species living on the margins and in deep water.

Marginal or emergent plants
Plants that have roots and sometimes stems that grow in shallow water, but with shoots, leaves and flowers above the water surface.

Oxygenators These important plants live beneath the surface and enrich the water with oxygen.

Water lilies and deep-water aquatics The roots of these plants are submerged, the leaves are on the surface, and the flowers are either on or above the surface.

Free-floating plants The leaves and stems are free-floating on the water surface. The roots are submerged and the flowers grow on or just above the water.

Bog plants These are plants that prefer to grow in permanently wet or waterlogged ground. Some species that flourish on pond margins can also be grown as bog plants.

Ponds should be shallow at one end to provide a bathing area for birds, and if possible have wet, muddy margins to attract birds needing a drink. Ponds also provide a unique visual focus, and have a restful quality that is hard to match.

POND PLANTS

Plants are essential to the health of any small area of water, enabling the habitat to achieve a correct water balance and provide surface cover on otherwise open water. Without them the water would, over time, probably start to resemble a thick pea soup, as algae – small, mostly microscopic plant-like organisms – will start to grow prolifically and ultimately colour the water. Plant leaves have the double action of absorbing both carbon dioxide and minerals from the water, which in turn starves the algae. Many natural bodies of still or slow-moving water have extensive cover of floating plants and their sides are also shaded by larger, bank-side or shallows vegetation.

In a garden pond it is easy to recreate this by ensuring that there are plenty of submerged plants, about half of the water surface is covered with foliage and that the margins have plants in them that are capable of surviving immersion in shallow water in order to achieve this balance. This will keep the water clear and will also make the pond attractive for birds and a host of creatures that are either residents or visitors.

Above: *Pond dipping is a good way to assess what wildlife you have in a pond. It is a great way to interest children in wildlife.*

BOG GARDENS

Usually specially constructed areas, bog gardens provide permanently waterlogged soil. They are often made in conjunction with a pond, and can support a range of unusual plants normally found in wetland habitats. Bog gardens are an important element of any mosaic, and can be a vital refuge for aquatic birds, such as coots and moorhens, and also amphibians, which will relish the cool, damp shelter.

POND PLANTINGS

Ideally, a pond profile will include shallow areas as well as deeper water. In the deeper reaches, the vegetation consists of plants able to live permanently underwater or those with roots that send up leaves which float on the surface. Shallow water will support plants capable of tolerating waterlogged conditions, and the remainder are free-floating on the surface.

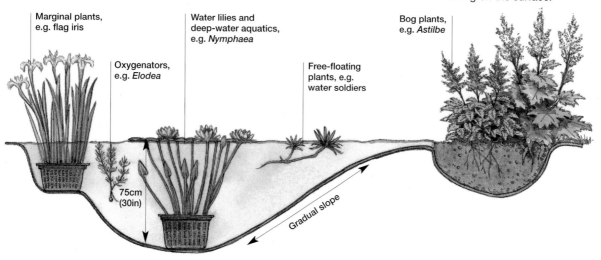

Marginal plants, e.g. flag iris

Oxygenators, e.g. *Elodea*

Water lilies and deep-water aquatics, e.g. *Nymphaea*

Free-floating plants, e.g. water soldiers

Bog plants, e.g. *Astilbe*

75cm (30in)

Gradual slope

MAKING A POND

Ponds are a real boost to wildlife gardens, providing a watering hole for birds and a complete habitat for other wildlife. They are relatively easy to construct, but need to be properly sited and designed to be useful habitats. Care and attention at the planning stage will boost the wildlife potential of your garden.

When choosing a site for your pond, look for an attractive, sunny place, sheltered from the prevailing wind. Try to avoid a site that is shaded by trees because they will cut out light, and their leaves will drop into the water, enriching it with nutrients and organic debris. This promotes green water and blanket algae in the warmer months.

In any garden where a water feature is planned, child safety is of paramount importance. If there is any risk that young children might fall in, consider delaying your plans until they are older. Children love water and the wildlife it attracts, but you should always weigh up the risks.

THE SHAPE AND SIZE OF A POND

As a general rule, 4m² (43sq ft) is the minimum area needed to create a balanced environment, with marginal shelves at least 25cm (10in) wide to support containers of emergent plants. Create the outline using sweeping curves with no sharp bends; a figure of eight or a kidney shape is often the best idea for smaller ponds. Then draw a rough cross-section of the pond to check how much depth you will get for your width. Aim to get at least 60cm (2ft) and ideally 90cm (3ft) or more in the deeper

Above: *Even a small garden pond may attract a kingfisher foraging for fish and molluscs, perhaps to feed its young.*

reaches to benefit a range of wildlife. The slopes should drop at a rate of one-third of the equivalent distance travelled across the top to assure stability.

CHOOSING A LINER

For small ponds, moulded or fibreglass pools can be used but are limited in terms of design, and do not always look very natural. A flexible liner, such as butyl rubber, is generally considered the best (if most expensive) option, although UV stabilized PVC can be a cheaper alternative. Both these materials are prone to puncture, for example by the sharp beaks of herons, and care must be taken to line the hole with soft sand and/or an underlay, such as old carpet (made of natural fibres), to avoid this. The liners are easy to lay, and can also be used when creating bog gardens.

HIDING THE EDGE

Both flexible and rigid liners need to be hidden if you want to promote a natural effect. There are many ways of doing this.

A cobbled edge is easily achieved by setting some large stones or cobbles into a bed of sand/cement laid on the liner, both below and above the eventual water surface on a shallow slope. The stones form a firm base, and other stones can be piled between, with the gaps providing sheltering space for small animals, while also providing a gently sloping 'beach' for birds to approach and drink.

A drystone wall, or alternatively a loose rock pile set on a mortar base on the liner, just below the water, can act as a retaining

CREATING DRINKING SHALLOWS

1 The shallow areas of ponds are important to allow birds to drink, but they can become muddy traps for smaller creatures and offer little protection or shelter for visitors.

2 Start by placing some larger stones or rounded rocks both in the shallow water and on the bank, arranging them in small groups of varying sizes to create a natural-looking effect.

3 Once the larger stones have been placed, the spaces between them should be filled with round cobblestones to create both shallow stony pools and drier beach areas.

4 The finished effect is very ornamental, and the strong shoreline provides hiding places for smaller creatures as well as a basking area and safe drinking site for birds.

wall for nearby planting, with the niches between the stones providing shelter for amphibians. Walls or rock features are best placed at the back of the pond so that they create a reflection on the water surface.

A planted edge is also an option with a 'planting pocket' being built on the liner. This involves running the liner about 10cm (4in) above maximum water level, and then burying it in the soil around the edge. It provides a simple and natural effect, with the overhanging plants hiding the edge, but the liner will show when the water level drops, and there is always the added danger of damaging a flexible liner when mowing or gardening near the pond.

Concrete or stone slabs laid on a sand/cement bed over the edge of the liner are a somewhat formal solution, but are very practical if you want to view the water up close. Try to avoid this all the way around, though, as very small animals, such as young frogs, may have difficulty climbing in and out over the stone edge.

PUTTING IN A BUTYL LINER FOR A POND

1 Start by marking out the outside edge of the pond using stakes or canes, and then mark out the locations of any shallow margins with spray paint.

2 Once marked out, begin digging the pond, starting with the deeper areas first, before digging out the margins and finalizing the edge of the pond.

3 Once you have excavated all of the pond to the required depth, establish the slopes on the side of the pond and the planting shelves within it.

4 To gain nicely smooth sides to the excavated pit, line the whole of the base and sloping sites with graded stone-free sand, fabric or old carpet.

5 Carefully lift the liner over the pit. Don't drag it because sharp stones may puncture it. Secure the corners using bricks or stones and start to fill the pond with water.

6 As the liner fills with water, it will mould to the shape you have excavated. Once the pond is nearly full, cut the edge of the liner, leaving a generous overlap.

7 As the water level continues to rise, fold the liner to create an even finish and avoid any unsightly creases across the pond bottom or sloping sides.

8 Once the water is almost up to the top, bury the edges of the liner by cutting and then lifting the turf edges of the pond and laying it under the cut turf.

9 The new pond can now be filled to the brim, then planted with various wetland species. Shallows can be created using stones of varying sizes.

PLANTING A POND

Naturally occurring ponds and wetlands are rich in plant life, much of which is specially adapted to grow in waterlogged ground, shallow water or even under the surface. By including a range of these plants, you will greatly improve the look of your water feature and also its value for birds and other wildlife.

Surprisingly, new ponds can seem initially quite stark and lifeless. Plants provide the magic to bring them to life and, once surrounded by vegetation, the whole feature becomes more attractive both to us and to birds and other wildlife.

To create a natural look, you could put a layer of soil on top of the liner for plants to root into, and creatures to hide in. This has the disadvantage, however, of introducing nutrients that can cause algal growth, and often means that you must be prepared to cull the plants regularly because aquatic plants can spread rapidly and choke the pond. Most people minimize the problem by using special aquatic plant containers that curtail excessive growth. Most pond plants are perfectly happy in clay loam. Provided you ensure that the soil used is free of pesticides or pollutants most heavy types are fine, but the best idea is to buy a proprietary brand. Planting is mostly the same as for other potted plants, but the soil needs to be firmed down a little more than usual, and it is a good idea to spread gravel and/or cobbles on top of the soil to keep the pot stable and keep the soil in the pot. The best time for planting is late spring as the water warms up. Don't give plants a shock by plunging them into icy water.

Above: *Water lilies, such as this* Nymphaea alba, *are a beautiful addition to any garden pond. Frogs are often seen on the leaves.*

PLANTS USUALLY BEST AVOIDED

These plants can become invasive in a garden pond and, if they escape into the wild, can become a severe problem in natural ponds, lakes and waterways. Avoid using them in favour of native species or non-invasive plants.

Note: If these plants are already in the pond, they should be disposed of carefully to prevent their spread either here or elsewhere.

- Australian swamp stonecrop (*Crassula helmsii*)
- Fairy moss (*Azolla filiculoides*)
- Floating pennywort (*Hydrocotyle ranunculoides*)
- Curly waterweed (*Lagarosiphon major*)
- Parrot's feather (*Myriophyllum aquaticum*)
- Kariba weed (*Salvinia*)
- Water hyacinth (*Eichhornia crassipes*) – a particularly invasive species
- Water lettuce (*Pistia stratiotes*)

CHOOSING POND PLANTS

There are three different types of plant that you need to attract wildlife. All are essential to a healthy pond because they constitute the range of habitats needed to support a diverse wildlife community.

Oxygenators spend the whole year submerged. These plants supply a steady infusion of oxygen, which is needed by the aquatic creatures that breathe through their gills. Oxygenators often grow densely and serve as egg-laying sites, nurseries and cover for many aquatic animals. The second type are deep-water aquatics, which have roots and stems in the deeper

FILLING A POND BASKET AND PLANTING IT UP

1 Pond plants are best planted in specially made crates. These are lined on the base with gravel and filled with specially formulated compost.

2 Once the base is covered with stones and soil, put your plants in the crate. Fill around the remaining gaps with more of the aquatic compost mix.

3 When the compost is up to the height of the top of your plant root-ball, dress the compost surface with more gravel to help keep it in place.

4 The pond plants should quickly establish in their new surroundings and will soon send up new shoots and flowers above the surface.

RENOVATING A BOG GARDEN

1 Thoroughly weed the bog garden, taking special care to remove all the roots of any persistent perennial weeds or unwanted plants.

2 Retain any useful specimens and dig in some organic matter to enrich the soil. Take a note of bare areas to calculate numbers of new plants needed.

3 Dig over the whole area to be planted, then set out the new plants and decide the best arrangement before planting them in their final positions.

4 Once the area is planted, give the garden a thorough watering to help the plants settle in. Take a note of all species planted in case replacements are needed.

Above: *Small sections of oxygenating plants, such as this* Elodea*, can be tied with a stone and placed into the pond to grow and start to oxygenate the water.*

reaches, but with floating leaves and flowers. They are especially important because they help to shade the water from too much sunlight in summer. Too much light entering the water can cause algae to become a problem, and ideally you need to cover about half the surface of the pond with these plants. Water lilies (*Nymphaea*) are a big favourite, being very decorative, relatively easy to grow and available in a wide range of colours and sizes. Other plants are also available, and you must ensure that the species chosen are not too vigorous for your pond size. A few species are entirely free-floating and include duckweed (*Lemna*), water fern (*Azolla*) and water hyacinth (*Eichhornia crassipes*), but they can be invasive and are best avoided.

The third class of aquatic plants, marginal or emergent plants grow in shallow water at the edge and offer shade and cover for birds and other animals, while greatly enhancing the visual appeal. They are used by dragonflies and nymphs to crawl out of the water and pupate.

MARSH AREAS

Bog gardens mimic areas of marshy ground found in wetlands. They provide ideal cover for amphibians as the soil in these areas is always wet. The need for permanently wet ground means they are lined in a similar way to a garden pond. Many species of marginal plants are equally at home in a bog garden, and careful planting in such situations can help hide the division where the water stops and the bog garden starts, thereby enhancing its look.

TOP PLANTS FOR WILDLIFE PONDS

There are various types of wetland plants. They are split into categories to make it easy to select the correct plants for different areas of the pond or wetland.

MARGINAL/EMERGENT PLANTS
Flowering rush (*Butomus umbellatus*)
Water forget-me-not (*Myosotis palustris*)
Marsh marigold (*Caltha palustris*)
Yellow flag (*Iris pseudacorus*)
Watermint (*Mentha aquatica*)

WATER LILIES/DEEP-WATER AQUATICS
Water lily (*Nymphaea alba*)
Water hawthorn (*Aponogeton distachyos*)
Japanese pond lily (*Nuphar japonica*)
Floating heart (*Nymphoides peltata*)
Golden club (*Orontium aquaticum*)

Flowering rush

Marsh marigold

Water lily

Golden club

OXYGENATORS
Curled weed (*Potamogeton crispus*)
Hornwort (*Ceratophyllum demersum*)
Milfoil (*Myriophyllum spicatum*)
Pondweed (*Elodea* spp.)
Water starwort (*Callitriche stagnalis*)

FREE-FLOATING PLANTS
Water soldier (*Stratiotes aloides*)
Lesser duckweed (*Lemna minor*)
Water lettuce (*Pistia stratiotes*)
Water fern (*Azolla filiculoides*)
Bladderwort (*Utricularia vulgaris*)

Hornwort

Pondweed

Water soldier

Water fern

ATTRACTING INSECT-EATING BIRDS

Insects offer a rich source of protein for birds and their young. Insectivorous birds are a familiar sight in gardens particularly in summer, when their activities help to control pests. Many of the species seen are summer migrants that visit to feast upon the abundance of insect life that appears at this time.

Insects and small invertebrates constitute an important food source for birds and particularly their young, especially in regions where insects are most plentiful. Swallows, martins and swifts pursue their insect meals while flying, often swooping down in pursuit, while woodpeckers can sometimes be seen – and more often heard – making holes in wood to find grubs. Even the flocks of starlings that walk across your lawn are systematically searching for insects.

INSECT-EATERS

Typical species Swallows, swifts, martins, wrens, woodpeckers, warblers, nuthatches, flycatchers.

Garden benefits Insect-eaters benefit gardeners by eating many pests. Incoming migrants help tackle the rocketing summer population.

Migratory species For insectivorous birds, with their high mobility, migration is the rule rather than the exception. For some, such as swallows and swifts, the journey covers thousands of miles.

Natural diet Insectivorous birds will often take a range of invertebrates. Because they gain most of their moisture from these, they drink less frequently than seed-eaters.

Resident species Very few insectivores remain as residents in higher latitudes. Those that do – mostly small birds such as the wren – are very susceptible to cold and therefore limited to mild regions.

Supplementary diet Mealworms are an excellent supplement and can be offered in a simple dish or a specialist feeder. In addition, many food suppliers now provide dried food for insectivores.

HABITAT PREFERENCES

While some birds are entirely insectivorous, others, including many common songbird species, eat insects only when raising young. Some of these feed the offspring entirely an insect diet, but only a small percentage of their own food is insects. This habit has the obvious advantage that they do not have to change their preferred habitat and can remain in a garden all year.

Some larger birds also eat insects as part of their diet when these are plentiful but revert to other foods at other times of the year. The swallow, on the other hand, is a well-known example of a species that feeds only on insects and so must make radical shifts in its habitat preferences within a single season by migrating vast distances to follow seasonal 'gluts' of its prey in different countries.

FEEDING STRATEGIES

Although there are many different species of insect-eating birds, they often adopt similar strategies for catching their prey. Most have fine, narrow beaks, although even this can vary greatly according to

Below: *Barn swallows* (Hirundo rustica) *migrate vast distances to follow seasonal abundances of insects.*

Above: *Wrens are among the smallest of garden birds, but are voracious predators of insects in the summer months.*

species. Ecologists therefore tend to divide insectivorous birds according to their hunting habits, or guilds.

These guilds consist of groups of species that, although not necessarily closely related, behave in similar ways. Leaf-gleaners, such as warblers, pick insects off leaves, whereas bark-gleaners, such as nuthatches, pick them off tree trunks. Woodpeckers are wood- and bark-probers because of their ability to dig out their prey from within the branch.

The air-salliers, including flycatchers, sit on a perch waiting for their prey to pass,

Above: Several species of woodpecker may visit gardens, all of which prefer to feed on wood-boring grubs.

THREATS

Pesticides Increased use of pesticides in both urban and rural settings means that insects are now relatively scarce. Many surviving insects carry small traces of poison which can accumulate in the bodies of insect-eating birds.

Predation Small birds are vulnerable to predation from larger species, both birds and mammals. Domestic cats are a big danger in urban gardens, and both squirrels and large birds, such as magpies, will take eggs and the young in the breeding season.

Territory If food becomes scarce, small birds are generally less able to compete with larger birds and become seasonal insectivores. Many need larger territories as a result, and the effort of defending this may use a lot of energy.

Urbanization Insect-eating birds often find it difficult to find enough food in very built-up areas. The lack of suitable vegetation means that insect prey is often relatively scarce. Vehicular pollution in the environment can also limit insect populations.

whereupon they fly out and catch insects on the wing. The final guild includes swallows, martins and swifts – gleaners of aerial plankton. These eat a large number of small insects while on the wing. In reality, however, most birds opt for more than one strategy, particularly if food becomes scarce. Most insectivorous birds consume several different kinds of insect, often switching their preferences through the season according to the abundance of species available.

MIGRATORY SPECIES

Birds that feed exclusively on insects often face seasonal food shortages if they remain in one place, and that's why they travel in search of food. Swallows and flycatchers in north-western Europe fly south in autumn to spend winter in Africa. It is easy to see why they do so because the cold, dark months offer little reward in terms of insects. What is less easy to understand is why they should return. The simple answer is that countries in high or low latitudes have a large seasonal glut of insects in summer. The birds move from place to place, so that it's always summer, and there's always plenty of food.

Migrating insect-eating birds also prosper because there are often not many resident insectivorous birds in their summer feeding grounds. This means that the migrants have an abundant food supply without facing competition from too many residents. Furthermore, feeding and raising their young in high or low latitudes means that they can use the longer hours of daylight to gather plenty of food, so they can potentially raise more young. A final advantage for migratory birds is that they avoid specialist predators trying to feed on them, because few of their predators make the same migratory journey.

Below: Lavender is an excellent plant for attracting insects such as bees and butterflies, which flock to the flowers in search of nectar. In turn, these creatures often become food for many birds.

PLANTS TO ATTRACT INSECT-EATING BIRDS

Evening primrose (*Oenothera biennis*)
Fern-leaved yarrow (*Achillea filipendula*)
Flowering rush (*Butomus umbellatus*)
Golden rod (*Solidago virgaurea*)
Honesty (*Lunaria annua*)
Lavender (*Lavandula angustifolia*)
Lemon balm (*Melissa officinalis*)
Tansy (*Tanacetum vulgare*)

Evening primrose

Golden rod

Honesty

Tansy

ATTRACTING SEED-EATING BIRDS

Seed-eaters include some of the most engaging of garden birds. Changes in agriculture have caused a decline in these birds, many of which were once very common. Fortunately, the increasing popularity of garden feeders has thrown the birds a lifeline, and many now prosper in a domestic setting.

The majority of birds using garden feeders will be seed-eaters for at least part of the year. However, comparatively few species are exclusively seed-eating, since most seed-eating birds hunt nutritious insects when they are feeding and raising their young. The main problem with being a seed-eater is that the majority of seeds ripen in summer and autumn. By the following spring, seed is in short supply and the birds must switch to a substitute food during winter or face a shortage. Feeding seed-eating species therefore helps them to survive this period, and ensures that they will be in peak condition, ready for the breeding season in spring.

HABITAT PREFERENCES

Recent years have seen a serious decline in many formerly common seed-eating birds. Intensification of agriculture has borne most of the blame, although realistically the shortage of food is the root of the disaster. The seed-eaters' numbers were previously probably artificially high as they prospered under traditional agricultural practices. If that sounds puzzling, note that large flocks

Above: *Although they have a variable diet, great tits are mostly dependent on seeds throughout the year, especially in winter.*

Above: *Goldfinches eat mostly seeds but will sometimes consume buds, sap and occasionally insects through a season.*

of seed-eaters were often seen feeding on winter stubble before moving on to land that was ploughed in late winter to find weed seed that had been thrown on to the surface. Before the widespread use of herbicides, crops had many weeds that left seed in the soil. It was these weeds that the seed-eating birds depended on,

and modern agricultural efficiency has largely removed them. A second problem is that seed-eaters can no longer feed on spilt grain in the stubble because fields are now ploughed soon after the autumn harvest.

Another traditional agricultural habitat that has declined is the hay meadow. Many were rich in plant species, but it is actually how they are managed that is important. In fact they do not have to have a great variety of plants to be important for birds, but those that contain dandelion and sorrel are especially useful for seed-eating birds, such as linnets, in summer.

Ironically, housing developments that spread over what was once farmland may yet help save some of these birds. The increasingly popular habit of feeding seed-eating birds has thrown them a lifeline, and many now prosper as a result. It is not the same for all species, however. The house sparrow, found in many towns and cities, was first attracted to our streets when the only form of transport was horse-drawn. The sparrows fed on the grain spilt in the streets and lived around the stables, common all over the city. The arrival of the motor car saw the decline in their numbers across much of their original range, although ironically they remain a pest in other areas where they were introduced.

SEED-EATERS

Typical species Finches including linnets, buntings, sparrows, tits, pigeons, doves, dunnocks.

Garden benefits Seed-eating birds are beneficial when they switch to hunting insects to feed their young. Foraging seed from the soil in winter also helps to reduce weed growth the next season.

Natural diet Seed-eating birds eat a range of seed, including grain, nuts and sunflowers. They will switch their preferences as a season progresses according to the availability of food.

Resident species Resident breeding populations of seed-eating birds are extremely dependent on the availability

of food, and almost all non-migratory species move between breeding and wintering areas in order to forage.

Migratory species The corn and snow bunting, brambling, siskin and other finches migrate in short hops in search of food. They do not always choose a regular destination, and often only a proportion of the birds migrate.

Supplementary diet Many seed-eating birds are choosy about what they eat, and prefer oil-rich, high-energy food. The best includes black sunflower hearts (seed with the husks removed), white proso millet, niger (thistle) and good quality peanuts, including peanuts in their shells.

**PLANTS TO ATTRACT
SEED-EATING BIRDS**
Amaranth (*Amaranthus caudatus*)
Dandelion (*Taraxacum officinale*)
Fat hen (*Chenopodium album*)
Field forget-me-not (*Myosotis arvensis*)
Millet (*Panicum miliaceum*)
Red clover (*Trifolium pratense*)
Sunflower (*Helianthus annuus*)
Teasel (*Dipsacus fullonum*)

Amaranth

Red clover

Sunflower

Teasel

Always try to provide as much natural food as possible to ensure that you preserve birds' natural behaviour patterns. Plants such as sunflowers (*Helianthus*), and a patch of wildflowers that includes thistles, knapweed (*Centaurea*) and teasel (*Dipsacus*) will help to attract seed-eaters.

Traditionally, feeding birds was limited to the winter, but recent evidence suggests that serious shortages are experienced in summer by many species when they are rearing their families. Summer feeding with

Below: *Knapweed is a common perennial weed with attractive flowers. The seeds are eaten by species such as finches.*

sunflower hearts and other seed can help the birds to lay more eggs and rear a healthier brood. However, note that not all commercial bird foods are formulated to meet all nutritional needs of seed-eaters.

FEEDING STRATEGIES
The seed-feeders generally have short, thick, strong beaks that are good for crushing or cracking open seed. They can take some time to learn which foods are safe or good for them to eat. They often have an instinctive wariness about any change in their habitat, and you will need to be patient when you try to feed them. Seed-eaters prefer their natural food sources, and when they come to the garden for the first time they may not actually recognize supplementary foods.

Try offering black sunflower, white proso millet, niger (thistle) and peanuts, but remember that most of these foods are supplements and can't always meet all of the birds' nutritional needs. Gradually add variety once they become accustomed to feeding at the site. They will soon overcome their caution and start to experiment.

Seed-eaters are naturally more gregarious in winter, probably because of their tendency to form large flocks at this time. This helps them locate food and feed more efficiently than when alone, and also makes them less vulnerable to predators.

MIGRATORY SPECIES
Seed-eaters tend to be resident species, however buntings, such as corn and snow buntings, and finches such as siskins do migrate in search of food, moving to areas

Below: *Dunnocks have a variable diet through the seasons but depend heavily upon small seeds during the winter months.*

Above: *Dandelions are generally regarded as weeds by gardeners but their seed is an ideal food for smaller seed-eating birds.*

where the climate is milder and food sources more accessible. These winter migrants return to their breeding grounds in spring, although in some bird populations, for example goldfinches, only part of the population migrates. Other species simply move to lower ground.

THREATS
Competition Winter is a time when birds naturally flock, and this can cause aggression and tension. Birds at a winter feeder are forced together, and aggression is likely. Try to spread food around, and for aggressive species such as robins, you should put food out separately to avoid conflict.

Habitat loss Intensification of farming has meant that many species of once common birds are in serious decline due to loss of habitat and food sources. Oil-rich wildflower seed is vital for these species, with many now remaining abundant only in gardens.

Herbicides Weedkillers have been used with increasing regularity in many countries, both to control crop weeds and also to improve the look of the garden. However, letting some weeds flourish is vital for the survival of foraging seed-eaters.

Predation The seed-eaters' habit of feeding on the ground makes them vulnerable to attack by cats, especially where the latter can hide and wait under garden bushes.

ATTRACTING FRUIT-EATING BIRDS

Fruit is an abundant and nutritious source of natural food, and one that many bird species have learned to exploit. In cooler climes, fruit tends to be a seasonal bounty, and so most fruit-eaters in these regions alternate their diet, eating other foods when fruit is not available.

Berries grow on a wide variety of plants including trees, bushes, climbing plants and even some herbaceous and ground-cover plants. When they are ripe, birds often descend on them and can clear a bush in a matter of hours, with some species, such as thrushes, switching almost totally to a fruit diet from late summer into autumn.

ROLE IN GARDENS
Birds and berries are a remarkable example of how plants and animals have evolved together, with one exploiting the other. The fleshy pulp of a berry is surprisingly nutrient-rich, and contains a good deal of starchy carbohydrate or sugars that conceal and protect the seed within. Most berries are also full of vitamins. The trade-off is simple. Birds benefit from the nutrients contained in the soft flesh. The berry-bearing plant benefits as birds spread its seed in their droppings.

The major limitation for most birds with a fruit diet, however, is that it is not available for enough of the year. Late winter to midsummer is a time when there is precious little fruit around, so birds must find an alternative. Most fruit-eaters switch

Below: *A blackbird feasts on the red fruit of a crab apple* (Malus sylvestris). *This fruit is a favourite of many birds.*

FRUIT-EATERS

Typical species Blackbirds, thrushes, starlings, waxwings, blackcaps.

Garden benefits Fruit-eating birds play an important role in dispersing seed, but are most useful in summer when they switch to insect-eating and thus help to control pests.

Natural diet Fruit rarely provides all of any bird's diet for the whole year, but it does form an important part of some species' diet from midsummer into the colder months. Even fruit specialists occasionally take alternative food types.

Migratory species While there are fewer migrant fruit-eaters, many bird species that move short distances in winter will eat fruit in winter. Waxwings, on the other hand, are unpredictable in their movements but travel long distances in search of food.

Resident species Birds often widen their territories to forage, and may even defend fruit sources. Many species flock together in winter and adopt a methodical feeding approach that is different to their summer behaviour.

Supplementary diet Fruit-eating birds will quite happily take substitutes for fruit, provided they are able to recognize what it is. Pieces of broken apple and dried raisins may prove popular, and specialist suppliers now sell dried fruit especially for these birds.

---

to eating insects or other protein-rich foods in summer. Even when fruit is plentiful, many fruit specialists still supplement their diet with insects or other animal protein to ensure that they maintain a balanced diet.

HABITAT PREFERENCES
Fruit availability varies according to the season and, in most temperate climates, is available from midsummer until late winter. The fruit of the guelder rose (*Viburnum opulus*) or currants (*Ribes*) are quite short-lived and, if not consumed immediately, will fall from the plant and rot. However, the fruit of the cotoneaster and holly (*Ilex*) remains on the plant for many months, being a vital food reserve for much of the winter.

Always choose a range of plants that produce fruit over a long period. Remember that most species of fruit-eating birds have their favourites that they will take first, and that some fruit will remain on the plant for a long time before it is taken. Early fruiting bushes, such as currants and wild strawberries, are just as important as the late berries, and even a small garden can accommodate some of these plants.

FEEDING STRATEGIES
Fruit is extremely important for many songbirds that switch from a summer invertebrate diet to a winter one based on berries. This is especially important when cold weather arrives and frozen ground

Below: *The scarlet berries of the rowan tree* (Sorbus aucuparia) *provide sustenance for many species of birds in autumn.*

Above: *Elderberry is an excellent source of berries in midsummer. The berries are especially liked by blackbirds and thrushes.*

prevents resident species foraging for worms, grubs or fallen seed. It is at these times of year, when food is short, that nourishing fruit is most vital.

Some birds tend to descend en masse to take berries when ripe. Starlings, for example, are highly systematic in their approach, methodically stripping bushes and trees from the top down. They also drop far fewer berries than other birds, and leave bushes picked clean. Thrushes, on the other hand, are well known for their tendency to defend their territory, and will often defend a berrying tree or shrub against all-comers. This acts as a larder that will see them through the winter, and if hard times do not materialize the birds gain a great advantage in having food to the end of winter, enabling them to nest early.

MIGRATORY SPECIES

As with most bird species, harsh winter weather is often a trigger for berry-eaters to move south. While most only move short distances, a few species cover much greater distances. The movements of berry-feeding birds are always inextricably linked to the availability of the fruit itself. Possibly the most famous migratory berry-eaters are the waxwings. In both Europe and North America these beautiful birds leave their forest homes and move to warmer climes, often descending on gardens to feast on berries. They are communal feeders, with individuals eating up to 500 berries each day, and in Holland they are called *pestvogel*, meaning invasion bird, due to their habit of appearing suddenly and clearing away all the fruit.

Flocks of some berry-eating birds show a high degree of co-operation when they feed. On trees or shrubs where slender twigs hold a supply of berries that only one bird can reach at a time, flock members have occasionally been observed lining up along the twig and passing berries from beak to beak so that each bird gets to eat.

PLANTS TO ATTRACT FRUIT-EATING BIRDS

Blackcurrant (*Ribes nigrum*)
Elderberry (*Sambucus niger*)
Herringbone cotoneaster
(*Cotoneaster horizontalis*)
Holly (*Ilex aquifolium*)
Guelder rose (*Viburnum opulus*)
Mezereon (*Daphne mezereum*)
Rowan (*Sorbus aucuparia*)
Wild strawberry (*Fragaria vesca*)

Cotoneaster

Holly

Mezereon

Rowan

Below: *The small berries of the blackcurrant* (Ribes nigrum) *are popular with birds such as blackbirds as well as people.*

Below: *Although naturally migratory, the availability of supplements in gardens means that some blackcaps overwinter.*

ATTRACTING OMNIVOROUS BIRDS

The need to survive has driven the majority of resident garden birds to adopt an omnivorous diet, which allows them to exploit various foods as they become available. It is a highly successful strategy, and the chief reason behind the success of many species in colonizing our towns and gardens.

Birds that eat anything digestible/edible are known as omnivores. This is not to say that an omnivorous bird will eat any item of food that is put in front of it, and in most cases omnivores have specific feeding needs that may vary seasonally or perhaps in response to local variations in their habitat. In fact the vast majority of birds tend to be somewhat omnivorous, although the tendency is usually most pronounced when their normal food source is in short supply.

Being an omnivore is usually the most successful survival strategy in rapidly changing environments, or in places subject to extreme seasonal variation. It is also noteworthy that many larger birds are omnivores because their body size makes specialization difficult unless their habitat – and therefore food supply – is very consistent all year round.

In time, successful omnivorous species can become very numerous. Members of the crow family, such as magpies and jays, will eat smaller birds and immature chicks, among other foods. This results in an unusually high number of these large birds.

Above: *Originally from Europe, chaffinches have also been introduced elsewhere. Their varied diet has contributed to their success.*

Above: *A familiar sight in many European gardens, blue tits exploit numerous food sources, especially during the winter.*

HABITAT PREFERENCES
The changing seasons bring times of alternate plenty and shortage for birds with highly specialized diets. Eating many different foods is usually a much more

successful strategy. Because omnivores will eat both plant and animal matter, they survive well in many environments and often prove highly adaptable. Some, like the seagull, have no problem adapting to living near humans and have recently started scavenging in landfill sites and city streets. This shouldn't be so surprising because modern cities are similar in many ways to tall, rocky cliffs, and as the seagulls often nest or roost on top of tall buildings, safe from predators, it is only natural that they should feed nearby.

As habitats change, those creatures that best adapt to them tend to prosper. Urban bird populations have changed over time, and pigeons have now reached epidemic proportions in many cities. Surprisingly, garden birds are often quite urban in their distribution, with higher densities in towns than in the surrounding countryside. The most common species of these urbanized populations are often omnivores, and the garden is an ideal habitat.

FEEDING STRATEGIES
Being omnivorous has obvious advantages, but various foods often require adaptations to the digestive system. Some omnivorous

---

OMNIVORES
Typical species Corvids including jays, crows and magpies, also thrushes, tits, finches, starlings and gulls.

Garden benefits Omnivores can be a mixed blessing in the garden, particularly if you have a vegetable patch. On the other hand, their varied diet includes many garden pests.

Resident species Resident omnivores often face a bleak prospect during winter. Food shortages, exacerbated by resident competitors and incoming winter migrants, means that there is a naturally high mortality rate.

Migratory species The vast majority of omnivores are able to avoid the necessity of migrating vast distances,

but many – including members of the thrush family – just travel short distances to escape harsh winter weather, and often take up temporary residence in gardens.

Natural diet Many omnivores have set patterns regarding exactly what and when they will eat. These species are often insect-eaters in the summer months, for example, before their digestive tracts adapt for their winter diet of berries and seed.

Supplementary diet Omnivores should be provided with a varied diet. Numerous mixes exist, and the best idea is to provide a full range of food types, including grain, small seeds, suet, fruit and even some live food.

PLANTS TO ATTRACT OMNIVOROUS BIRDS
Blackthorn (*Prunus spinosa*)
Bramble (*Rubus fruticosus*)
Evening primrose (*Oenothera biennis*)
Gooseberry (*Ribes uva-crispa*)
Hawthorn (*Crataegus monogyna*)
Ivy (*Hedera helix*)
Juneberry (*Amelanchier lamarkii*)

Blackthorn

Bramble

Gooseberry

Hawthorn

bird species lengthen the digestive tract in winter to get more out of relatively poor quality food. This allows them to be mostly vegetarian in winter, switching to an insectivorous diet in summer.

The beaks of omnivorous birds are usually relatively long and unspecialized, although this can vary considerably according to their evolutionary history. Feral ring-necked parakeets in the UK, for example, are much more omnivorous than

Below: *Ivy (*Hedera helix*) berries are eaten by many species including pigeons, doves, jays, thrushes and waxwings.*

the original wild populations in Africa and Asia that eat fruit, berries, nuts and seed. This is likely to be a result of their foraging in domestic gardens where meat and bacon rinds are often left out on bird tables. It is this ability to adapt, learn new tricks and exploit unfamiliar food sources that differentiates omnivores from other birds with more restrictive diets.

MIGRATORY SPECIES
Omnivores, like most birds, will migrate if food becomes scarce. They rarely undertake the huge journeys so characteristic of insectivores, however, with starlings or European robins simply travelling a few hundred miles and, even when they do migrate, it will not always be the whole population that does so. In fact the most likely migrants in a normally resident bird population are invariably the females and young. Many common species move from one area to another, while others simply move into the towns from the countryside. Some species regarded as non-migratory will sometimes move large distances when faced with harsh winter conditions, and because these newcomers look just like the residents, their arrival often goes largely unnoticed.

Robins, thrushes, skylarks and blackbirds all tend to undertake short flights to warmer areas, and blackbirds that live in Scandinavian countries fly south-west to spend the winter in countries with a less severe winter. In fact blackbirds often change their habits and distribution over

Below: *Corvids such as the rook are highly adaptable feeders. Flexible eating has enabled them to become numerous.*

Above: *The sweet, edible fruits of juneberry* (Amelanchier) *mature in midsummer and are eaten by a wide variety of birds.*

the year, raising families and feeding in gardens during the spring and summer where they can raise up to three broods. After the breeding season, they must 'feed up' for the coming winter, and move out into the surrounding countryside to do so.

THREATS
Competition Omnivores are adaptable and able to exploit new situations, but this brings them into contact with new competitors. Some urban birds are highly aggressive, and often chase away newcomers.

Disease Any increase in population raises the chances of disease spread. Omnivorous birds often congregate where there is a food source, and disease becomes more prevalent than for birds following a more solitary life.

Habitat changes As changing habitats favour certain incoming species, others are less favoured and some omnivorous birds that were formerly common in cities – such as the raven in London – are now scarce or absent, having been unable to adapt to modern city life.

Predation All birds face predators in either the garden or their natural habitats, but they are usually numerous enough to cope with any losses. In gardens, cats are usually the main threat, although other birds (including birds of prey) can also take their toll.

PLANTING GUIDE FOR BIRDS

The species listed below are just a small selection of the many varieties that can be planted to attract birds. Your choice will depend on personal preference and on the space available, soil type and the position, whether in sun or shade. A good rule is to choose the widest variety of plants possible.

TREES

The trees listed here provide foods such as fruits or insects, and also make good nesting sites for birds. If space allows, large trees such as oaks and maples will support a wealth of insect life.

Crab apple *Malus sylvestris*
Height: 10m/33ft. Spread: 10m/33ft.
This small woodland tree grows in fertile, well-drained soil in gardens. It prefers full sun or partial shade. In late spring this deciduous tree produces white flowers. In autumn it bears red fruits which are eaten by birds such as finches and thrushes. The cultivated apple (*Malus domestica*) is also highly attractive to birds.

False acacia *Robinia pseudoacacia*
Height: 25m/80ft. Spread: 15m/50ft.
This quick-growing tree is a native of North America, where it is also called the black locust. It needs a sunny position, and will grow in poor soil, but not waterlogged ground. Scented, drooping white flowers

Below: *Waxwings (shown here) and fieldfares are among the birds that feast on rowan berries during the autumn period.*

Above: *The crab apple* (Malus sylvestris) *is often found growing wild in hedgerows and along woodland edges.*

appear in late spring or early summer. This deciduous tree with dark-green leaves attracts seed-eaters such as finches.

Mountain ash (Rowan) *Sorbus aucuparia*
Height: 15m/50ft. Spread: 8m/26ft.
This small deciduous tree has delicate, frond-like leaves. It requires light, moist soil which can be acidic, and prefers full sun or partial shade. In autumn the rowan produces small scarlet berries which provide food for many birds. The whitebeam (*Sorbus aria*) and wild service tree (*S. torminalis*) are related.

Lodgepole pine *Pinus contorta*
Height: 15–25m/50–80ft.
The lodgepole pine is native to North America, as are the Monterey pine (*P. radiata*) and black pine (*P. nigra*). These evergreen conifers have needle-like leaves and bear cones that ripen in their second year. All three prefer full sun and moist soil. The dense evergreen foliage provides shelter for nesting birds, while the cones provide food for seed-eaters.

Bird cherry *Prunus padus*
Height:15m/50ft. Spread: 10m/33ft.
The bird cherry is a small deciduous tree which produces white scented flowers in

Above: *The common oak is renowned for supporting larger numbers of invertebrates than any other European tree.*

spring. Its black cherries are eaten by birds such as finches in autumn. It prefers full sun and needs well-drained soil. Many *Prunus* species attract birds, including the wild black cherry (*P. serotina*), the choke cherry (*P. virginiana*) and the cultivated plum (*Prunus domestica*).

Oak *Quercus robur*
Height: 30–40m/100–133ft.
Spread: 25m/83ft.
This large deciduous tree is suited only to large gardens. It requires well-drained soil and is a slow-grower. The oak supports a huge range of insects whose caterpillars provide food for nesting birds. It produces acorns in autumn. Relatives include the fast-growing red oak (*Quercus rubra*), and live oaks, which have evergreen leaves.

Cappadocian maple *Acer cappadocicum*
Height: 20m/70ft. Spread: 15m/50ft.
This native of Asia is now found in Europe. The leaves of this deciduous tree turn bright orange in autumn. It needs sun or partial shade and fertile, well-drained soil. Winged fruits and insects living on the tree provide food for birds. Relatives include the red maple (*A. rubrum*), the silver maple (*A. saccharinum*) and the sugar maple (*A. saccharum*).

SHRUBS

Seed-bearing shrubs will attract birds such as finches and sparrows, while berry-bearers nourish thrushes and warblers. Dense shrubs provide cover and safe sites for birds to nest.

Barberry *Berberis vulgaris*
Height: 2m/6ft. Spread: 3m/10ft.
This evergreen shrub bears scarlet berries that are eaten by many birds. Sharp spines make it a good hedging plant. It grows in sun or partial shade in most well-drained soils. *Berberis thunbergii* grows in similar conditions, but is deciduous, with leaves that turn orange in autumn. This produces pale flowers in spring, followed by bright red berries in autumn.

Guelder rose (Viburnum) *Viburnum opulus*
Height: 4m/12ft. Spread: 4m/12ft.
This deciduous shrub produces white flowers in spring and red berries in autumn. It requires sun or semi-shade and well-drained soil. Relatives include Laurustinus (*V. tinus*) which bears white flowers and black fruits. Black haw (*V. prunifolium*) is popular with birds, as are nannyberry (*V. lentago*) and arrow-wood (*V. dentatum*).

Hawthorn (May) *Crataegus monogyna*
Height: 10m/30ft. Spread: 8m/25ft.
This deciduous, spiny bush is common in European hedgerows. It prefers sun but will tolerate shade. Its white blossoms are attractive in spring. The crimson berries are eaten by birds such as starlings, tits and thrushes in autumn. Dense foliage provides good cover for nesting birds.

Below: *Hawthorn is often found growing wild in hedges. Many birds eat the berries, and wood pigeons eat the leaves.*

Above: *Tits and cuckoos are among the species that harvest caterpillars and insects from buddleja blooms.*

Pyracantha (Firethorn) *Pyracantha coccinea*
Height: 2m/7ft. Spread: 2m/7ft.
This evergreen shrub is sometimes grown as a hedge or along a wall. It grows in sun or partial shade and any well-drained soil. It has dark-green leaves and produces white flowers and clusters of scarlet berries. The dense, spiny foliage provides safe nesting sites for birds, while thrushes, pigeons and other species eat the berries.

Common elder (Elderberry)
Sambucus nigra
Height: 10m/30ft.
This deciduous shrub does well in partial shade. It provides good cover for nesting birds. The pale blossoms of early summer are followed by drooping clusters of small black berries which attract birds. The American elderberry (*S. canadensis*) and red-berried elder (*S. racemosa*) are also popular with many birds.

Cotoneaster *Cotoneaster microphyllus*
Height: 1m/3ft 4in. Spread: 2m/7ft.
This evergreen shrub has rigid, drooping branches. The dense foliage provides safe nesting sites for birds, while in autumn, the berries are eaten by species such as thrushes. It prefers full sun. A relative known as wall-spray (*C. horizontalis*) provides similar attractions for birds and will grow along walls, banks or the ground.

Dogwood *Cornus sanguinea*
Height: 4m/13ft. Spread: 3m/10ft.
The bright red stems of this deciduous shrub provide colour in winter. It needs sun and grows well in chalky soil. The small black berries are eaten by birds in autumn. Many *Cornus* species are attractive to birds, including Siberian dogwood (*C. alba*), the red osier (*C. stolonifera*), and flowering dogwood (*C. florida*), a small tree.

Buddleja (Butterfly bush) *Buddleja davidii*
Height: 5m/15ft. Spread: 5m/15ft.
This sprawling deciduous shrub requires full sun and well-drained soil. In midsummer it produces drooping spikes of scented lilac flowers which attract butterflies. In turn the insect life attracts insect-eaters such as tits. Buddleja can look untidy and should be pruned back severely in spring.

Serviceberry (Juneberry) *Amelanchier lamarckii*
Height: 6m/20ft. Spread: 3m/10ft.
The green or tawny leaves of this deciduous shrub turn red or orange in autumn, providing a blaze of colour. It needs full sun or semi-shade and prefers slightly acidic soil. The berry clusters are eaten by many types of birds. Related species such as *A. arborea* and *A. canadensis* are also popular with birds.

Dog rose *Rosa canina*
Height: 3m/10ft.
This deciduous rambling shrub grows wild in European woods and hedgerows. It prefers sun and fertile soil. The pale pink flowers open in summer, following by juicy red hips that are eaten by many birds. Many species of cultivated shrub roses, such as *Rosa rugosa*, also attract insects, insect-eaters and fruit-eating birds.

Below: *Dog rose flowers give off a delicate scent. Blackbirds and thrushes are among the birds that eat the fruit.*

Above: *Honeysuckle blooms produce more scent toward evening. The fruit is eaten by warblers and blackbirds.*

Above: *Blackberry plants flourish on waste ground. The berries feed wood pigeons, crows, starlings and finches.*

Above: *Virginia creeper is a highly ornamental climber, particularly in autumn. It can be grown up buildings and walls.*

CREEPERS AND CLIMBERS

Leafy climbers offer sheltered nesting sites for birds. Some species provide foods such as autumn berries, nectar, or a wealth of insects to eat.

Honeysuckle *Lonicera periclymenum*
Height: 7m/23ft.
This deciduous climber grows well up garden walls. It requires sun or partial shade and fertile, well-drained soil. The sweet-scented pink or yellow flowers attract insects and insect-eaters, while some types of birds sip the nectar. The red berries are enjoyed by warblers and finches. The Amur honeysuckle (*L. maakii*) is also attractive to birds.

Blackberry (Bramble) *Rubus fruticosus*
Height: 3m/10ft. Spread: 3m/10ft.
This prickly deciduous climber runs wild in hedgerows and on waste ground. It grows in either sun or partial shade. Small white flowers in summer are followed by black fruits that are enjoyed by birds and people. Other *Rubus* species such as dewberry (*R. caesius*), cloudberry (*R. chamaemorus*) and raspberry (*R. idaeus*) produce edible fruits.

Virginia creeper *Parthenocissus quinquefolia*
Height: 15m/50ft or more.
This fast-growing, deciduous climber clings to walls with its tendrils. Its foliage provides cover for nesting birds. The leaves turn crimson or purple in autumn, when the plant also produces dark-blue berries which are eaten by crows and thrushes. This creeper grows best in sun or semi-shade in fertile, well-drained soil.

Grape vine *Vitis vinifera*
Height: 30m/100ft.
This woody, deciduous climber is grown for its juicy green or purple fruits, which are enjoyed by birds as well as humans. The fleshy fruits are used in wine-making. The vine's green, scented flowers open in early summer. It needs full sun or semi-shade and fertile, well-drained soil, and can be grown against walls and trellises.

Below: *The grape vine can be a useful screening plant when grown up a trellis. There are hundreds of varieties.*

HERBACEOUS PLANTS

Flowering plants provide foods such as seeds and insects and their caterpillars. Some attract slugs, snails and other invertebrates which also feed some types of birds. As with other types of plants, old-fashioned and native plants should predominate, but non-native species can play an important role too.

Sunflower *Helianthus annuus*
Height: 3m/10ft. Spread: 60cm/2ft.
This native of North America grows wild on wasteland. A leggy annual, the long green stem bears a single large, deep-yellow flower with a massive seedhead. The seeds

Below: *Sunflowers are often seen growing as a crop. Many bird varieties, including this great tit, enjoy eating the seeds.*

feed doves, nuthatches, crows and other birds. The plant requires full sun and fertile, moist but well-drained soil. It may need to be staked when in bloom.

Michaelmas daisy *Aster novi-belgii*
Height: 1m/3ft 4in. Spread: 50cm/20in.
This North American plant grows wild on waste ground and damp sites. A tall perennial, it has branching stems and likes sun or partial shade and fertile, well-drained soil. Purple, daisy-like flowers with yellow centres appear in autumn. These attract insects such as bees and butterflies. The seeds also provide food. Many other asters are also popular with birds.

Cornflower *Centaurea cyanus*
Height: 1m/3ft 4in. Spread: 30cm/1ft.
This tall perennial has slim, grey-green leaves. It requires a sunny position and fertile, well-drained soil. The flowers appear in late autumn – most commonly deep blue, but also pink, red, purple or white. These attract insects which feed birds. Cornflower seeds are eaten by tits, finches and members of the crow family.

Yarrow *Achillea millefolium*
Height: 60cm/2ft. Spread: 60cm/2ft.
This perennial herb grows wild in hedgerows, grasslands and meadows. With its delicate, frond-like leaves, it needs

Below: *Insect-eaters feed on aphids attracted to the yarrow. Sparrows, finches and tits eat the seeds.*

full sun and moist, well-drained soil. It produces clusters of pale flowers in summer or autumn. These attract insects which provide food for birds, as do the yarrow's seeds.

Dill *Anethum graveolens*
Height: 90cm/3ft.
This slender plant is often found on waste ground. It prefers full sun and sandy soil. The seeds are used in cooking, so it makes a good kitchen-garden plant. The tall stems support flattened clusters of yellow flowers in late summer. The seeds provide food for birds, while slugs attracted to dill plants feed species such as thrushes.

Marigold *Calendula officinalis*
Height: 60cm/2ft. Spread: 30cm/1ft.
This quick-growing plant with light-green, scented leaves is often found growing wild on waste ground. It requires a sunny position but will grow in any well-drained soil. Cultivated varieties bear yellow or orange, daisy-like blooms from spring to autumn. The plant attracts insects and slugs which provide a source of food for invertebrate-eating birds.

Foxglove *Digitalis purpurea*
Height: 1–1.5m/3–5ft. Spread: 60cm/2ft.
This tall, upright plant grows wild in woods and heathland. It grows best in semi-shade and needs moist, well-drained soil. In summer the foxglove produces tall spikes of bell-shaped flowers which may be purple, pink or white. These attract bees which provide food for insect-eaters. The seeds also nourish birds.

Above: *The many varieties of marigold brighten gardens with their single- or double-headed flowers.*

Coreopsis (Tickseed) *Coreopsis grandiflora*
Height: 45–120cm/1½–4ft.
The many varieties of coreopsis produce bright yellow, daisy-like flowers from early summer to autumn. These long-lasting blooms provide colour and attract insects, which in turn draw insect-eating birds. *Coreopsis* species require full sun and fertile, well-drained soil.

Below: *Foxglove flowers attract bumblebees which are hunted by flycatchers. Some birds eat the seeds.*

MAKING BIRD FEEDERS, BIRDBATHS AND NEST BOXES

Perhaps it is the opportunity to create a world in miniature, while simultaneously giving nature a helping hand, that has ensured the continued popularity of nest-box construction. Bird boxes and also feeders and birdbaths can be plain, pretty or fanciful without affecting their primary function. Having satisfied the basic requirements, the finish is up to the individual. The projects in this book present a wide variety of ways to provide your local feathered community with food, drink and nesting sites.

Left: *Although highly embellished, this house still retains its practical function, providing a safe, dry site for birds to nest.*

Above: *From rudimentary woodwork to more complex projects, bird-feeder construction can suit every skill level.*

Above: *Simple feeders such as this one look very attractive when filled with foods with different colours and textures.*

Above: *Even unoccupied nest boxes make charming decorative features that enhance many different garden settings.*

BUILDING MATERIALS

Bird boxes, feeders and baths for garden species can be constructed using a wide variety of materials. The garden shed will probably provide many suitable items, such as sticks, string, garden wire, paint, varnish and offcuts of wood. You may be able to improvise using materials not listed here.

ALUMINIUM MESH

Useful for making bird feeders, this is available from hardware shops and some hobby suppliers. Birds can peck food through a coarse mesh, while a fine gauze can be used to line the base of a feeder to enable rain to drain away.

CLAY

A birdhouse moulded from potter's clay will need to be fired in a kiln. Self-hardening clay does not need firing, and is available in various colours, including stone and terracotta. You will need to varnish the clay to make it water-resistant.

COCONUT

Birds love fresh coconut, and when they have eaten the contents you can use the half shells as parts of a birdhouse or fill them with bird pudding. Never put out dry, shredded coconut.

CORRUGATED ROOFING MATERIAL

Any offcut that you are able to purchase from a DIY shop would be enough to cover a large birdhouse. You will need to buy special screws to attach it.

Below: *Paintbrushes will be useful for decorating projects. You will need medium-sized brushes as well as very fine ones.*

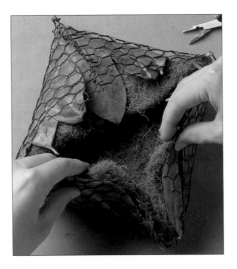

Above: *Hanging basket liners can be purchased in various colours, including green, which blends with garden settings.*

HANGING BASKET LINERS

Basket liners are available in a soft green with a texture that resembles moss. They can be cut to size and moulded over chicken wire.

PAINT AND VARNISH

Use exterior quality paint with a satin or matt finish. If you use emulsion paint, it will need to be protected with a varnish designed for exterior use, such as yacht varnish. For fine work, use craft enamels or artist's acrylics.

PAINTBRUSHES

You will need a range of small household paintbrushes, together with medium and fine artist's brushes for detailed decoration. Clean brushes in white spirit if you are using oil-based paints.

PALETTE

A white ceramic tile, or an old plate, is useful for mixing paint colours.

READY-MADE BIRDHOUSES

As an alternative to making your own birdhouse, you can buy ready-made houses inexpensively and customize them to suit the style of your garden.

Above: *Shells provide a decorative finish to projects. Collect them responsibly – by recycling old necklaces, for example.*

ROOFING SLATES AND TILES

Beautiful old roofing slates and tiles can often be purchased from architectural salvage yards and make excellent weatherproof roofs for birdhouses.

SELF-ADHESIVE ROOF FLASHING

This material is tough and waterproof. It looks like lead and makes an invaluable covering for birdhouse roofs.

SHELLS

These make pretty decorations. You can buy them from craft shops or, better still, use an old shell necklace.

STICKS

Garden canes are available in a range of colours. Thick stakes can be used to support some houses. Withes are willow stems used for weaving. They are available stripped or unstripped, and become very pliable once soaked. Straight hazel twigs can be gathered in the garden or hedge.

STRING

Ordinary household string is useful for many projects, as well as for hanging up feeders. Green garden string and natural raffia make good binding materials and

garden string has also usually been treated for outdoor use to help it last longer. Sea grass string is both strong and decorative.

WIRE
Plastic-coated chicken wire is attractive and easy to work with, as it will not scratch your hands. Garden wire is also plastic-coated and comes in various gauges. Galvanized wire is useful for constructing and suspending birdhouses. Florist's wire is much thinner and is useful for binding.

WOOD
For long-lasting, weatherproof houses, use timber that is at least 15mm/⅝in thick. Planed pine is easily available in a wide range of widths. For outdoor use, treat it with preservative, or paint or varnish it. Tongue and groove or ship-lap boards make attractive walls for larger birdhouses. Marine or exterior quality plywood is easy to cut with a fretsaw for decorative panels. A birdhouse made from a hollowed-out log looks good in natural surroundings.

Clockwise from top left: *Natural and planed wood, a ready-made birdhouse, natural and treated willow, aluminium mesh and wire sheets, galvanized and plastic-coated wire, a range of paints, paintbrushes, string, liner, roof slate, coconut, self-adhesive flashing, clay, sticks and shells.*

BUILDING EQUIPMENT

No special equipment is needed for building bird boxes and feeders, and only basic carpentry skills will be required. Take care when using new equipment; you might like to practise on a scrap first. Before cutting, always recheck against the template, or double-check your measurements.

ADHESIVES
Glue all joints in wooden birdhouses, using wood glue, before nailing or screwing them together. Masking tape can be useful for holding wood together while glue is drying. Two-part epoxy resin glue makes a strong bond when you are joining disparate materials. Small stones or shells can be embedded in ready-mixed tile cement for a decorative finish. Always use exterior grade glue, especially when you are working with PVA.

BROWN PAPER
Heavy craft paper makes a good protective covering for your work surface when painting or gluing. Old newspaper is also ideal as protective covering.

CRAFT KNIFE AND SCISSORS
Always use a sharp blade in a craft knife and protect the work surface with a cutting mat. When using self-adhesive flashing, cut with a sharp knife, rather than scissors.

DRILL AND BITS
A drill will be needed to make holes for screws and other fixings. Spade bits can be used to make entry holes up

Below: *Drill holes using a clamp to keep your work steady. If you use countersink screws, you will need a countersink bit.*

Above: *Glue can be spread using a gun, simple spatula or even a matchstick. Wipe off any excess glue before it dries.*

to 2.5cm/1in. Hole saws, which fit on to a drill, are available in a range of sizes to cut larger entry holes for birdhouses. You can also cut an entry hole using a fretsaw and jigsaw, if a hole saw is not available.

GLOVES
Wear gardening gloves to protect yourself from scratches when you are handling, bending or cutting wire. You could wear

Below: *Pliers will be useful to bend and mould wire, and also to cut it. Protect your hands by wearing thick gloves.*

Above: *Hammer steadily and gently, taking care to keep your free hand well away from the hammer head.*

a pair of latex gloves to keep your hands clean whenever you are painting or varnishing, or using modelling clay.

HAMMER AND NAILS
Use galvanized nails or plated moulding pins, which will not rust.

PENCIL AND RULERS
Use a sharp pencil and ruler for accurate marking out of wood. Use a metal ruler when cutting with a craft knife.

PLIERS AND CUTTERS
General-purpose pliers and small, round-nosed ones will be useful for working with wire. You will also need wire cutters. Lead flashing, for roofs, can be cut using tin snips.

SANDPAPER
Smooth the edges of the wood after cutting using medium-grade sandpaper wrapped around a wooden block. Roll a piece of sandpaper around your finger to smooth the edges of entry holes.

SAWS
Use a tenon saw for square cutting, unless you are making large cuts, in which case you will need a panel saw. Curved shapes can

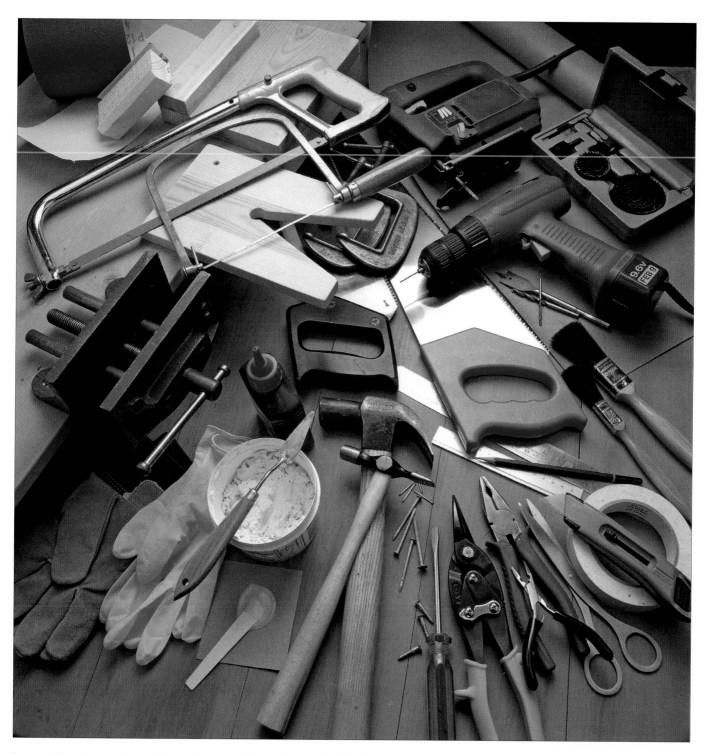

be cut using a jigsaw. Use a fretsaw to cut small, intricate shapes. When cutting, you should always support the wood on a V-board screwed to the workbench. Use a hacksaw to cut metal.

SCREWS AND SCREWDRIVER
Screws rather than nails should be used to make secure fixings in large, heavy structures. Buy Pozidriv screws for outdoor use, as these tend to be plated and therefore will be less inclined to rust.

VICE AND CLAMPS
A vice or adjustable workbench will be essential for holding wood steady when you are sawing it, and can also help when you are gluing. A bench hook will be helpful when you are cutting timber with a tenon saw, because it is useful for cutting strips to length. You will need to clamp a coconut in a vice to saw it in half. Clamps of various sizes, and even clothes pegs can be useful for holding your work together while you are assembling it.

Clockwise from top left: *Sandpaper and wooden blocks, panel and tenon saw, drill kit and bits, brown paper, hacksaw, paintbrushes, pencil and ruler, craft knife and masking tape, scissors, pliers and cutters, screwdriver and screws, hammers and nails, epoxy resin glue, wood glue and spatula, latex and fabric gloves and vice.*

BIRD FEEDERS AND BIRDBATHS

Many species of garden birds have suffered quite serious declines in recent years. By providing food and water you will help the local bird population to remain fit and healthy, so that the birds are more likely to breed successfully when the mating season comes around.

Even a well-stocked garden can be an unforgiving place for birds as winter draws in. Late autumn marks the time when many birds will visit your garden, seeking extra supplies of food. However, feeding can be beneficial throughout the year, especially in spring when the young are born and adults must find food for their growing families. By supplementing bird diets with extra food, you are arguably maintaining a falsely high population of birds in your garden, but this in turn helps some species to survive when their natural habitats have been reduced by human activities.

FEEDERS

Different species of birds have different feeding habits. Hanging food is ideal for members of the tit family, placed high enough up so that cats can't get at it.

Above: *Feeders are available in a wide range of shapes and sizes, and make attractive additions to the garden.*

Above: *Small perching birds, such as this juvenile great tit, are able to take advantage of hanging feeders, safe from competition.*

If the food is too exposed, however, the birds may be in danger from sparrowhawks, unless there is nearby cover, such as trees and hedges. Trees, large shrubs or even a dead branch, firmly planted in the ground, can act as a support for feeders. Securely attach your feeders to the branches using thin, pliable wire.

PONDS AND BIRDBATHS

Birds need a constant supply of water, for both bathing and drinking. It is essential for them to keep their feathers in good condition for insulation during the long and bitter nights of winter. Some birds, such as blue tits, may drink more in winter because the seasonal diet of dry nuts is not sufficient to hydrate them. Seed-eaters in general also need plenty of water to compensate for the lack of moisture in their diet.

Ponds, of course, provide water all year round for bathing and drinking, and will also attract many other types of wildlife to your garden. We are not all fortunate enough to have the space or facilities for ponds or larger water sources, but a birdbath is an attractive option which will enhance your garden as well as proving extremely useful to local birds.

DIFFERENT TYPES OF FEEDER

By using a wide range of bird feeders, you can provide a greater variety of food items. In doing this, you will increase the chances of more species visiting your garden.

Bird feeder table
Tables are excellent for a wide range of small garden birds and also for larger birds that perch or stand in order to eat their food. Food placed on the table supplies birds in the critical winter season, in spring when birds are nesting, and throughout the year.

Glass/plastic feeder
These types of feeders are usually filled with mixed seed, which is made accessible to birds through a series of small hoppers in the side.

Half a coconut
A coconut sliced in two is an excellent way of providing food for small, clinging birds. Can be filled with suet or seeds.

Squirrel-proof feeder
To discourage squirrels, make bird food inaccessible. This type of feeder has a cage to protect the seed.

Wire feeder
These are mostly for peanuts, and are useful because they prevent birds from choking on whole nuts.

Bird feeder table

Glass feeder

Half a coconut

Squirrel-proof feeder

as appealing to human visitors. You can also create your own exclusive birdbath using the projects given here.

Whatever the birdbath, make sure that it has either sloping sides or a ramp if the sides are steep, so that birds can easily walk in and out, and small animals do not become trapped. Don't forget to keep the birdbath clean and filled with fresh water, and crack any ice which forms on the surface in winter.

Left: *Like all birds, sparrows benefit from a dip in a birdbath. Seed-eaters like these need plenty of drinking water too.*

Below: *Pieces of broken crockery make a wonderful mosaic pattern. The sloping sides provide easy access to the water.*

A birdbath need not be an elaborate affair. A puddle is the simplest form of all. You could make a more permanent watering hole by scraping out a shallow puddle-shape in a flower bed, lining it with plastic and securing the plastic in place with stones. Another simple and unobtrusive option might be an inverted dustbin lid securely placed on bricks.

There are many commercially available birdbaths which not only serve a useful purpose to the birds, but add a point of interest to any garden. Fountains, or any form of dripping water, make ponds and baths even more enticing to birds as well

Below: *A traditional stone birdbath makes an atmospheric addition to any garden, as well as benefiting birds.*

NEST BOXES

In recent years, nest boxes have become a familiar sight in many gardens, chiefly because people like to see birds raising their young. Nest boxes have proved extremely valuable for a variety of birds because they provide alternative, artificial nesting sites for many species.

Before you erect a nest box, decide what type of bird you are trying to help. Different species have different needs. Choosing the wrong type of box or putting it up in an inappropriate place may mean that it is not used. If a box is to be used immediately, it needs to be in place by the start of the breeding season, and that usually means late winter. However, there is never a wrong time of year to put one up, and they often provide winter shelter. A box so used is more likely to be used again next season.

READY-MADE BOXES

There has been a rapid increase in the range of commercially produced bird boxes, and numerous designs are now available to suit a range of garden birds from martins and swifts, tawny owls and wrens, to starlings, sparrows and tits. Small-scale specialist producers of bird boxes can be found on the Internet.

The best designs are usually solid and simple. In general, beware fussy, overly ornate boxes, as they can be useless. If you are buying a box, it needs to be waterproof, but it must have a drainage

Below: *Swallows usually build mud nests under the eaves of houses. This adult has been induced to nest in a whimsical box.*

Above: *The sight of a bird, such as this blue tit, feeding a brood of chicks is a wonderfully rewarding sight in a garden.*

hole in the bottom to allow any water that blows or seeps in to escape. If there's any standing water, it will make the box cold, might lead to disease, and will increase the chances of rotting the box. For the same reason, make sure that the base of the box is inside the sides and not fixed to the bottom or water will seep straight into the base. The lid must fit tightly,

Above: *Doves roost in dovecotes with ledged entrances. However, in general, an outside ledge can attract predators.*

preferably with a hooked catch to prevent predators, such as squirrels or cats, from getting in and eating the chicks. Boxes with a perch under the entrance hole should be regarded with caution, as they can be used by hungry (predatory) squirrels to stand on. Lastly, avoid using any boxes that have been heavily treated with preservative. The fumes will be off-putting to birds, and what is more, they could prove poisonous to the adults or chicks.

When you buy bird boxes, make sure that they are accompanied with instructions and other useful information regarding their positioning to maximize the chances of birds taking up residence. The best brands may also offer advice on how you can improve your garden to suit particular species. Buying a bird box from a reputable supplier is probably the simplest (if most expensive) way to achieve success.

FIXING A BIRD BOX

It is not difficult to fix a bird box, but choosing the right position is important. It must be fixed securely so that it doesn't fall when occupied, particularly when well-grown nestlings become more active.

DIFFERENT TYPES OF NEST BOX

There is no standard design for a bird box. What birds really need is a secure and weatherproof home, safe from predators.

Do remember, though, that different bird species have different preferences regarding the type and location of a box.

With a front hole The size and shape of the hole varies with the species you intend attracting. Small birds such as tits and sparrows need round holes around 2.8cm/1⅛in wide whereas larger birds such as woodpeckers and pigeons need rectangular holes that are 6cm/2¼in or more.

With an open front Many birds, including European robins, wrens, wagtails and thrushes, prefer this design, and the opening width varies accordingly, from 4cm/1½in for wrens to 12cm/4¾in for flycatchers and thrushes.

Duck box Usually large and square, these are attached to poles sunk in water to keep predators away. The rectangular entrance is reached via a ramp-like ladder.

Communal box Birds such as house sparrows form communal nests, commonly in the eaves of houses. Modern energy efficiency means that many former nest sites have been sealed off, however, and the house sparrows often have difficulty in breeding. A communal nest box can help to boost numbers of these species. It is best attached as high as possible on the shady side of a building.

Martin box Swallows and house martins can have difficulty finding nest sites, and the smooth walls of modern buildings often cause nests to fall, sometimes with the young inside. Near roads, vibration caused by heavy vehicles may also shake nests loose. Artificial nests, made of a wood and cement mix, are sometimes supplied attached to an artificial overhang and ready for immediate use.

Owl box These vary considerably in their design and are often more of a tube rather than a box. Smaller owl boxes are used by other large birds as they are often at least three times the size of a standard bird box. While there are many designs, all need a well-drained floor and easy access for cleaning at the end of the season, and are best placed in a large tree in the lower to mid canopy.

Tree creeper box Tree creepers build nests that have contact with the trunks of thick-barked trees such as oak (*Quercus*), alder (*Alnus*), poplar (*Populus*) or pine (*Pinus*), and so the boxes must be open at the back. They are fixed to the tree using wire attached to each side or with wooden blocks. The entrance holes face downward and are located at the side of the box.

| Open-fronted box | Duck box | Communal box | Martin box | Owl box | Tree creeper box |

Although boxes can be fixed at 1.8m/6ft above ground, they can be placed higher than this, and a height of 3.7m/12ft or more will defeat many predators.

When positioning a bird box, make sure that it is protected from prevailing cold winds and hot sun, preferably giving it a shady aspect or wall that faces away from the strong midday or afternoon sun. Try to ensure that the birds have a fairly clear flight path to and from the nest, and try to angle the box slightly downward to help exclude rain. Remember that birds are often territorial and, in most cases, don't like being crowded together. Leave some space between the boxes unless providing for communal species such as sparrows. There may be natural possibilities already in your garden that, with a little thought, can be turned into good nest sites. Birds may nest in an old shed that has had the door left purposely ajar, or make their homes in a hole in the eaves of a house or outbuilding.

MAINTENANCE

Inspect the box in late summer or early autumn, and remove any nest material or other debris. This helps reduce parasites. You could add some clean straw if you want small birds to use it over winter. In late winter, clear the box out again ready for the nesting season. Finally, provide nesting materials such as string, cloth, wool, dried grass and excess hair from your cat or dog.

Right: *If you find a nestling on the ground, leave it alone. The parents will not be far away, and may abandon it if you intervene.*

WIRE BIRD FEEDER

*Small aluminium drinks cans and aluminium mesh form the basis
for these simple feeders which, when filled with seeds or peanuts,
will attract a range of species, including tits.*

1 Cut a small aluminium drink can in half,
then draw a decorative scalloped border
around each half and cut out using
scissors. Trim off any jagged edges.

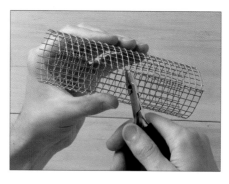

2 Cut a rectangle of mesh to fit, rolled up,
inside the can. Roll the mesh around a
bottle. Join the edges by hooking the cut
ends through and bending them with pliers.

3 Pierce a hole in the bottom of the can.
Fit the mesh cylinder into the two halves of
the can, then thread them on to galvanized
wire. Twist the lower end of the wire into a
flat coil so that the feeder cannot slide off.

4 Leave enough wire above the top so you
can slide the top off for refilling, then allow
an extra 7.5cm/3in. Cut the wire. Twist the
end into a flat coil, then make a hook by
bending the wire over a marker pen.

YOU WILL NEED
small aluminium drink cans
old scissors, wire cutters
aluminium mesh
straight-sided bottle
small pliers, bradawl
galvanized wire
permanent marker pen

TYPICAL FOOD
peanuts, sunflower seeds

TYPICAL VISITORS
tits
greenfinches

Above: *Greenfinches are among the birds
that will visit feeders filled with various
types of nuts, scraps or larger seeds.*

BOUNTY BOWER

In winter, the food you provide can make the difference between life and death for birds. Once you have started, continue to put food out each day, but for a real treat offer this gourmet selection.

1 Skewer an apple and thread it on to a long piece of garden wire. Wind the end around the base of the apple to prevent it slipping off. Embed sunflower seeds into the flesh of the apple. You can adjust the quantities to suit the number of birds that call at your bower.

2 Screw metal eyelets into the base of a selection of pine cones. Thread them with string and tie the cones together in size order. Hang the string on an existing bower.

3 Tie a selection of millet bunches with raffia. Using a darning needle and strong thread, thread unshelled peanuts to make long strings. Saw a coconut in half. Drill two holes near the edge of one half and thread a piece of wire through them. Twist the ends of the wire together.

4 When the seeds have been pecked out of the cones, you can revamp them by filling with unsalted, unroasted smooth peanut butter and dipping in small mixed seeds.

YOU WILL NEED
skewer
garden wire
wire cutters
metal eyelets
string
scissors
raffia
darning needle
strong thread
hacksaw
drill
unsalted, unroasted smooth peanut
    butter (from health food shops)

TYPICAL FOOD
apple
millet bunches
whole coconut
peanuts in their shells
sunflower seeds
mixed birdseed
niger (thistle)
pine cones

TYPICAL VISITORS
goldfinches
hawfinches
grosbeaks

COCONUT FEEDER

A plastic tube, made from a recycled cosmetic bottle, makes a practical seed-dispenser. The half-coconut roof lifts off to the side, allowing you to refill the plastic tube. Tits are particularly adept at using this kind of feeder and their acrobatics can be entertaining.

Above: *While not as acrobatic as tits, redpolls (Carduelis flammea) will still use feeders such as this one. This species is named after the red patch on the forehead which both sexes posses, though the male's is brighter in hue.*

YOU WILL NEED
2 coconuts
drill
hole saw
knife
hacksaw
4cm/1½in diameter straight-sided
    plastic bottle
scissors
florist's wire
twigs
small pliers
string
bead

TYPICAL FOOD
sunflower seeds
mixed seed

TYPICAL VISITORS
robins
sparrows
redpolls
tits

1 Drill two holes in the top of each coconut and drain the milk. Cut two 5cm/2in holes from one on opposite sides and a third at the top. Remove the flesh with a knife.

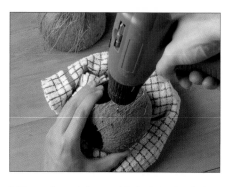

3 Beneath each large side hole in the first coconut, drill two tiny holes on either side. These will be used for holding the perches. Drill two further holes on each side for attaching the roof.

5 Attach a perch beneath each side hole by threading florist's wire through the small drilled holes and around a twig, twisting it to form a cross over the centre. Using small pliers, twist the ends of the wire together inside the coconut to secure it.

2 Saw the second coconut in half. Remove the flesh from one half to form the roof of the feeder. Make a small hole in the top and two holes on each side near the rim.

4 Remove the top and bottom of a plastic bottle to make a tube. Cut two semicircles at the bottom on opposite sides to allow seeds to spill out. Place the tube in the first coconut through the large hole at the top.

6 Attach the roof to the base by threading string through the side holes in the coconuts. Tie a bead to a doubled piece of string, to act as an anchor, and thread the string through the central hole of the roof for hanging the feeder.

BOTTLE FEEDER

This elegant and practical seed feeder keeps the contents dry. You will be able to regulate the flow of seed by adjusting the height of the bottle, but don't forget to cover the opening while you insert the filled bottle into the frame, to avoid spilling any seed.

Above: *House sparrows (Passer domesticus) are among the most common visitors to seed feeders. In recent years this species has declined, but putting out seed for birds can help to reverse the trend.*

YOU WILL NEED
bottle
pierced galvanized metal L-shaped
    bracket
hacksaw (if needed)
galvanized wire
pliers
13cm/5in tart tin with
    removable base
aluminium gauze
old scissors
epoxy resin glue
florist's wire

TYPICAL FOOD
black sunflower seeds
striped sunflower seeds
mixed seed

TYPICAL VISITORS
blue tits
great tits
sparrows
finches
dunnocks

1 Measure your chosen bottle against the metal bracket and, if the bracket is too long, cut off the excess metal using a hacksaw. However, it does not matter if a little of the bracket shows above the top.

3 Place the bottle in position on the bracket and wrap the wire around it, forming a criss-cross shape. Secure the wire by threading it through a hole on the bracket at the back.

5 Remove the bottom of the tart tin and use it as a template to cut out a circular piece of aluminium gauze. Use epoxy resin glue to stick the gauze into the bottom of the tin.

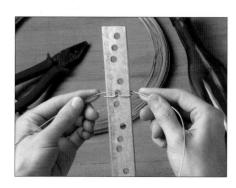

2 Cut a piece of wire long enough to wrap around the bottle in a criss-cross fashion. Thread both ends of the wire through an appropriate hole positioned near the top of the bracket.

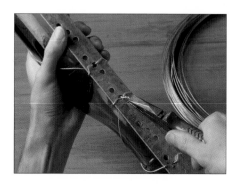

4 Repeat the process at the neck of the bottle, so that the bottle is held in place by two lots of crossed wire. Twist the ends of the wire together at the back of the bracket using a pair of pliers.

6 Using florist's wire, attach the tin to the arm of the bracket by wiring through the aluminium gauze. The gap between the bottle neck and the pan should be wide enough to allow seeds to trickle through.

RUSTIC BIRD TABLE

A basic table is one of the simplest ways of dispensing food to birds. One of the advantages is that it can take many different kinds of food. You can make this attractive rustic table quite simply from two pieces of rough timber, nailed together with battens to strengthen the structure. The lip around the edge is designed to stop nuts and seeds rolling off. String is tied to a hook in each corner so that the table can be hung in a tree, out of reach of predators.

Above: *Finches are among the species that benefit from bird tables. The chaffinch* (Fringilla coelebs) *is one of our most attractive small birds.*

YOU WILL NEED
rough timber, 25 x 13 x 1cm/
   10 x 5 x ½in (x 2)
battens, 25 x 2.5 x 2.5cm/
   10 x 1 x 1in (x 2) and
   28 x 5 x 1cm/11 x 2 x ½in
   (x 4)
nails
hammer
wood preservative
paintbrush
4 brass hooks
2m/2yd sisal string
scissors

TYPICAL FOOD
varied, including seeds, bread

TYPICAL VISITORS
finches
sparrows
tits

1 Join together the two pieces of rough timber by positioning them side by side and placing the two 25cm/10in battens across the wood, one at each end. Nail the battens securely in place to make the base.

2 Nail the four 28cm/11in lengths of batten around the edges of the flat side of the table, creating a lip of at least 2.5cm/1in. This will ensure the food is not spilled.

3 Lightly paint all the surfaces of the table with wood preservative and leave to dry.

4 Screw a brass hook into each corner of the table to attach the string.

5 Cut the sisal string into four equal lengths and tie a small loop in one end of each piece. Attach each loop to a hook, then gather up the strings above the table and tie in a loop for hanging.

KITCHEN BIRD TABLE

This original bird table uses cooking and cleaning equipment in ingenious ways, and makes an offbeat sculpture at the same time. The sieves allow rain to drain away, and the finial is the head of a balloon whisk, into which a fat ball can be inserted.

1 Clamp the sieve handle under a wooden block and bend it through 90 degrees. Then bend it further by hand to fit around the broom handle. Repeat the same process with the other sieves.

2 Nail a piece of scrap wood to the bottom of the broom handle and firmly anchor this in the bucket using large beach pebbles.

3 Position the sieves along the length of the broom handle and hold each one in place by threading a wooden spoon into the bent handle. Once you are happy with the arrangement, sand grooves into the broom for the spoons to fit into.

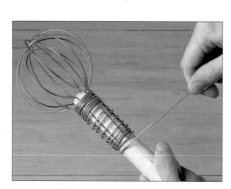

4 Using either a hacksaw or wire cutters, remove the handle of a balloon whisk and attach it to the top of the broom handle using a length of galvanized wire. This provides a holder for a fat ball.

YOU WILL NEED
clamps
metal sieves
wooden block
scrap wood
protective gloves
broom handle
nails
hammer
galvanized bucket
beach pebbles
wooden spoons
sandpaper
balloon whisk
hacksaw or wire cutters
galvanized wire

TYPICAL FOOD
fat ball
sunflower seeds
mixed seed
shelled peanuts
leftovers and kitchen scraps

TYPICAL VISITORS
doves
starlings
thrushes
jays
sparrows

PALLADIAN BIRD TABLE

This classical-style feeding table looks elegant and impressive but is actually relatively simple to make. It will not only attract birds that enjoy eating seeds, fat and scraps, but will also beautify any garden setting. It can be mounted on a pole, hung from a branch or fixed to a wall using a large bracket.

Above: *The siskin (*Carduelis spinus*), a member of the finch family, can be drawn to bird tables holding seeds and scraps.*

YOU WILL NEED
12mm/½in medium-density
    fibreboard (MDF) or exterior-grade
    plywood (for the base)
6mm/¼in medium-density
    fibreboard (MDF) or exterior-grade
    plywood
ruler, pencil
saw
glue gun and glue sticks
8 threaded knobs, 30mm/1¼in
    diameter x 20mm/¾in deep
4 dowels, 120 x 16mm/4¾ x ⅝in
drill and 3mm/⅛in bit
exterior-grade filler
fine-grade sandpaper
medium paintbrush
off-white emulsion paint
exterior-grade varnish

TYPICAL FOOD
varied, including seeds, fat, scraps

TYPICAL VISITORS
tits
finches

1 Mark and cut out all the pieces, following the template given at the back of the book. Assemble the base and steps with wood glue. You could apply hot glue using a glue gun if you possess one.

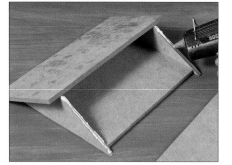

3 Glue each half of the roof on to the top of the gable triangles. Make sure each roof half overlaps the ceiling by the same amount at the sides and each end.

5 Glue the threaded cupboard knobs in position at each corner mark on the base and the ceiling. Allow to dry thoroughly. Meanwhile drill each end of the dowel columns to accommodate the protruding thread of the knobs.

2 Mark the positions of the columns at each corner of the top step and on the underside of the ceiling. Glue the main gable triangles in place on each end of the ceiling piece.

4 Allow enough time for the roof glue to dry thoroughly. Next, glue the decorative gable triangle in place centrally on the face of the front gable.

6 Apply glue to each thread and assemble the dowels between the base and the roof. Fill any gaps with exterior-grade filler. Rub down with fine-grade sandpaper and paint with off-white emulsion followed by several coats of exterior-grade varnish.

SEASIDE BIRD TABLE

The pretty decorative details and distressed paintwork of this bird table are reminiscent of seaside architecture. You can use plain dowelling – or a broom handle – to make the supports for the roof, or recycle the turned legs from an old piece of furniture.

Above: *Robins* (Erithacus rubecula) *are among the tamest species to visit gardens, and enjoy feeding from bird tables.*

YOU WILL NEED
2cm/¾in pine board
pencil, ruler
jigsaw or scroll saw
drill
wood glue
4 screws
screwdriver
fretsaw
4 x 20cm/8in lengths of 2cm/¾in dowelling
4mm/⅙in plywood
sandpaper
plated moulding pins
hammer
watercolour paints
paintbrushes
petroleum jelly
white emulsion paint
blowtorch
satin yacht varnish
water bowl

TYPICAL FOOD
varied, including kitchen scraps

TYPICAL VISITORS
starlings
sparrows
robins

1 Using the templates, mark out the base, roof base and roof ends on pine board. Cut out using a jigsaw. Drill a 2cm/¾in hole in each corner of the two bases. Glue and screw the roof ends to the roof base.

2 In the base, drill a starter hole for the fretsaw. Cut out a 7.5cm/3in diameter hole, 5cm/2in in from one short side. Glue the four dowelling supports in place on the frame and base. Leave to dry overnight.

3 From the 4mm/⅙in plywood, cut five strips 2.5cm/1in wide for each roof end panel. Cut seven 2.5cm/1in strips for each side of the roof. Cut out the scalloped edging pieces, four strips for the eaves and two lozenges for the finials. Sand surfaces.

4 Glue the plywood strips across the roof ends and nail in place with the pins. Attach the roof slats along the sides of the roof, and the scalloped frills all around the roof edge and the base. A piece of cardboard can hold the pins steady while hammering.

5 Paint the bird table with a dilute mixture of cobalt blue and burnt umber watercolour paint. Leave to dry, then smear on a thin layer of petroleum jelly with your fingers. Apply white emulsion paint and dry it with a blowtorch to make the paint crack.

6 To age the paintwork, apply a dilute, equal mixture of yellow ochre and burnt sienna watercolours. Leave to dry, then finish with a coat of satin yacht varnish. Attach to a ready-made stand and place a water bowl on the table.

BAMBOO BIRD TABLE

It is a real treat to watch birds feeding, and seeing them at close range from the comfort of your armchair is even better. This bamboo structure is designed to hang on a wall from two cup hooks. Position it near a window so that you can see the birds easily.

Above: *With his bright pink chest, the male bullfinch (Pyrrhula pyrrhula) is one of the most attractive members of the finch family. The female has duller plumage.*

YOU WILL NEED
tenon saw
timber offcut
pencil
ruler
drill
bamboo canes
clips
garden string
scissors
scrap roofing material
baking tin
2 clothes pegs
wire whisk

TYPICAL FOOD
fat ball
peanuts in their shells
sunflower seeds
breadcrumbs
kitchen scraps

TYPICAL VISITORS
tits
goldfinches, bullfinches and
    other finches

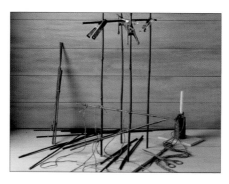

1 Mark and cut out a rectangle 12 x 16cm/ 4½ x 6¼in on the timber offcut. Drill a hole in each corner and push in four 90cm/36in canes. Cut two short lengths of cane and clip them diagonally at the top to hold the uprights in place.

3 Tie on the roof supports on each side, again using the templates given at the back of the book as a guide. Use garden string or twine to tie the supports.

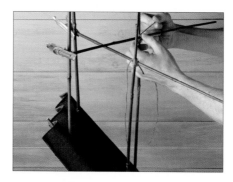

5 To attach the roof, drill four holes in the roofing sheet. Unclip the top diagonals and push the roof down over the uprights until it is resting on the roof supports. Tie on the long top diagonals.

2 Using the templates at the back of the book as a guide, tie on the horizontal canes, using garden string. These will hold the baking tin firmly on each side. Add two diagonal canes on each side as shown, to reinforce the structure.

4 Join the two sides of the structure, first attaching the bottom diagonal canes, then with two pieces running straight across at the level of the feeding tray.

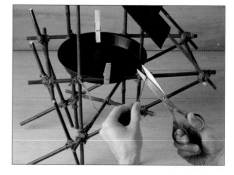

6 Snip off the long ends of the string and attach the feeding tray with two clothes pegs. Use the top long diagonals to hang food from, such as a whisk as a fat ball holder, or nuts.

RUSTIC FEEDERS

These two feeders in different styles originate from the same basic shop-bought model. One has been sanded and given a driftwood-style paint effect, while the other has been camouflaged beneath found objects, including a rusty tin sheet and a short length of plasterer's angle bead.

Above: *With its long, sharp bill, the great spotted woodpecker is well equipped to harvest nuts from feeders such as these.*

1 Paint the first feeder and allow to dry. Rub down with sandpaper to give the surface a weathered, driftwood effect. Apply clear glue to the roof and sprinkle sand over it. Twist lengths of stub wire around a pencil and weave natural twine through them to imitate coils of rope.

2 Add natural objects found either in the countryside or on the seashore, such as shells, twigs and moss, to decorate and personalize the feeder. Shells can be attached with glue. Use cut-off corks to seal the feed chambers, and tie a loop of florist's wire to suspend the house.

3 For the second feeder, wearing protective gloves, snip pieces of old tin to make a roof. Remove all sharp edges and glue in place. Glue moss around the base.

4 Make the roof ridge from plasterer's angle bead sprayed with black paint. Glue it firmly to the house. Plug the feed holes with corks and suspend with wire as before.

Left and right: *Two very different results can be achieved using the same basic shop-bought feeder. You can experiment with different materials and applications to create your own designs. You could be very creative with the choice of found objects you use, to give your personalized feeder a flavour of whatever is in its immediate environment. This will help it to harmonize with the garden setting. Or you could use materials such as shells, collected while on holiday, to produce a delightful memento.*

YOU WILL NEED
2 wooden bird feeders
light grey emulsion paint
medium paintbrushes
sandpaper
clear glue
sand
stub wire
pencil, corks
natural twine
shells, twigs or moss
craft knife or scalpel
thick florist's wire
protective gloves
sheet of old tin
tin snips or saw
glue gun and glue sticks
plasterer's angle bead
black spray paint

TYPICAL FOOD
shelled peanuts

TYPICAL VISITORS
woodpeckers
tits

GLASS GAZEBO FEEDER

Constructed from recycled tin cans and small pieces of glass,
this converted lantern makes a highly attractive feeder, which
will shine, jewel-like, from among the surrounding dark foliage.

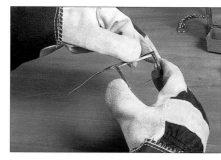

1 This lantern required extra glass to be installed. If this is the case, measure the areas required and reduce all measurements by 6mm/¼in to allow for the metal border around each panel. Using a chinagraph pencil, mark the reduced measurements on the glass, then cut out by running a glass cutter in a single pass along a ruler, while pressing firmly. Tap along the score line to break the glass. It is always advisable to wear protective gloves when handling glass.

2 Still wearing gloves, cut 9mm/⅜in strips of metal from a used tin can using tin snips. Wrap a strip of metal around each edge of each glass panel. Trim, then smear a small amount of soldering flux on to the adjoining surfaces of each corner joint.

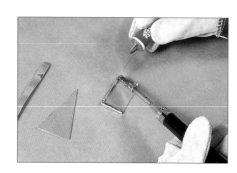

3 Solder the corner joints of each panel. Heat up a joint using a soldering iron and apply solder until it flows between the surfaces to be joined. Remove the heat source. The solder will set in seconds, but the metal will remain hot for some time.

4 Measure openings for the hoppers and fold sections of metal, using a try-square or ruler to keep the folds straight. Solder the meeting points of each hopper. Cut a base from fine wire mesh, then solder the base, panels and hoppers in place.

YOU WILL NEED
glass lantern
tape measure (optional)
thin glass (optional)
chinagraph pencil (optional)
try-square (optional)
glass cutter (optional)
ruler
protective gloves
shiny tin can (not aluminium),
    washed and dried
tin snips
flux and soldering iron
solder
fine wire mesh

TYPICAL FOOD
shelled peanuts
black sunflower seeds
striped sunflower seeds

TYPICAL VISITORS
tits
sparrows
finches
starlings

WOVEN WILLOW FEEDER

Made from the supple branches of unstripped willow, this woven basket feeder will look very picturesque placed in the garden. It could be used to dispense foods such as peanuts. The conical roof is packed with moss: as well as adding weight, this will provide valuable nesting material for breeding birds.

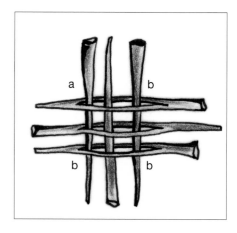

YOU WILL NEED
about 150 withes
knife or bodkin
clothes peg
secateurs
bradawl (optional)
pencil or pen, string
6 long strands ivy, moss
glycerine (optional)
garden twine

TYPICAL FOOD
shelled peanuts or seeds

TYPICAL VISITORS
warblers
buntings

Left: *The willow warbler* (Phylloscopos trochilus), *a common summer visitor, is a shy, drab bird easiest identified by its song.*

1 Trim six withes to a length of 23cm/9in from the butt (thick) end. Pierce the centre of three of these rods using a knife or bodkin and push the other three withes through them to form a cross. The rods should be arranged with the butt ends pointing in alternate directions. Push the rods together.

2 The cross you have made will form the centre of the base of the feeder. Insert the tips of two long withes into the slits to the left of the short rods and hold them in place by gripping the slit rods. Take one long withe in front of the three uprights, and behind the next three rods. Take the second withe behind the first three rods and in front of the next three, crossing its partner at b. Continue this weave for two complete rounds. Prise the rods apart to form the spokes of a wheel and continue weaving. Try to keep the weaving as tight as possible.

3 Continue to weave the base of the feeder basket, adding new weavers either butt to butt or alternatively tip to tip. The new one is placed to the left of, and under, the old end, which should finish resting on a bottom rod, while the new weaver carries on over it. Join both new weavers at the same time, on neighbouring bottom rods. Continue with your weaving until the base of the basket measures about 18cm/7in, finishing with tips. Temporarily secure the ends with a clothes peg and then trim the bottom rods flush with the weaving.

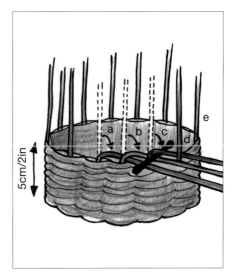

4 Having finished the base, you can now start to fashion the uprights which will support the cone-shaped roof of the bird feeder. Start by selecting 12 new withes. Trim the butt ends of the rods by slicing down the back of each one with a sharp knife, to make a thin wedge-shape. Insert each new willow stick to the left of a bottom rod. You may need to loosen the weave first, using a bodkin or bradawl, before you can fit in the new rod if you have woven the base very tightly.

5 Using your thumb nail or the blade of a knife, make an indentation in each of the new willow sticks where they join the base, then gently bend each one up to form the uprights and temporarily tie them all together at the top with string. You can now start to make the sides of the basket. Begin by inserting three new willow sticks, tip end first, to lie to the right of three consecutive uprights. Take the left-hand weaver in front of two uprights, behind the third and out to the front again.

6 Repeat with the second and third. Continue this pattern, pushing the weavers down, until the side of the basket measures 5cm/2in. Join in new weavers butt to butt or tip to tip, laying the three new rods to the right of the three old rods. To finish the basket, make a kink in each upright over a pencil or pen about twice the diameter of the rod. Bend the first rod (a) behind the second (b) and round to the front. Bend (b) over and behind (c), then bend (c) over and behind (d) and round to the front.

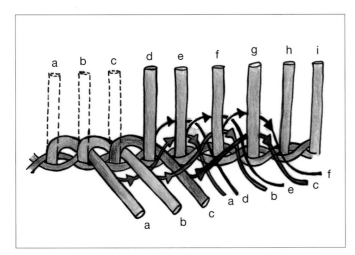

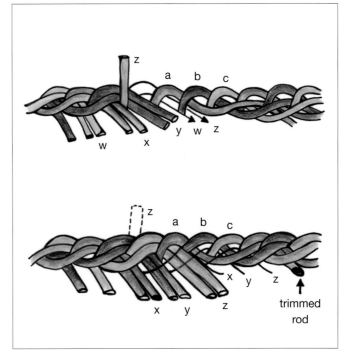

7 To finish off the border: rod (a) travels in front of (c) and (d) and behind (e) and lies in front. (d) bends down and lies beside and to the right of (a). Rod (b) travels in front of (d) and (e) and behind (f) and lies in front. (e) bends over and lies beside and to the right of (b). Rod (c) travels in front of (e) and (f) and behind (g) and lies to the front. Rod (f) lies down beside and to the right of (c). There are now 3 pairs of rods (ad), (be) and (cf). Continue the work always weaving with three pairs of rods until the end of the border. Always start with the far left pair of rods (ad) but use the right-hand rod (d), (e) and (f) and make each rod do the same journey (in front of two uprights, behind one) and pull down the next upright (g), (h) and (i), until there is only one upright left.

8 To finish the border, starting with the far left pair as before, each right-hand rod goes in front of two rods (which are not now upright) and behind the third, coming out through the original 'arches' made with a, b and c. Pull all the rods well down into place, lying tightly together. Trim the ends neatly all round the basket.

9 To make the frame for the roof, select 12 rods and trim them to 30cm/12in. Tie them securely together, 5cm/2in from the tips, using ivy. The ivy can be stripped of its leaves, or you can preserve the leaves by soaking them in glycerine, diluted half and half with water, for several days. Bend a withe into a circle a little larger than the basket. To secure the rods for the roof to the circular frame, take two long ivy stems, stripped of leaves, and tie them to the left of an upright. Wind one length around the upright above the frame and the other around the upright below the frame. Take both pieces around the frame to cross between the first and second uprights, then around the frame to the second upright. Repeat the pattern.

10 Weave the roof using the same pattern as for the sides of the basket using two sets of three rods, then change to a pairing weave, going in front of one upright and behind the next. Near the top, use a single rod weaving in and out and go as high as you can. Stuff the roof with moss.

11 To hold the moss in place, tie garden twine across the base of the roof, connecting each upright with the ones on the opposite side to make a star pattern. Cut four rods 20cm/8in long and trim both ends of each into flat wedges. Push them, equally spaced, into the weave of the roof and into corresponding positions in the basket, using a bodkin to open the weave if necessary.

COPPER BIRDBATH

You will have endless pleasure watching many different species of birds drinking from or preening and cleaning in this beautiful yet eminently practical beaten copper birdbath.

1 Using a chinagraph pencil and a piece of looped string, mark a 45cm/17¾in circle on the 0.9mm/20 SWG copper sheet.

2 Wearing protective gloves, cut out the circle with a pair of tin snips. Carefully smooth any sharp edges using a file.

3 Put the copper on a blanket and hammer it lightly from the centre. Spread the dips out to the rim. Repeat, starting from the centre each time, to get the required shape.

4 Continue hammering until you have achieved a shallow dish shape that will allow birds to enter and leave the water without difficulty. To make the perch, cut 1m/1yd copper wire, loop and hold the ends in a vice. Insert a cup hook into the chuck of a hand drill or slow-speed power drill. Put the cup hook through the loop. Run the drill to twist the wire. Drill three 3mm/⅛in holes around the rim of the bath.

5 Bend a knot into one end of each of three 1m/1yd lengths of wire. Thread the wires through the holes from beneath the bath. Slip the twisted wire over two of the straight wires to form a perch, and hang in a suitable position.

6 Maintain a constant supply of fresh drinking water all year round to help ensure the health of your local bird population. Once the birds have got used to this new feature, many different varieties will visit to bathe and drink.

YOU WILL NEED
chinagraph pencil
string
0.9mm/20 SWG copper sheet
protective gloves
tin snips
file
blanket or carpet square
hammer
medium copper wire, 4m/13ft
cup hook
drill and 3mm/⅛in bit

TYPICAL VISITORS
blackbirds
tits
finches

CHROME BIRDBATH

The gently sloping sides of a dustbin lid allow smaller birds to paddle, while larger birds can have a good splash in the middle without emptying the water. A night light fitted under the bath will prevent the water freezing over on winter days.

1 Using a hacksaw, saw across the middle of the dustbin lid handle. Bend back both sides of the severed handle using pliers.

2 Wearing protective gloves, remove the handle from the cheese grater using pliers. Once you have managed to detach one side of the handle from the securing rivet, the other will work free more easily.

3 Push the narrow end of the cheese grater on to the post and secure it with nails through the holes left by the handle rivets.

YOU WILL NEED
hacksaw
galvanized dustbin lid
pliers
protective gloves
cylindrical metal cheese grater
round fence post to suit size of grater
galvanized nails
hammer

TYPICAL VISITORS
sparrows
starlings
blackbirds
redpolls
robins

Above: *Blackbirds (*Turdus merula*), are among the most frequent visitors to birdbaths, splashing to wet their feathers.*

4 Squeeze the two sides of the lid handle together to insert them into the wide end of the grater. Place a night light inside the grater. This can then be lit to provide an interesting garden feature and prevent the water from freezing on cold days.

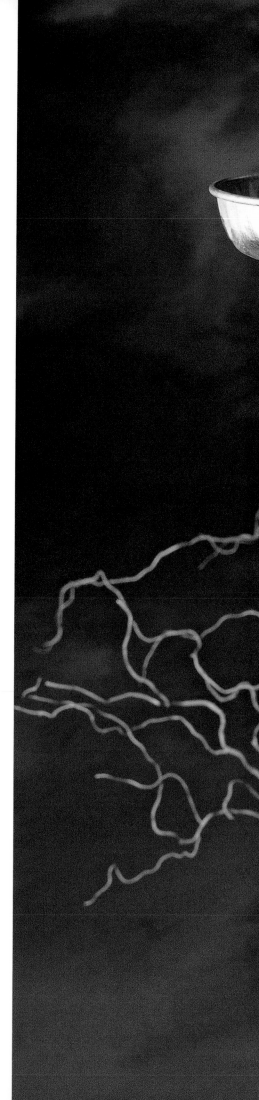

NESTING MATERIALS DISPENSER

This sculptural container will not only look elegant in your garden but will encourage birds to build their nests nearby. At nest-building time, keep the dispenser topped up with nesting materials such as scraps of wool, fur, fabric, straw, feathers and even hair, all of which will be most welcome to garden birds.

Above: *The domed nest of the long-tailed tit (*Aegithalos caudatus*) is an amazing structure, made of feathers bound together with strands of cobweb. The outside is disguised with lichen to conceal it from predators. Most birds build the basic nest structure using tough plant fibres such as twigs, leaves and dry grass. The interior is lined with soft, warm materials such as moss, hair and feathers. By providing nesting materials, you will give birds a helping hand to raise their young.*

YOU WILL NEED

chicken wire, approximately
    25cm/10in wide
protective gloves
wire cutters
small pliers
thin and thick garden wire
plastic picnic plate
bradawl
coffee jar lid
epoxy resin glue
large wooden bead

TYPICAL VISITORS

finches
sparrows
tits

1 Cut a rectangular piece of chicken wire and roll it into a cylinder. Join the wire along the edges by carefully twisting the cut ends together. Using a pair of pliers, pull the bottom of the cylinder to draw the wires together into a tight roll.

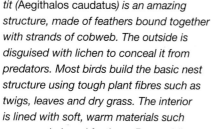

3 Splay out the rim of the container at the top. Bind the bottom with thin green garden wire. Secure both ends of the wire.

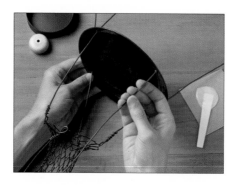

5 Make holes to match the positions of the wires around the edge of a plastic plate using a heated bradawl. Thread the plate, upside down, on to the wires. Glue a coffee jar lid to the plate to make a container for food or water.

2 Now start to shape the wire into an elegant vase shape. A third of the way from the top, form a neck by squeezing the wires together with the pliers. To create the belly of the container, pull the holes further open to fatten out the shape.

4 Attach four lengths of thicker wire, evenly spaced, around the rim of the container. Loop them through and secure the ends.

6 Connect the four wires to a single wire threaded with a large bead. Twist the wires neatly into position. Now you are ready to hang the dispenser from a tree or large shrub, so that nesting birds can pluck the contents at will.

ENCLOSED NEST BOX

This box will attract small birds to nest in your garden. The small, round entrance hole is designed to suit species such as tits. Once birds have taken up residence, they could return year after year.

1 The timber used in nest boxes should preferably be of hardwood, such as oak. Softer woods such as pine can also be used, but will start to rot more quickly. Whatever wood you use will last longer if you give the finished box a coat of exterior-grade varnish.

2 Measure the dimensions on the timber, referring to the template at the back of the book, and mark them clearly using a pencil and carpenter's square. Always double-check your measurements before cutting. Mark the names of each section in pencil.

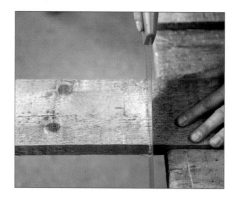

3 Cut the pieces using a sharp carpentry saw and put them to one side. Sand off any splintered edges to the wood.

4 Carefully screw the sections together. Don't use nails as these can cause the wood to split, allowing water into the box.

5 On the front face of the box, make a hole with a large drill bit. Attach the roof, using the rubber strip as a hinge. Varnish and fix the bird box in the garden, choosing a suitable spot out of direct sun and high enough to be out of reach of predators.

YOU WILL NEED

length of wood, 142 x 15 x 1cm/
   56¾ x 6 x ½in
pencil
ruler
carpenter's square
saw
sandpaper
screws
screwdriver
drill with 3cm/1¼in drill bit
rubber strip (for hinge)
varnish
paintbrush

TYPICAL INHABITANTS
tits
house sparrows
nuthatches
starlings – could use the box if you
   enlarge the entrance hole

OPEN-FRONTED NEST BOX

Not all of the birds that may nest in your garden like boxes with small entrance holes. Open-fronted boxes are designed to suit robins, wrens, spotted flycatchers and pied wagtails, and if you made the dimensions bigger, you could attract blackbirds and maybe even kestrels.

Above: *A nest box with a large, square entrance hole as shown in this project will attract robins and wrens. However, spotted flycatchers* (Muscicipa striata) *(above) will nest in a similar box with an entirely open front. This species begins nesting later than many other garden birds, using twigs, grass and moss bound with cobwebs to make the basic structure. The nest is then lined with feathers. An entirely open-faced box could also attract pied wagtails, while blackbirds may nest in an open-faced box of larger dimensions.*

YOU WILL NEED
length of timber 15mm/⅝in thick
wood glue
hammer
nails or panel pins
pencil
strip of sacking or rubber (for hinge)
varnish
paintbrush

TYPICAL INHABITANTS
robins
wrens
spotted flycatchers and pied wagtails
– will nest in a similar box with an
entirely open front

1 Cut out the timber using the template given in the back of the book. Arrange the pieces of wood in position to make sure that they all fit properly.

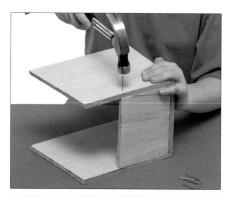

3 Glue on the other side and nail all the pieces together. Position the box on the rear board, and draw round it in pencil.

5 Your nest box will last longer if you give it a coat of exterior-grade varnish both inside and out. Leave the box overnight to let the varnish dry completely.

2 Glue the low front of the box to the base. Give the glue a little time to dry. Now add one of the side pieces of your nest box. Glue it in place carefully.

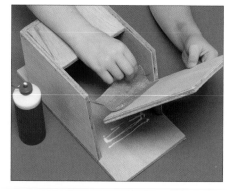

4 Using your pencil guidelines, nail the rear to the box. Add the roof by gluing and nailing on the sacking hinge.

6 Nail your box to a tree, shed or post, about 2m/7ft from the ground. Face the box away from any direct sunlight, as this may harm very young birds.

CUSTOMIZED NEST BOX

*Ready-made nest boxes are available in every shape and size.
An inexpensive birdhouse can be transformed with a lick of paint
and a few decorative touches. The Shaker-style paintwork on this
birdhouse uses leftover paint, the finial is cut from scrap timber
and the perch is an apple-tree twig.*

Above: *Studies have shown that tits
(Paridae) are opportunistic birds, quickly
able to adjust to new situations and turn
them to their advantage. Members of this
family are the species most likely to nest
in an enclosed nest box such as this one.
To ensure that the nest box gives you
maximum pleasure, position it so it can
be seen from the house.*

YOU WILL NEED

nest box
emulsion paint in 2 colours
paintbrush
permanent marker pen
decorative finial cut from a piece
   of scrap pine
PVA glue
drill
apple-tree twig

TYPICAL INHABITANTS

tits
house sparrows
nuthatches
woodpeckers
jackdaws and pigeons – will nest in
   a larger box of this type

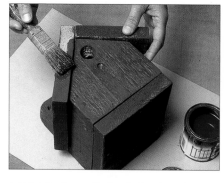

1 Paint the box with the first colour of
emulsion paint and set it aside to dry.
Draw the door and heart motifs using
the permanent marker pen.

2 Fill in the design and the finial with the
second colour of emulsion paint and leave
to dry completely. Glue the finial in place at
the front of the roof ridge using PVA glue.

3 Drill a hole of the same diameter as the
apple-tree twig beneath the entrance hole.
Apply a little glue to the twig and push it
in position. Allow the glue to dry.

DECORATED BIRDHOUSES

Inexpensive ready-made plain boxes can be customized to suit your taste. Paint makes for the simplest transformations – an alpine chalet and a Shaker-style dwelling are pictured here. You could also create a leafy hideaway using fabric shapes. Paint each house with primer before you begin, and allow to dry.

YOU WILL NEED
ready-made birdhouses
paintbrushes
emulsion paints
matt varnish and brush
pencil, paper and scissors
self-adhesive roof flashing
waterproof green canvas
staple gun
waterproofing wax (optional)

TYPICAL INHABITANTS
tits

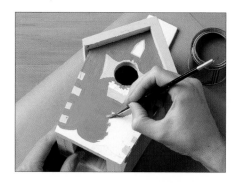

1 To create an alpine chalet, draw the design on the box. Paint the roof, shutters and other details in blue. When this is dry, paint the walls of the house in rust red.

2 Add details on the gable, shutters and stonework in white and grey. Paint flowers, grass and leaves along the front and sides in yellow and green. Varnish when dry.

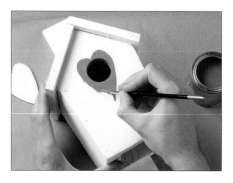

1 To make a Shaker-style dwelling, cut a heart out of paper and position it over the entry hole. Draw around it in pencil and paint the heart rust red.

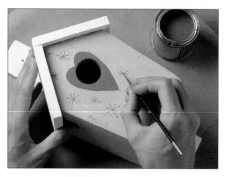

2 Paint the walls in duck-egg blue using a larger paintbrush. When this layer is dry, paint on little starbursts in rust red using a very fine artist's brush.

3 Cut a piece of roof flashing to fit the birdhouse roof. Cover the roof, folding the edges under the eaves. Protect the paintwork with matt varnish.

1 To make a leafy hideaway, paint the birdhouse a colour complimentary to your green canvas, such as mid-blue, and leave to dry. Cut the canvas into 4cm/1½in bands and scallop one edge. Staple the bands on to the house, starting at the base and allowing the scallops to overhang.

2 Staple more canvas bands around the front and sides, with each layer overlapping the last. When you reach the entry hole, snip the top of the canvas and glue it down inside. Staple on the next band, then trim back the central scallop to form a few small fronds above the entry hole.

3 Overlay strips on the side of the roof. Cut the top strip double the width, with a scalloped edge along both sides, so that it fits over the roof ridge. Finally, staple bands along the gable ends. Spray the finished house with waterproofing wax, if not using a waterproof fabric.

LAVENDER HIDEAWAY

This hand-painted project takes only a short time to make using a ready-made birdhouse. Even the heaviest shower pours freely off the lead roof, leaving the occupants warm and dry inside.

1 Paint the birdhouse with lilac emulsion and allow it to dry. Sketch out the decorative design using a pencil. Fill in the sketch using acrylic or watercolour paints. When dry, cover the whole house with several coats of exterior-grade matt varnish.

2 Make a paper pattern to fit the roof, using the template at the back of the book as a guide. Allow 12mm/½in extra for turning under each side and the rear, and 32mm/1¼in extra for the scallops.

3 Transfer the design on to a piece of thin sheet lead and cut it out using tin snips or a craft knife. Wash your hands thoroughly afterward if you have touched the lead.

YOU WILL NEED
wooden birdhouse
lilac emulsion paint
medium and fine paintbrushes
pencil
acrylic or watercolour paints
exterior-grade varnish
paper
scissors
thin sheet lead
tin snips or craft knife
soft hammer or wooden mallet

TYPICAL INHABITANTS
house sparrows
wrens
nuthatches

Above: *Nuthatches (*Sitta europaea*) are hole-nesters and are well suited to this box.*

4 Hold the lead roof in place and mould to shape by tapping the lead with a soft hammer or wooden mallet until the correct fit is achieved. Turn the 12mm/½in allowance under at the back and at the eaves to secure the roof in place.

FOLK-ART TIT BOX

This box is simple to make, but with its traditional weathered look, it makes the perfect springtime retreat for blue tits and other hole-nesters, such as nuthatches and house sparrows. Mounted on a post in a quiet spot, it should be safe from prowling predators such as cats.

1 Mark and cut the basic house on MDF or plywood following the template at the back. Mark a vertical line on the front panel. Mark a horizontal line across at the base of the triangle. Where the two lines cross, draw a 32mm/1¼in circle using compasses. Cut out the hole by first drilling a pilot hole, then enlarging it with a padsaw. Assemble the front, back, sides, base and the smaller roof piece of the hut using PVA glue and panel pins hammered down flush with the surface of the wood.

2 Paint the whole house, including the loose roof piece, with blue-grey emulsion paint. When dry, paint the walls of the house white. When these are dry (about 2–3 hours), distress the surfaces by rubbing with medium-grade sandpaper until the undercoat shows through.

3 Wearing protective gloves, cut a strip of lead the depth of the roof by 50mm/2in using tin snips. Staple this to the loose roof half. Position the roof halves together, bend the lead to fit and staple through the lead into the fixed roof half.

4 Drill two small holes just below and to either side of the entrance hole. Bend a piece of copper wire into a flattened loop slightly wider than the distance between the holes. Pass the two ends of the wire through the holes and turn them down just inside the box to hold the perch in place.

Above: *The blue tit, our most common tit, is identified by its blue-and-yellow plumage and the thin dark stripe across the face.*

Above: *This tit box can be adapted with different embellishments. It can be fixed on a pole or hung from a tree.*

YOU WILL NEED

6mm/¼in medium-density fibreboard (MDF) or exterior-grade plywood
small piece of timber (for base)
saw
pair of compasses
drill, padsaw
PVA glue
panel pins
hammer
emulsion paint: blue-grey and white
medium paintbrush
medium-grade sandpaper
protective gloves
lead sheet, tin snips
staple gun and staples
copper wire and wire cutters

TYPICAL INHABITANTS

tits
nuthatches

ROCK-A-BYE BIRDIE BOX

This box constructed from plywood is made to suit small, acrobatic birds such as wrens and tits.
The removable roof is covered with flashing to repel rainwater. The box hangs on stout string, though
if you have a problem with predators, it would be safer to use greased wire.

Above: *The wren is one of our most common breeding birds. Its small size means that it is often overlooked.*

YOU WILL NEED
paper
pencil
scissors
6mm/¼in plywood
drill
sandpaper
fretsaw
V-board
18 x 6mm/¾ x ¼in D-shaped
    moulding
tenon saw
wood glue
nails
hammer
scrap wood
varnish
paintbrush
self-adhesive roof flashing
knife
cutting mat
string or wire

TYPICAL INHABITANTS
tits
wrens

1 Copy the templates at the back of the book, cut out and use to mark out the shapes for the base and roof on thin plywood. Drill an entry hole in one side of the top and sand the edges.

3 Glue and then nail the lengths of moulding around the base, with the flat side facing outward. You'll find the easiest way of working is to start with the central strip and then work out.

5 Mark a line around the base, about 6mm/¼in below the top edge of the sides, and trim back the mouldings to this level to allow the roof to overlap the base. Apply a coat of varnish to the box.

2 Cut out the plywood shapes using a fretsaw and V-board. Next, cut the D-shaped moulding into 10cm/4in lengths to make the base and 15cm/6in lengths to make the roof.

4 Make a simple template to the width of the box from a piece of scrap wood and use it to space the sides of the roof. Attach the roof slats as before, allowing for an overlap on each side.

6 Cut a strip of 15cm/6in-wide roof flashing, long enough to cover the roof, and smooth it over the moulding strips. Hammer the surface if you wish. Attach a length of string for hanging.

SLATE-ROOFED COTTAGE

As long as a birdhouse is weatherproof and sited in a safe, sheltered position, its external appearance will not affect the inhabitants. This sturdy-looking house, which will suit sparrows, is actually made of wood faced with self-hardening clay and roofed with slate.

Above: *As its name suggests, the house sparrow usually nests near buildings. It is well adapted to living alongside humans.*

YOU WILL NEED

pencil
ruler
2cm/¾in pine board
tenon saw
drill
wood glue
nails, hammer
enamel paints
paintbrushes
paper
scissors
terracotta self-hardening clay
board
rolling pin
knife
epoxy resin glue
blunt-ended modelling tool
acrylic paints
satin exterior varnish
varnish brush
slate
face mask
hacksaw

TYPICAL INHABITANTS

sparrows
tits

1 Using the templates at the back of the book, cut out the birdhouse pieces from the board. Drill an entry hole in one side only. Glue and nail the box together. Draw, then paint, the door and window on the front.

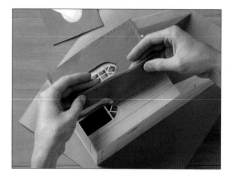

3 Cover the whole of the front of the house with a layer of epoxy resin glue, but take care to avoid the painted door and window. Now carefully lay the clay over the front. You may need to adjust it slightly to fit it in the exact position.

5 Paint over some of the bricks using acrylic paints to imitate the varied colours of real brickwork. Leave it to dry, and then coat with a satin exterior varnish.

2 Make paper patterns of the sides and front. Cut out the entry hole, front door and window. Roll out the clay to a depth of 8mm/⅜in thick. Lay the patterns on the clay and cut around them.

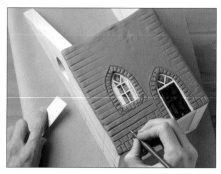

4 Inscribe the fancy brickwork around the window and door using a blunt-ended modelling tool, then use a ruler to press in horizontal lines as a guide for the standard brickwork. Inscribe the brickwork with the modelling tool. Repeat on the side walls.

6 Cut a piece of slate to size, wearing a face mask. It helps to saw through each side edge before cutting across. Drill four holes for nails and nail the roof to the sides.

RIDGE TILE RETREAT

This elegant birdhouse is divided into two. With an entry hole at each end, it is made to suit larger birds, such as starlings, which live in colonies. An old ridge tile makes an excellent roof.

1 Using the templates at the back of the book, mark and cut out the components for the birdhouse, adapting the pitch of the roof to fit your tile. Drill an entry hole in each end.

2 Sand all the surfaces. Now glue and then nail the floor to the sides. Next measure and mark the centre line of the box and glue the dividing wall in position.

3 Glue and nail each gable end piece to the sides. Paint the outside of the birdhouse and leave it to dry thoroughly.

4 Place the ridge tile in position on top of the birdhouse. This house can be erected on a post or simply placed at medium height in a quiet location.

Below: *Starlings* (Sturnus vulgaris) *are gregarious birds that feed and roost in flocks. This box will suit two pairs of birds.*

YOU WILL NEED
pencil, ruler
2cm/¾in pine board
tenon saw
drill
hole saw
sandpaper
wood glue
galvanized nails
hammer
paint
paintbrush
ridge tile

TYPICAL INHABITANTS
starlings
jackdaws

SWIFT NURSERY

Swifts build their nests in wall crevices, under the eaves of houses or in tunnel-shaped boxes. Although they will sometimes take to boxes with front-facing access holes, an entrance hole underneath is better, as it prevents house sparrows and starlings taking over the box.

Above: *Swifts* (Apus apus) *spend almost their entire lives on the wing, but touch down to nest, often high up on walls.*

1 Using the templates at the back of the book, mark and cut out all the pieces for the box, except the front, from pine board. Cut lengths of batten for the front. Cut a paper pattern for the entry hole at one end of the base and cut it out using a fretsaw.

2 Glue and nail the base to the back of the box. Glue and nail the ends in place and add the top batten. Cut the tongue-and-groove board into 15cm/6in lengths. Glue and nail to the front of the box, attaching it to the batten and the edge of the base.

YOU WILL NEED
pencil, ruler
carpenter's square
2cm/¾in pine board
tenon saw
2cm/¾in square pine batten
paper
fretsaw
V-board
hammer
nails
wood glue
tongue-and-groove board
drill
sandpaper
emulsion paint in cream
  and black
varnish
paintbrushes
self-adhesive roof flashing
scissors

TYPICAL INHABITANTS
swifts

3 Allow the glue time to dry. Then drill a 15mm/⅝in hole at each joint, placing a piece of scrap timber behind the tongue-and-groove to prevent it splitting. Now trim the lower edge of each board to form a chevron shape. Drill two holes in the back of the box for fixing to a wall. Sand and paint the box, then leave to dry. Paint the outside with varnish to protect the wood.

4 Cut two battens for the roof, using the template at the back. Mark positions for the battens on the underside of the roof using the box as a guide. Fix the battens with short nails. Paint the underside black. Cover the top of the roof with strips of self-adhesive flashing and fit the roof on to the box. Overlap the last strip of flashing to the back of the box. Fix the box on to a wall.

POST BOX

Thick wooden stakes can be hollowed out and turned into unusual nest boxes for small birds such as tits. The boxes can be sited on their own or form part of a garden fence. The cover of roof flashing protects the box from the elements and also helps prevent the wood from splitting.

Above: *Great tits (Parus major) can be distinguished from their smaller cousins, blue tits (Parus caeruleus), by their size, and also by their broad black chest stripe. Another distinguishing feature is the blue-black cap, which extends down as far as the eyes.*

YOU WILL NEED

drill and 25mm/1in bit
fence post of 10cm/4in diameter
chisel
mallet
self-adhesive roof flashing
craft knife
cutting mat
protective gloves
lead flashing
pair of compasses
pencil
ruler
scrap wood
vice
pliers
nails
hammer

TYPICAL INHABITANTS

tits
wrens
nuthatches

1 Using a 25mm/1in bit, drill an entry hole into the side of the post 5cm/2in from the end, then drill out the end to a depth of about 15cm/6in.

3 Cover the end of the post with self-adhesive roof flashing. Pierce the flashing in the centre of the entry hole and cut back to the edges. Now turn back the flashing inside the hole, but take care not to significantly reduce the size of the entry hole which the birds will use.

5 Wearing gloves, bend the lead to a cone shape. Then join the seam by squeezing the edges together with pliers. Flatten the seam against the cone.

2 Use a chisel and mallet to remove the waste wood left in the end of the post after drilling. Work to create a roughly circular cavity at least 15cm/6in deep.

4 Wearing protective gloves, cut out a circle of lead flashing for the lid and remove one quarter of the circle, using the template at the back of the book. Clamp the lead between two pieces of scrap wood and fold one cut edge at 90 degrees. Fold the second edge over twice at 90 degrees, as shown.

6 Attach the roof to the post using two nails, but leave one not fully nailed in so that it can be removed to give access to the box when you need to clean it out.

CLAY POT ROOST

For this project you will need access to a kiln (perhaps through a local education centre or school), but you do not need to be skilled in pottery. Cut the entry hole to suit your choice of potential resident, and site the pot in a sheltered position, out of reach of predators.

Above: *The domestic pigeon (*Columba livia*) is a common sight in towns and gardens in many parts of Britain. This species may shelter or nest in the pot roost if you make the dimensions and entry hole a little bigger. The dimensions given here will provide a roost for wrens, tits, nuthatches and house sparrows.*

YOU WILL NEED

paper
pencil
scissors
latex gloves
clay
rolling pin
craft knife
length of 10cm/4in diameter plastic
    plumbing pipe
round cutter
bradawl
fresh leaves, to decorate
kiln

TYPICAL INHABITANTS

wrens
tits
nuthatches
house sparrows
street pigeons
starlings

1 From the paper, cut a circle 12cm/4½in across, a rectangle 12 x 17cm/4½ x 6½in, and a semicircle 38cm/15in across. Roll out the clay to 8mm/⅜in thickness and cut out the shapes. Cover the pipe in paper and roll the rectangle of clay around it.

3 Keeping the pipe inside the clay cylinder, add the circular section to make the base, and join on to the side by smoothing the edges together. Remove the pipe.

5 Mould a small bird from leftover clay to decorate the top of the lid. Model the wings separately and then moisten them before pressing them on to the body. Draw the feathers and eyes using a bradawl.

2 Seal the joint at the side by wetting the overlap slightly and then smoothing it down with your thumb. Now cut an entry hole 25mm/1in in diameter, positioned about a third of the way down from the top, using a plain round cutter.

4 To make the lid of the roost, curl the semicircle of clay into a cone shape. Join the edges as before by moistening and then smoothing them with your fingers.

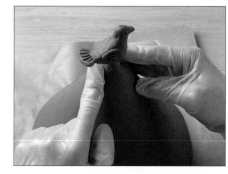

6 Attach the bird by smoothing a little clay over the base of the bird and the top of the lid. Fire the base and the lid separately in a kiln. To decorate, press fresh leaves into the clay before firing.

EDWARDIAN NEST BOX

Inspired by Edwardian seaside architecture, this pretty box is designed for small birds such as tits and nuthatches. Fretwork is satisfying to make, but it does require practice and patience. However, your efforts will be rewarded once you see your creation hanging on the garden wall.

Above: *Position the box high in a tree if you want to provide a nest site for nuthatches* (Sitta europaea), *which are woodland birds.*

YOU WILL NEED
ruler, pencil
jigsaw
2cm/¾in pine board
tenon saw
plane
8mm/⅜in dowelling
4mm/⅙in plywood
fretsaw
V-board
drill
sandpaper
wood glue
plated moulding pins
hammer
nails
watercolour paints in cobalt blue,
    burnt umber, turquoise, yellow
    ochre, burnt sienna
paintbrushes
petroleum jelly
2 butterfly hinges, with screws
tourmaline antiquing medium
white emulsion paint
blowtorch
satin yacht varnish
screwdriver and screws

TYPICAL INHABITANTS
tits
nuthatches

1 Using the templates at the back of the book, mark and cut out the base, back, sides and lid from 2cm/¾in pine. Cut the notches in the side pieces. Plane the edges of the base and lid to line up with the sides. Cut a length of dowelling for the perch.

2 Mark out the back plate, front, circular frame for the entry hole and the decorative panel for the lid front on 4mm/⅙in plywood and cut out using a fretsaw and V-board. Cut out a 2.5cm/1in entry hole in the front panel. Sand all the surfaces.

3 Glue the sides, base and back support together and secure with moulding pins. Glue and nail the fretwork panel to the front edge of the lid. Drill a hole for the perch below the entry hole, and glue into place, then glue and nail the front to the sides.

4 Paint the box with a dilute mixture of cobalt blue and burnt umber watercolour paints, in equal proportions. Leave to dry, then smear on a thin layer of petroleum jelly with your fingers. To age the hinges, paint with tourmaline antiquing medium.

5 Treating one surface at a time, apply a coat of white emulsion paint and dry it with a blowtorch to make the paint crack. Add a little turquoise and yellow ochre watercolour to the emulsion to make green for the entry hole frame and backboard.

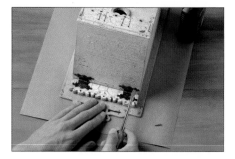

6 Glue and nail the back panel on to the box. To age the paintwork, apply a dilute mixture of yellow ochre and burnt sienna watercolour until you achieve the desired effect. Leave to dry, then finish with varnish. Screw on the hinges to attach the lid.

DUCK HOUSE

You don't need a very large pond to provide a home for ducks such as mallards. If possible, the house should be positioned on an island or raft to provide protection from predators. The ramp for this desirable house has horizontal struts to make sure the occupants don't slip. Post caps on each leg will protect the wood on dry land. If it is to stand in water, use timber pressure-treated with preservative.

YOU WILL NEED
2cm/¾in pine board
45mm/1¾in square pine batten
20 x 45mm/¾ x 1¾in pine batten
rebated ship-lap boards
pencil
ruler
carpenter's square
tenon saw
jigsaw
sandpaper
wood glue
nails
hammer
exterior paint
paintbrush
corrugated roofing sheet
polystyrene filler
roofing screws and cups
screwdriver
timber decking or treated timber
flat work surface

TYPICAL INHABITANTS
ducks, including mallards and
    shovellers

Left: *The mallard (Anas platyrhynchos) is the most widespread and familiar duck in Britain. These waterbirds sometimes nest in gardens near lakes or rivers, that contain thick vegetation to provide cover for the nest site. The appearance of the male differs quite markedly through the year. In the breeding season the handsome green head, white collar and brown chest distinguish him from the female. In late summer he moults into eclipse plumage, which quite closely resembles the female's in its drab hues.*

Left: *Shovellers (Anas clypeata) have a broad bill that enables these waterfowl to feed more easily in shallow water. They typically swim with their bill open, trailing through the water to catch invertebrates, although they also forage both by up-ending themselves and catching insects on reeds. These ducks choose wet ground, often some distance from open water, as a nesting site. Like the young of other waterfowl, the young birds take to the water soon after hatching.*

1 Mark out and cut out all the components for the duck house using the templates given at the back of the book. Carefully cut out the curved roof battens and then the arched opening using a jigsaw. Sand all the edges.

2 On a large, flat work surface, lay out two of the legs parallel to one another. Position the cross rail on top of the legs, using the carpenter's square to make sure all three parts are at right angles to one another. Now attach the cross rail using wood glue and nails.

3 Turn the leg assembly over and attach the first curved roof batten. Repeat the process with the other two legs.

4 Connect the front and back with the two lower cross rails. These are nailed to the inner side of the legs.

5 Nail and glue the upper side rails at both sides. These rails are attached to the outside of the legs. This completes the basic framework of the house.

6 Ship-lap the back and sides of the house, starting at the top. Glue and nail the top piece in place, but don't drive the nails in fully. Only do so after the lower piece has been glued and nailed in place.

7 Ship-lap the front in the same way, securing the door sides first. Make sure that you align the door sides carefully to give a straight, clean line when the duck house is assembled.

8 Finish off the house walls by attaching the four corner pieces. Paint the house inside and out, and allow it to dry. Put in the floor, which rests in place on the cross rails.

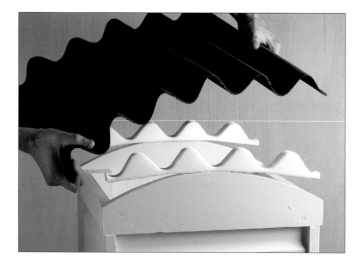

9 Cut a piece of roofing sheet to the measurements given at the back of the book, and cut two strips of polystyrene filler to fit the arched front and back walls. Offer up the roof, locating it centrally.

10 Attach the roof to the front and back walls of the house, using special roofing screws and cups.

11 Make a simple ramp by joining two planks of timber decking with cross pieces. Nail an extra cross piece to the back of the ramp at the top to hook over the batten under the door.

RUSTIC CABIN

This charming cabin is constructed around a basic box with a sloping roof. Faced with 'logs', it will harmonize well with any garden setting, offering a nursery for hole-nesting birds.

YOU WILL NEED

6mm/¼in medium-density
    fibreboard (MDF) or exterior-grade
    plywood
ruler, pencil
hammer, nails
saw
twigs and branches
axe or small-scale log splitter
glue gun and glue sticks
dark grey emulsion paint
medium paintbrush
drill
padsaw
100 x 12mm/4 x ½in coach
    bolt
moss or moss-covered branch

TYPICAL INHABITANTS

sparrows
tits

1 Mark and cut out the basic house in MDF or plywood following the template at the back of the book. Make 'logs' from small branches by splitting the branches lengthways so there is a flat side for sticking to the box and a rounded surface with bark for the outside.

2 Assemble the basic box with glue and nails. Paint it with dark grey emulsion paint so that any small gaps between the logs will not show when they are attached.

3 Glue the logs to the front. To make the entry hole, cut through the logs and the box below using a drill and then a padsaw.

4 Cut a 12mm/½in hole and insert a coach bolt for the 'chimney'. Continue to fix logs to the rest of the house, shaping them to fit and making the roof logs overlap the walls slightly as an added protection against rain. Neaten the corners of the walls by trimming the individual log ends with a saw. Glue a piece of moss or moss-covered branch to the opening as a perch.

Left: *Tree sparrows* (Passer montanus) *are mainly birds of farmland, but they can sometimes be encouraged to nest in your garden. This species is now rare in many parts of Britain.*

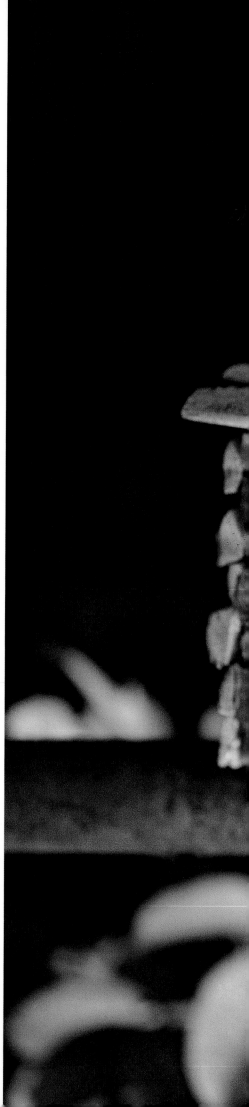

ROBIN'S LOG CABIN

Designed for robins and wrens, which like open-fronted nest boxes, this log cabin-effect box will blend in well with the natural environment. Position it low down in a well-hidden site, preferably surrounded by thorny shrubbery, and well away from any other birdhouses.

Above: *One of the best-loved garden birds, robins (*Erithacus rubecula*) are actually quite aggressive, defending a feeding territory for much of the year. Robins breed from March to August, fashioning a cup-shaped nest from grass and leaves, and lining it with hair. Females lay 4–6 eggs. Both parents help to feed the young and may raise two broods within a season.*

YOU WILL NEED

sticks – newly-cut hazelwood from
    coppiced woodland is best, as
    the coppiced stems can be cut to
    length to produce short, strong,
    straight sticks
ruler
pencil
tenon saw
bench hook
hammer
short, fine nails or sturdy panel pins
10cm/4in square plastic tray
piece of turf
knife

TYPICAL INHABITANTS

robins
goldfinches
wrens

1 Select evenly sized, straight sticks and cut them to length, using a tenon saw and bench hook. You will need 4 sturdy uprights 15cm/6in long, 10 sticks to make the base 12cm/4¾in long, and about 50 sticks for the sides, 10cm/4in long.

3 Attach the two sides by nailing more small sticks across the back. You may need to brace the structure. Work from bottom to top, hammering nails into the uprights at an angle, to keep the structure strong.

5 Build up the top of the box by adding two more of the shorter sticks to each side, on top of the existing pieces. Gently nail the new sticks on top of the walls.

2 Construct the first side by nailing 10cm/4in lengths to two of the uprights. Use short, fine nails or sturdy panel pins. Nail on the two end sticks first to make a rectangle, then fill in with other sticks. Repeat to make the other side.

4 Turn the box over. Attach one stick at the top of the front, then leave a gap of about 5cm/2in for the entrance hole before completing the rest of the front. Use the 12cm/4¾in sticks to make the base.

6 Fit the tray into the top so that it rests on the uprights, or so that the lip rests on top of the walls. Cut a piece of turf to fit and place it in the tray to make the roof.

THATCHED BIRDHOUSE

As long as the basic box requirements are fulfilled, the finish is up to you. Tailor-made for sparrows, who will take to almost any hole, this box should be sited somewhere quiet, as sparrows are easily disturbed during the nesting period. Leave the house out during winter for use as a snug roost.

Above: *House sparrows breed between April and August, building their nests in holes in buildings, often under roof tiles.*

YOU WILL NEED
pencil, ruler
carpenter's square
6mm/¼in medium density fibreboard
(MDF)
tenon saw
drill
wood glue
masking tape
small metal eyelet and hook
craft knife
cutting mat
metal ruler
self-adhesive roof flashing
ready-mixed tile cement
palette knife
aquarium gravel
sisal hanging-basket liner
PVA glue
paintbrush
raffia
large-eyed needle
clothes pegs
diluted brown watercolour paint
matt varnish
varnish brush

TYPICAL INHABITANTS
sparrows
tits

1 Following the templates at the back of the book, mark and cut out the component parts from MDF. Drill an entry hole in the front wall and, if required, drill a small hole in the back wall for hanging.

3 Cut a strip of roof flashing 13cm/5in wide to the length of the roof ridge. Position the two roof pieces side by side, leaving enough of a gap to allow the roof to hinge open. Remove the backing and cover the ridge with the flashing.

5 Coat the sisal with diluted PVA glue and leave to dry. Cut a rectangle 28 x 14cm/ 11 x 5½in for the thatch and a strip 15 x 7.5cm/6 x 3in for the ridge. Stitch two rows of large cross-stitch in raffia along the sides of this strip, then glue and stitch it across the thatch.

2 Glue the base and walls together and then hold the structure in position with masking tape until the glue is quite dry. Screw in an eyelet 1cm/½in from the top back corner of the right-hand wall.

4 Working on a small area at a time, spread ready-mixed tile cement over the house walls. Embed aquarium gravel firmly into the cement, choosing darker stones to outline the entry hole. Cover the walls of the house completely.

6 Glue the thatch to the roof. Secure it with clothes pegs until dry. Screw in the hook at the back of the roof, then glue the other side of the roof to the walls, securing it with masking tape until quite dry. Wash the cement with brown watercolour and, when dry, give it a coat of varnish.

NESTY NOOK

This cosy home, made to imitate a wren's nest, is formed from plastic-coated chicken wire covered with moss. Place the nest in a hidden position, low down in thick undergrowth or even in the bank of a stream beneath overhanging roots, as long as the site is dry.

Above: *Wrens (Troglodytes troglodytes) are easily overlooked because of their tiny size and skulking habits, however their song is surprisingly loud. They also produce a ticking sound. These little birds breed from March to July, constructing a domed structure in thick vegetation, where the female lays 5–8 eggs. The young hatch after 16–17 days and take a similar time to fledge from the nest structure.*

YOU WILL NEED
chicken wire
wire cutters
large leaves
sisal hanging-basket liner
scissors
pliers
hair net
moss
sea grass string
garden wire

TYPICAL INHABITANTS
wrens
tits
sparrows
jackdaws – will use a nest of this type
    with slightly larger dimensions,
    placed in a high position

1 Cut a square of chicken wire measuring about 30cm/12in. Line it with large leaves. Cut a square of hanging basket liner made of sisal to the same size and lay it down on top of the leaves.

2 Fold the four corners into the centre and join the sides by twisting the ends of the wires together. Leave the centre open. Tuck in the wire ends to ensure that there are no sharp bits poking out to harm the bird.

3 Pull at the wire structure from the front and back to 'puff' it out and create a larger space inside for the bird to nest.

4 Carefully stretch a hair net over the whole nest structure. Take care to keep the entrance hole clear.

5 Stuff moss evenly between the nest and the hair net to cover the chicken wire completely. Work on one part at a time until you are satisfied with the look of the whole.

6 To define the entry hole, form a ring of sea grass string and secure it by twisting garden wire around it. Wire it into position around the hole.

SCALLOP SHELTER

This little nest designed for house martins and swallows is made of papier-mâché. It is easily replaced each season, though the chicken wire container will last longer. Attach it to the wall with two cup hooks, in a dry place under the eaves. The scallop shell is purely decorative.

Above: *House martins originally nested in caves but now are most often seen near human dwellings, building their little cups of mud under the eaves. These migrants are seen in Britain from April to September.*

YOU WILL NEED
newspaper
bowl of water
plastic bowl
wallpaper paste
brush
scissors
corrugated cardboard
pencil
masking tape
acrylic paints
paintbrush
chicken wire
protective gloves
wire cutters
small pliers
drill
scallop shell
florist's wire

TYPICAL INHABITANTS
martins
swallows
tits

1 To make the papier-mâché, tear a newspaper into small squares and soak it in water. Cover one half of a plastic bowl with a layer of wet, unpasted pieces of paper. The pieces should slightly overlap.

2 Brush paste liberally over the first layer and add more pieces, pasting each layer, until you have built up about six layers. Leave it to dry out in a warm place such as an airing cupboard.

3 When the papier-mâché is completely dry, remove it from the plastic bowl and trim the rough edges to make a neat half-bowl shape. Now cut out a semicircle of corrugated cardboard, which will form the backing for the nest.

4 Attach the cardboard to the papier-mâché bowl shape using masking tape, then reinforce the structure by adding a few layers of pasted paper over the back and edges. Leave the nest in a warm place to dry out thoroughly.

5 Paint the nest in variegated muddy tones. Cut a piece of chicken wire using wire cutters. Wrap it around the nest and join the wire ends together at the sides.

6 Squeeze the chicken wire with the pliers to shape it to the form. Drill two small holes in the top of the scallop shell and one at the bottom, and wire it on to the frame.

WILLOW STICK NEST

Half coconuts are just the right shape and size to make snug nests for small birds. Two halves are wedged into a bunch of withes, and a woven sea grass wall completes the nest.

1 Soak the withes overnight to make them pliable. Wedge them around a stick using a napkin ring. Saw a coconut in half and scrape out the contents. Using raffia, tie the withes together at the top.

2 Insert the coconut halves. Starting by the rim of the lower half, weave sea grass string around the withes for three rounds.

3 Create a gap by doubling the string back on itself and changing the direction of the weaving for about four rounds.

YOU WILL NEED

about 15 withes
straight stick or bamboo pole
wooden napkin ring
coconut
saw
knife
raffia
sea grass string
scissors

TYPICAL INHABITANTS

wrens
tits

4 Complete the weaving with three more rounds. Wedge the top of the coconut into position above the weaving and secure it by re-tying the withes at the top if necessary.

Left: *Coal tits are small woodland birds that build cup-shape nests made out of vegetation. They also use human-made nests such as this willow-stick construction.*

HOLLOW LOG NEST BOX

Choose an appealing log for this nest box. Depending on its size, you can adapt it to suit the type of bird you want to attract, from tits to woodpeckers. Mossy logs look beautiful, as do chunks of silver birch. Avoid pieces of wood with knots or branches, as they are difficult to split neatly.

Above: *Place the nest box high in a tree to attract woodpeckers, such as this great spotted (Dendrocopos major). These birds use their short, stiff tails to balance upright on the trunk while they extract grubs from beneath the bark. They usually nest in tree holes excavated with their sharp beaks.*

YOU WILL NEED
2 logs
pencil
ruler
straight-edged chisel
mallet
drill
saw
hammer
nails
garden wire
scissors
pliers

TYPICAL INHABITANTS
starlings
woodpeckers
tits

1 Mark out a square on the end of one log. Use a mallet and straight-edged chisel to split off the first side, making sure that you work evenly along the line.

2 Repeat this process to remove all four sides of the square. Drill an entrance hole through one of the sides, making a sizeable hole if you want to attract woodpeckers.

3 Saw a 20mm/¾in slice off one end of the centre of the log to form the base.

4 Using the base piece, reassemble the log by nailing the four sides together.

5 Wrap a length of garden wire around the top of the box, twist the ends to tighten it and hold the sides securely together.

6 Split the second log to make a roof for the nest box. Attach it using one long nail, so that the roof can easily swivel open.

NEST-IN-A-BOOT

An old boot provides the basis for this original nest box. It is half-filled with gravel to stabilize it, and a small basket makes a perfect foundation for the nest itself. Try to find an interesting seed pod or other natural decoration for the roof. The birds won't need the little ladder, but children will love it.

Above: *Blue tits are the small birds most likely to use nest boxes. They breed between April and May, having constructed a nest of moss, dry grass and twigs in a crevice or nest box.*

YOU WILL NEED
rubber boot
scissors
gravel
small round basket
bradawl
string
small sticks
epoxy resin glue
wooden curtain ring
protective gloves
chicken wire
wire cutters
small pliers
sisal hanging-basket liner
large-eyed needle
raffia
interesting seed pod
garden wire

TYPICAL INHABITANTS
tits
sparrows
starlings – may use this nest with
    a larger entry hole

1 Cut down the boot to a suitable size and cut out a small entry hole toward the top. Fill the bottom of the boot with gravel, then wedge a small round basket into position below the entry hole.

3 To make the roof, cut a semicircular piece of chicken wire, using wire cutters and wearing protective gloves. Curve the wire to form a cone. Join the sides by twisting the ends of the wire together using pliers.

5 Sew cross-stitch along the join using string and a large-eyed needle. Now cross-stitch around the bottom with raffia. Insert the seed pod decoration into the point of the roof and glue in place.

2 Make two small holes below the entry hole to either side. Thread a long piece of string through these and tie on little sticks to form a ladder. Glue on a wooden curtain ring over the entry hole as reinforcement.

4 Wrap a piece of the sisal hanging-basket liner around the cone of chicken wire, pressing the wire rim firmly into the matting. Turn in the edges of both the matting and the chicken wire.

6 Make four pairs of holes, evenly spaced around the rim of the boot. Attach the roof to the boot using four lengths of garden wire and twist the wires together. Snip off any excess wire.

DOVECOTE

This beautiful structure will make a comfortable roost for up to half a dozen doves, but it could be adapted to accommodate more birds by increasing the number of tiers. The dovecote is probably best sited on the side of a building, but it can also be mounted on a stout post.

Above: *Collared doves (*Streptopelia decaocto*) only began to breed in Britain in the 1950s, but are now quite common. Their call is a gentle cooing sound.*

YOU WILL NEED
pencil
ruler
carpenter's square
12mm/½in and 6mm/¼in plywood
jigsaw
20mm/¾in pine board
tenon saw
2 x 4.5cm/¾ x 1¾in pine batten
sandpaper
wood glue
nails
hammer
drill
screws
screwdriver
paint
paintbrush
self-adhesive roof flashing
craft knife
cutting mat
metal ruler

TYPICAL INHABITANTS
doves

1 Using the template at the back, mark and cut out the backboard from 12mm/½in plywood with a jigsaw. Cut the roof shapes and front arches from 6mm/¼in plywood.

3 Join the sides and centre by gluing and nailing on the front battens. Fit the back battens into the notches cut in the centre piece. Attach by nailing in the centre of the batten and at each end.

5 Cover the small roof sections with self-adhesive roof flashing. Cover the main roof with horizontal strips of flashing. Start from the bottom of the roof and overlap each section, allowing some overlap on the final piece to attach to the backboard.

2 Mark and cut out all the pine timber parts from 20mm/¾in thick planks, following the templates provided. The sides and centre will require wide boards. Sand all surfaces.

4 Drill pilot holes for the screws in the backboard. Attach the backboard to the frame using glue and screws. Paint the frame and the arched fronts and leave to dry. Attach the fronts using glue and nails.

6 Using nails, assemble the last parts in the following order: first the small roof sections; then the floors; then the main roof. Attach the dovecote to a wall by screwing through the backboard from the inside. Take care when fixing, as the structure is heavy.

CLAPBOARD HOUSE

This smart-looking New England-style house is suitable for hole-nesters such as tits and sparrows. It will add a decorative feature to any garden as well as providing small birds with a nesting site.

Above: *Tree sparrows breed between April and July, with females laying up to three clutches of eggs. The young birds hatch out after 11–14 days and leave the nest 15–20 days after hatching.*

YOU WILL NEED
6 mm/¼in medium-density
    fibreboard (MDF) or plywood
pencil
ruler
saw
PVA glue
hammer
panel pins
birch veneer
coloured woodstain
scalpel or craft knife
1.5 x 19mm/¹⁄₁₆ x ¾in balsa
    wood strips
pair of compasses
emulsion paint: off-white, dark brown
    and brilliant white
medium and fine paintbrushes
exterior-grade varnish
drill with 3mm/⅛in bit
50 x 50mm/2 x 2in wooden post
screwdriver
75mm/3in screw, plus smaller
    screws

TYPICAL INHABITANTS
tree or house sparrows

1 Mark and cut out the basic house on to MDF or plywood following the template at the back. Assemble using glue and panel pins. Mark a sheet of veneer into 19 x 38mm/ ¾ x 1½in shingles and rub randomly with woodstain. Cut out the shingles with a scalpel or craft knife. Glue them in overlapping rows to the roof of the house.

2 Cut balsa wood strips to length to use as clapboarding. Glue in position. Set a pair of compasses to transfer the cutting angles or make paper templates to show the shapes to be cut. Paint the clapboarding with off-white emulsion and dark-brown windows. Paint window frames and doors using a fine brush and white emulsion. Varnish.

3 Cut a base 200 x 125mm/8 x 5in from plywood. Drill pilot holes at each corner and in the centre. Fasten to the top of the post with a central 75mm/3in screw. Screw through the corners into the house.

DIRECTORY OF GARDEN BIRDS

A great many people derive pleasure from watching garden birds. This pastime can be enjoyed without special equipment, although binoculars, a sketchpad, notebook or similar items can add to your understanding. To help you identify the birds that visit your garden, the following pages present illustrations and in-depth profiles of 80 of the most commonly sighted British species, giving details of distribution, size, habitat, nests, eggs and food, together with descriptions of songs and behaviour. The order here reflects the standard order used in bird classification. Happy birdwatching!

Left: *The robin's jaunty breast and trusting nature make it popular with garden birdwatchers. It is a member of the thrush family.*

Above: *Chaffinches (Fringilla coelebs) usually feed on the ground, pecking at a range of seeds and invertebrates.*

Above: *Tits are the species most likely to visit feeding stations and use nest boxes. This is a coal tit (Parus ater).*

Above: *Small, brownish birds such as the chiffchaff (Phylloscopus collybita) are often easiest identifed by their songs.*

SEABIRDS AND DUCKS

Gulls are linked in many people's minds with the seaside, but some species have adjusted to living alongside people, and generally profiting from the association. A number of gulls have now spread inland. Ducks are freshwater birds whose appearance and distribution can differ through the year.

COMMON GULL

Mew gull *Larus canus*

Common gulls often range inland over considerable distances, searching for earthworms and other invertebrates to feed on. In sandy coastal areas they will seek out shellfish as well. There is a distinct seasonal variation in the range of these gulls. At the end of the summer they leave their Scandinavian and Russian breeding grounds and head farther south in Europe, to France and various other locations in the Mediterranean. Here they overwinter before migrating north again in the spring. In spite of its rather meek appearance, this species will bully smaller gulls and garden birds to steal food from them. When venturing inland, common gulls show a preference for agricultural areas and grassland, but they will also enter gardens in search of food.

Identification

White head and underparts with yellow bill and yellowish-green legs. Wings are greyish with white markings at the tips, which are most visible in flight. Flight feathers are black with white spots. Tail is white. Dark eyes. Greyish streaking on the head in winter plumage. Sexes are alike. Young birds have brown mottled plumage, and it takes them more than two years to gain adult coloration.

Distribution Iceland and throughout Europe, with breeding grounds in Scandinavia and Russia. Extends across Asia to western North America.
Size 46cm (18in).
Habitat Coasts and inland areas close to water.
Nest Raised nest of twigs and other debris.
Eggs 2–3, pale blue to brownish-olive in colour, with dark markings.
Food Shellfish, fish and invertebrates.

BLACK-HEADED GULL

Larus ridibundus

These gulls are a common sight not only in coastal areas but also in parks and gardens with or near lakes and ponds, including in cities. They move inland during winter, where they can often be seen following ploughing tractors searching for worms and grubs in the soil. Black-headed gulls nest close to water in what can be quite large colonies. Like many gulls, they are noisy birds, even calling at night. On warm, summer evenings they can sometimes be seen hawking flying ants and similar insects in flight, demonstrating their airborne agility.

Right: *The black feathering on the head is a transient characteristic, appearing only in the summer (far right).*

Identification

Throughout the summer, this gull has a distinctive black head with a white collar beneath and white underparts. The wings are grey and the flight feathers mainly black. In the winter, the head is mainly white except for black ear coverts and a black smudge above each eye, while the bill is red at its base and dark at the tip.

Distribution Greenland eastward around Iceland and throughout Europe, south along the coast of north-western Africa and into Asia.
Size 39cm (15in).
Habitat Coastal areas.
Nest Scrape on the ground lined with plant matter.
Eggs 2–3, pale blue to brown with darker markings.
Food Typically molluscs, crustaceans and small fish.

HERRING GULL

Larus argentatus

Distribution The northern Atlantic including north of Iceland and south to northern Africa and the Mediterranean. Also present in the North Sea and Baltic areas to northern Scandinavia and Arctic Russia.
Size 60cm (24in).
Habitat Coasts and inland.
Nest Small pile of vegetation.
Eggs 2–3, pale blue to brown with darker markings.
Food Fish and carrion.

These large gulls are often seen on fishing jetties and around harbours, searching for scraps. They have also moved inland and can be seen in areas such as rubbish dumps, where they scavenge for food, often in quite large groups. Herring gulls are noisy by nature, especially when breeding. They frequently nest on rooftops in coastal towns and cities, a trend that began in Britain as recently as the 1940s. Pairs can become very aggressive at breeding time, swooping menacingly on people who venture too close to the nest site (and even including the chicks once they have fledged).

Identification
White head and underparts, with grey on the back and wings. Prominent large, white spots on the black flight feathers. Distinctive pink feet. Reddish spot toward the tip of the lower bill. Some dark streaking on the head and neck in winter. Sexes are alike. Young birds are mainly brown, with dark bills and prominent barring on their wings.

Above: *The herring gull's pink legs are a distinctive feature.*

MALLARD

Anas platyrhynchos

Distribution Occurs throughout the northern hemisphere and resident through western Europe. Also occurs in north Africa.
Size 60cm (24in).
Habitat Open areas of water.
Nest Usually a scrape lined with down feathers.
Eggs 7–16, buff to greyish-green in colour.
Food Mostly plant matter, but some invertebrates.

These ducks are a common sight by lakes, rivers and canals in towns and cities. They are also seen in gardens with or near ponds and streams. They may congregate in quite large flocks, especially outside the breeding season, but are most evident in the spring, when groups of unpaired males chase potential mates. The nest is often constructed close to water and is frequently hidden under vegetation, including in urban gardens. These birds feed both on water, upending themselves or dabbling at the surface, and on land.

Identification
Metallic green head with a white ring around the neck. Chest is brownish, underparts are grey, and a blackish area surrounds the vent. Bluish speculum in the wing, most evident in flight, bordered by black-and-white stripes. Hen is brownish-buff overall with darker patterning, and displays the same wing markings as drake. Hen's bill is orange, whereas that of male in eclipse plumage (outside the breeding season) is yellow, with a rufous tinge to the breast.

AQUATIC BIRDS

Coots, moorhens and rails all belong to the group of crakes. These water-loving birds can often be observed out in the open, but when frightened will usually scuttle away to the safety of reeds or dense vegetation by the water's edge. Dippers are found exclusively near fast-flowing rivers and streams.

EURASIAN DIPPER

Cinclus cinclus

Dippers are sometimes seen in gardens near streams or rivers in northern and western Britain. The bird's name comes from the way in which it bows, or 'dips' its body, often on a boulder in the middle of a stream, rather than describing the way it dives into the water. Dippers are very adept at steering underwater with their wings, and can even elude birds of prey by plunging in and disappearing from view, before surfacing again farther downstream. They feed mainly on aquatic invertebrates caught underwater, sometimes emerging with caddisfly larvae and hammering them out of their protective casings on land. Breeding pairs work together to construct their nest, which may be concealed under a bridge or in a hole in a rock. The hen usually sits on the nest alone, and the youngsters will fledge after about three weeks.

Distribution Much of Scandinavia and parts of the rest of Europe, but not central and eastern England. Range extends south to parts of northern Africa. Also present in Asia.
Size 20cm (8in).
Habitat Stretches of fast-flowing water.
Nest Domed mass made from vegetation.
Eggs 1–7, white.
Food Aquatic invertebrates and also small fish.

Identification

Prominent white throat and chest. Brown on head extends below the eyes, rest of the plumage is dark. Young birds are greyish with mottling on their underparts. Some regional variation, usually relating to the extent of chestnut below the white of the chest. Dark bill, legs and feet. Sexes are alike.

WATER RAIL

Rallus aquaticus

Water rails frequent ponds, reed beds and bog gardens, but their skulking habits make them hard to notice. Being naturally very adaptable, these rails have an extensive distribution, and are even recorded as foraging in tidal areas surrounded by seaweed in the Isles of Scilly off south-west Britain. In parts of their range they migrate to warmer climates for the winter. They are very territorial when breeding and, as in other related species, their chicks hatch in a precocial state. Calls include squealing and pig-like grunts.

Identification

Prominent, long, reddish bill with bluish-grey breast and sides to the head. Narrow brownish line extending over the top of the head down the back and wings, which have black markings. Black-and-white barring on the flanks and underparts. Short tail with pale buff underparts. Sexes are alike.

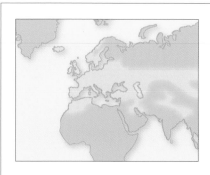

Distribution Extensive, from Iceland throughout most of Europe, south to northern Africa and east across Asia to Siberia, China and Japan.
Size 26cm (10in).
Habitat Usually reed beds and sedge.
Nest Cup-shaped, made from vegetation.
Eggs 5–16, whitish with reddish-brown spotting.
Food Mainly animal matter, but also some vegetation.

COOT

Eurasian coot *Fulica atra*

Distribution Range extends from Britain eastward throughout Europe, except the far north, south into northern Africa and eastward to Asia. This species is also present in Australia and New Zealand.
Size 42cm (16½in).
Habitat Slow-flowing and still stretches of water.
Nest Pile of reeds at the water's edge.
Eggs 1–14, buff to brown with dark markings.
Food Various kinds of plant and animal matter.

Coots may set up home by large ponds and lakes in parks and gardens. Open stretches of water are important to them, enabling them to dive in search of food. During the winter, these birds may sometimes assemble in flocks on lakes that are unlikely to freeze over.

Coots may find their food on land or in the water, although they will dive only briefly in relatively shallow water. Pairs are very territorial during the breeding season, attacking the chicks of other coots that venture too close and even their own chicks, which they grab by the neck. The young usually respond by feigning death, and this results in them being left alone.

Identification

Plump, sooty-grey body with a black neck and head. Bill is white with a white frontal plate. The iris is a dark brownish colour. White trailing edges of the wings evident in flight. Long toes have no webbing. Sexes are alike.

MOORHEN

Common moorhen *Gallinula chloropus*

Distribution From Britain east through Europe except for the far north. Occurs in parts of Africa, especially the south, and also through much of South-east Asia and parts of the Americas.
Size 30cm (12in).
Habitat Ponds and other areas of water edged by dense vegetation.
Nest Domed structure hidden in reeds.
Eggs 2–17, buff to light green with dark markings.
Food Omnivorous.

Even a relatively small garden pond can attract moorhens, and they may nest in gardens with dense vegetation near the pond. Although usually found in areas of fresh water, they are occasionally seen in brackish areas. Their long toes enable them to walk over aquatic vegetation. These birds feed on the water or on land and their diet varies according to the season, although seeds of various types make up the bulk of their food. If danger threatens, moorhens will either dive or swim underwater. They are adept divers, remaining submerged by grasping on to underwater vegetation with their bills. In public parks, moorhens can become quite tame, darting in to obtain food provided for ducks.

Identification

This aquatic bird has a slate-grey head, back and underparts. Greyish-black wings. A prominent white line runs down the sides of the body. The area under the tail is white and has a black central stripe. The greenish-yellow legs have a small red area at the top. The bill is red apart from a yellow tip. Sexes are alike.

GARDEN PREDATORS

Kestrels, peregrine falcons and sparrowhawks are agile aerial predators. These opportunistic birds of prey rely on strength and speed to overcome their prey, which frequently includes garden birds. Buzzards are bulkier, with hooked bills and powerful talons. They target small mammals as well as birds.

KESTREL

Common kestrel *Falco tinnunculus*

These common birds of prey can frequently be seen hovering at the side of busy roads, largely undisturbed by the traffic close by. Roadsides provide them with good hunting opportunities, and their keen eyesight enables them to spot even quite small quarry such as grasshoppers on the ground. They also hunt songbirds in parks and gardens, including in towns. In the winter, they may resort to hunting earthworms drawn to the surface by heavy rainfall.

Identification

Bluish-grey head, with a black stripe under each eye and a whitish throat. Dense black spotting on the pale brownish chest, extending to the abdomen. Wings are chestnut-brown with black markings. Rump and tail feathers are grey with black tips. Hens are similar but have browner heads and distinct barring across the tail feathers.

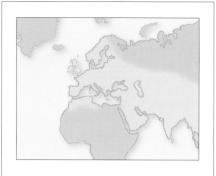

Distribution Range extends throughout western Europe across to South-east Asia and North Africa. Also breeds in Scandinavia.
Size 37cm (14½in).
Habitat Open countryside.
Nest Platform of sticks in a tree or agricultural building.
Eggs 3–7, pale pink with dark brown markings.
Food Invertebrates and small mammals and birds.

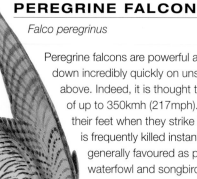

PEREGRINE FALCON

Falco peregrinus

Peregrine falcons are powerful aerial predators, swooping down incredibly quickly on unsuspecting birds from above. Indeed, it is thought that they can dive at speeds of up to 350kmh (217mph). The impact made by their feet when they strike is so great that their quarry is frequently killed instantaneously. Pigeons are generally favoured as prey, although they also hunt waterfowl and songbirds. These falcons are highly adaptable hunters and can very occasionally be sighted in cities, where apartment blocks replace the crags from which they would normally fly on hunting excursions.

Identification

Dark grey upperparts. A broad blackish stripe extends down below each eye, and the surrounding white area extends right around the throat. The barring on the chest is lighter than on the abdomen. Darker markings on the grey feathers of the back and wings. The tail is barred, with paler grey feathering at the base. The legs and feet are yellow. Wings appear relatively narrow when seen in flight. Hens are much larger than male birds.

Distribution Resident throughout most of western Europe and much of Africa, except for the Sahara Desert and the central rainforest band. One of the most adaptable and widely distributed birds of prey, occurring on all continents.
Size 38–51cm (15–20in).
Habitat Near cliffs, also open ground.
Nest Cliff ledges.
Eggs 3–4, whitish with red-brown markings.
Food Birds.

SPARROWHAWK

Eurasian sparrowhawk *Accipiter nisus*

Distribution Resident throughout most of Europe (except the far north of Scandinavia). Also occurs in North Africa and the Canary Islands. Migratory birds overwinter around the Red Sea. Range also extends eastward to Asia.
Size 28cm (11in).
Habitat Light woodland.
Nest Made of sticks.
Eggs 4–6, pale blue with reddish-brown markings.
Food Mainly birds.

These hawks favour preying on ground-feeding birds, and males generally take smaller quarry than females, reflecting the difference in their respective sizes. Even females rarely take birds much larger than pigeons, although they will prey on thrushes. Pairs nest later in the year than many garden birds, so there are plenty of nestlings to prey on and feed to their own chicks. Sparrowhawks have short wings and are very agile in flight, able to manoeuvre easily in wooded areas. They approach quietly with the aim of catching their target unawares, seizing their prey using their powerful clawed feet.

Identification
This hawk has a grey head, back and wings, with darker barring on the grey tail. The underparts are also barred. Bare yellow legs and feet, with long toes. Cock birds are smaller than hens and have pale rufous areas on the lower sides of the face, extending to the chest, while the barring on their underparts is browner.

Below: *Young male sparrowhawks fledge several days before their heavier siblings.*

COMMON BUZZARD

Eurasian buzzard *Buteo buteo*

Distribution Resident in western Europe. Summer visitor to parts of Scandinavia and across Asia. Migratory European birds overwinter in southern and eastern Africa.
Size 57cm (22in).
Habitat Areas with trees.
Nest Platform of sticks, usually in a tree, or in a shrub on a cliff ledge.
Eggs 2–4, white.
Food Small mammals and other prey.

With its rather broad and stocky appearance, the common buzzard's silhouette in flight helps to confirm its identity. Buzzards are capable of soaring for long periods, before suddenly swooping down to seize a rabbit or songbird. They also take the nestlings of garden and woodland birds. Buzzards can sometimes be observed hunting invertebrates, walking purposefully on the ground in search of their quarry. They may occasionally be spotted on roads too, feeding on road kill, even placing themselves in danger from the passing traffic. However, buzzards remain one of the most common raptors in Europe, thanks largely to their adaptable feeding habits.

Identification
This predatory bird is mainly dark brown, with a variable amount of white plumage around the bill and on the underparts. The tail is barred, with paler plumage around the vent. The legs and feet are yellow, and the bill is yellow with a dark tip. White predominates in the pale morph of this species. Hens are often larger than the males.

POND AND GARDEN PREDATORS

Aerial agility is a feature associated with birds of prey, particularly those that hunt other birds. Kites and harriers are nimble predators whose diet includes small birds and also carrion. Herons and kingfishers generally hunt by water. Both are opportunistic feeders, going after fish and other aquatic creatures.

GREY HERON

Ardea cinerea

Grey herons sometimes hunt in gardens with ponds soon after dawn. These opportunistic hunters are shy and can be difficult to spot. They are usually seen in flight, with their long necks tucked back on to their shoulders and their legs held out behind their bodies. They fly with relatively slow, quite noisy wing beats. Grey herons are very patient predators. They stand motionless, looking for any sign of movement in the water around them, then lunge quickly with their powerful bills to grab any fish or frog within reach. During winter, when their freshwater habitats are frozen, grey herons will often move to river estuaries in search of food. These birds frequently nest in colonies, and some breeding sites may be used for centuries by successive generations.

Identification

This tall predatory bird has a powerful yellow bill and a white head, with black above the eyes extending to long plumes off the back of the head. Long neck and chest are whitish with a black stripe running down the centre. Grey wings and black shoulders. Underparts are lighter grey. Long yellowish legs. Sexes are alike.

Distribution Throughout most of Europe into Asia, except for the far north. Also in Africa, but absent from the Sahara and the Horn.
Size 100cm (39in).
Habitat Water with reeds.
Nest Large platform of sticks built off the ground.
Eggs 3–5, chalky-blue.
Food Fish, amphibians and any other aquatic vertebrates.

KINGFISHER

Common kingfisher *Alcedo atthis*

A flash of colour may be all you see of a kingfisher visiting your garden pond. These birds are surprisingly difficult to spot, as they perch motionlessly while scanning the water for fish. Once its prey has been identified, the predator enters the water, where a protective membrane covers its eyes. Its wings provide propulsion, and having seized the fish in its bill it darts out of the water and back onto its perch with its catch. The whole sequence happens incredibly fast, taking just a few seconds. The kingfisher then stuns the fish by hitting it against the perch, then swallows it head first. It regurgitates the bones and indigestible parts later.

Identification

Bluish-green extends over the head and wings. Back is pale blue, with a blue flash on the cheeks. The throat is white, and there are white areas below the orange cheek patches. Underparts are also orange, and the bill is black. In hens, the bill is reddish at the base of the lower bill.

Above: *Kingfishers dive at speed into the water, aiming to catch their intended quarry, such as fish and amphibians, unawares.*

Distribution Occurs across most of Europe, but absent from much of Scandinavia. Also present in northern Africa, ranging eastward through the Arabian Peninsula and South-east Asia as far as the Solomon Islands.
Size 18cm (7in).
Habitat Slow-flowing water.
Nest Tunnel excavated in a sandy bank by the water.
Eggs 6–10, white.
Food Small fish. Also preys on aquatic insects, molluscs and crustaceans.

RED KITE

Milvus milvus

Distribution Patchy range includes Wales, the Iberian Peninsula and the adjacent area of North Africa. Extends north-eastward across Europe as far as the Baltic and southern Sweden, and also found in Russia.
Size 66cm (26in).
Habitat Light woodland.
Nest Large nest of sticks, built in a tree and usually well concealed.
Eggs 1–4, white with reddish-brown markings.
Food Small birds, mammals and carrion.

The red kite in a rare visitor to gardens, where it may take songbirds up to the size of crows. Although very agile hunters, these kites also seek carrion such as dead sheep. This behaviour has resulted in their persecution in some areas because of misplaced fears that they actually kill lambs. When seeking prey, red kites circle repeatedly overhead, relying on their keen eyesight to spot movement on the ground. They will then drop and sweep low, homing in on their target. Up until the 1700s, flocks of red kites were common scavengers on the streets of London, where they were sufficiently tame to swoop down and steal food from children. It was their willingness to scavenge, however, that led to a reduction in their numbers, since they were easily killed using carcasses laced with poison.

Identification
Predominantly reddish-brown, with a greyish head streaked with darker markings. Darker mottling over the wings, with some variable streaking on the underparts as well. Feet are yellowish with black talons. White areas under the wings and forked tail can be clearly seen in flight. Sexes are alike.

HEN HARRIER

Northern harrier *Circus cyaneus*

Distribution Throughout much of the Northern Hemisphere. Extends across most of Europe, including Scandinavia, east to Asia. Often moves south for the winter as far as North Africa.
Size 52cm (20in).
Habitat Moorland.
Nest On the ground among vegetation.
Eggs 3–5, whitish.
Food Mainly small mammals and birds.

These birds occasionally visit gardens to prey on songbirds, while in the winter months hen harriers may be forced to feed largely on carrion. They are very distinctive hunters, flying low over moorland, seeking not only small mammals but also birds. Their preference for hunting grouse has led to persecution by gamekeepers in various parts of their range. Their range extends farther north than those of related species, into the tundra region, but they are not resident in far northern areas throughout the year, and will head farther south before the start of winter. Hen harriers are unusual in not only roosting on the ground but also breeding on the ground. Once the breeding season is over they will often congregate at communal sites, which may be used for several generations.

Identification
Mainly chestnut overall, streaked with white. Darker over the wings. Narrow white band around each eye, with a solid brown area beneath. Tail is barred. The bill is dark, and the legs are yellow. Hens are larger.

OWLS AND NIGHT-TIME HUNTERS

More likely to be heard rather than seen, owls and the nightjar become more active after dark. Nightjars feed on night-flying insects, while the diet of most owls includes rodents. It is possible to determine the diet of owls by examining their pellets, which are the indigestible remains of their prey.

TAWNY OWL

Strix aluco

The distinctive double call notes of these owls reveal their presence, even though their dark coloration makes them difficult to spot. Tawny owls prefer ancient woodland and nearby gardens, where trees are large enough to provide hollow nesting cavities. They will, however, adapt to using nest boxes, which has helped to increase their numbers. Nocturnal by nature, these owls may nevertheless occasionally hunt during the daytime, especially when they have chicks in the nest. They usually sit quietly on a perch, waiting to swoop down on their quarry. Young tawny owls are unable to fly when they first leave the nest, and at this time the adults can become very aggressive in protecting their offspring.

Identification
Tawny-brown, with white markings across the wings and darker striations over wings and body. Slight barring on tail. Distinctive white stripes above facial disc, which is almost plain brown. Some individuals have a greyer tone to their plumage, while others are more rufous. Bill is yellowish-brown. Sexes similar, although females are generally larger and heavier. Females also distinguished by their higher-pitched song.

Distribution Across Europe (not Ireland) to Scandinavia and eastward into Asia. Also occurs in North Africa.
Size 43cm (17in).
Habitat Favours ancient woodland.
Nest Tree hole.
Eggs 2–9, white.
Food Small mammals, birds and invertebrates.

LITTLE OWL

Athene noctua

Little owls can be seen resting during the daytime, on telegraph poles and similar perches in the open. Introduced to Britain in the 1800s, they have since spread right across southern England, where they venture into gardens near farmland. They hover in flight, but are rather ungainly when walking on the ground. One factor which has assisted their spread is their adaptability in choosing a nest site – disused factories and even rabbit warrens may be used. The hen sits alone for the incubation, which lasts 24 days. Both adults feed the young, who fledge after five weeks, and are independent in a further two months.

Identification
White spotting on the head, white above the eyes and a whitish moustache. Heavy brown streaking on a white chest. Larger whiter spots on the wings, barring on flight feathers and banding across tail. Whitish legs and feet. Bill yellowish, irides yellow. Young lack white spotting on forehead. Sexes alike, but hens usually larger.

Distribution Range extends from southern Britain and throughout most of Europe at a similar latitude (not as far as Scandinavia) eastward into Asia. Also present in northern parts of Africa, extending to parts of the Middle East.
Size 25cm (10in).
Habitat Prefers relatively open country.
Nest Tree hole or a cliff hole.
Eggs 3–5, white.
Food Invertebrates and small vertebrates, including birds.

BARN OWL

Tyto alba

Distribution Range extends pretty much worldwide, including throughout western Europe, Africa (except the Sahara) and the Middle East.
Size 39cm (15in).
Habitat Prefers relatively open countryside and farmland.
Nest Hollow tree or inside a building.
Eggs 4–7, white.
Food Rodents (especially voles) and amphibians, and also invertebrates.

Barn owls seek out dark places in which to roost, using buildings. They may be seen in gardens near open country or swooping over farmland, and will sometimes nest in large oblong boxes placed high in outhouses. Males in particular will often utter harsh screeches when in flight, which serve as territorial markers, while females make a distinctive snoring sound for food at the nest site. They pair for life, which can be more than 20 years. Barn owls have adapted to hunting along roadside verges, but here they are in real danger of being hit by vehicles.

Identification
Whitish, heart-shaped face and underparts. In much of Europe, underparts more yellowish-orange. Top of the head and wings greyish-orange with spots. Eyes black. Males often paler than females.

NIGHTJAR

European nightjar *Caprimulgus europaeus*

Distribution Most of Europe and north-west Africa, east to Asia. Northern European birds overwinter in south-eastern parts of Africa, while southern European birds migrate to western Africa.
Size 28cm (11in).
Habitat Heathland and relatively open country with undergrowth.
Nest Scrape on the ground.
Eggs 2, buff-coloured, with darker markings.
Food Invertebrates.

Nightjars are regular summertime visitors to heathlands and nearby gardens in Britain, but their small size and cryptic coloration mean that they are seldom noticed. Perhaps even more significantly, these birds are nocturnal by nature, which makes them extremely difficult to observe. However, they have very distinctive calls, likened both to the croaking of a frog and the noise of a machine, which are uttered for long periods and carry over a distance of 1km (⅝ mile). During the daytime, nightjars spend much of their time resting on the ground, where their mottled plumage provides them with excellent camouflage, especially in woodland. Additionally, they narrow their eyes to slits, which makes them even less conspicuous. Nightjars are sufficiently agile in flight to catch moths and other nocturnal invertebrates, flying silently and trawling with their large gapes open. If food is plentiful, breeding pairs of nightjars may rear two broods in succession, before beginning the long journey south again to reach their African wintering grounds.

Identification
This small insect-eater is distinguished by its very small bill and long wings. Greyish-brown and mottled in overall appearance, with some black areas, especially near the shoulders. There are white areas below the eyes and on the wings, although the white spots on the wings are seen only in cock birds.

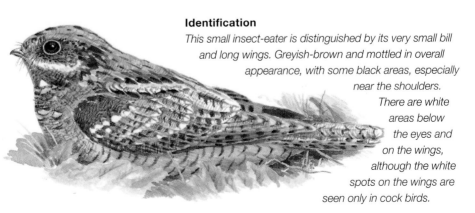

PHEASANTS, PIGEONS AND DOVES

Introduced and bred for sport, pheasants are game birds. Pigeons and doves have adapted well to living alongside people, although their presence is sometimes unwelcome. Large flocks of feral pigeons now inhabit urban areas. Their adaptability is shown by their ability to breed through much of the year.

COMMON PHEASANT

Ring-necked pheasant *Phasianus colchicus*

Common pheasants occur naturally in Asia. Introduced to Europe by the Romans, they have been widely bred and released for shooting, and are now commonly seen in British gardens, including in towns, especially in autumn and winter. Common pheasants usually live in groups comprised of a cock bird with several hens. They forage on the ground, flying noisily and somewhat clumsily when disturbed, and may choose to roost off the ground.

Identification

Cock bird has prominent areas of bare red skin on each side of the face, surrounded by metallic dark greenish plumage. Variable white area at the base of the neck. The remainder is mainly brown, with underparts chestnut with dark blotching. Hens are lighter brown, with darker mottling on the back and wings.

Below: *Mottled plumage provides the pheasant hen with good camouflage.*

Distribution Range now extends through most of western Europe, except much of Spain and Portugal, and in a band east across central Asia to Japan. Also introduced to the United States, Australia and New Zealand.
Size Cock 89cm (35in); hen 62cm (24in).
Habitat Light woodland.
Nest Scrape on the ground.
Eggs 7–15, olive-brown.
Food Plant matter including seeds and shoots, also invertebrates.

COLLARED DOVE

Streptopelia decaocto

The collared dove only appeared in north-western Europe in the 1940s. Since then its spread has been dramatic, to the extent that these are now a common sight in British gardens. These birds were recorded in Hungary in the 1930s, and then moved rapidly over the next decade west across Austria and Germany to France, and also north to the Netherlands and Denmark. The species was first sighted in eastern England during 1952, and a pair bred there three years later. The earliest Irish record was reported in 1959, and by the mid-1960s the collared dove had colonized almost all of the UK. No other bird species has spread so far and so rapidly in recent times, to the extent that the collared dove's range now extends right across Europe and Asia.

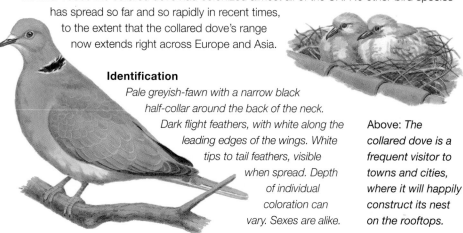

Identification

Pale greyish-fawn with a narrow black half-collar around the back of the neck. Dark flight feathers, with white along the leading edges of the wings. White tips to tail feathers, visible when spread. Depth of individual coloration can vary. Sexes are alike.

Above: *The collared dove is a frequent visitor to towns and cities, where it will happily construct its nest on the rooftops.*

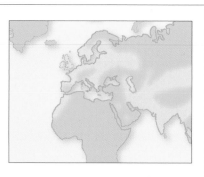

Distribution Across much of Europe but not including the far north of Scandinavia and the Alps, ranging eastward into Asia. More localized on the Iberian Peninsula and in northern Africa particularly.
Size 34cm (13in).
Habitat Parks and gardens.
Nest Platform of twigs.
Eggs 2, white.
Food Mostly eats seeds and other plant matter.

FERAL PIGEON (ROCK DOVE)

Columba livia

True rock doves have a localized range, favouring cliffs and ruined buildings as breeding sites. In the past, these doves were kept and bred by monastic communities, where the young doves (known as squabs) were highly valued as a source of meat. Inevitably, some birds escaped from their dovecotes and reverted to the wild, and their offspring gave rise to today's feral pigeons, which are a common sight in gardens and streets in almost every town and city, scavenging whatever they can from our leftovers. Colour mutations have also occurred, and as well as the so-called 'blue' form there are now red and even mainly white individuals today.

Left: *The rock dove nests on loose twigs.*

Identification
Dark bluish-grey head, slight green iridescence on the neck. Light grey wings with two characteristic black bars across each wing. Feral pigeons often have longer wings than rock doves. Reddish-purple coloration on the sides of the upper chest. Remainder of the plumage is grey with a black band at the tip of the tail feathers. Sexes are alike.

Distribution The rock dove occurs naturally in northern areas of Scotland and nearby islands, and in western Ireland. It is also found around the Mediterranean. The feral pigeon's range now extends throughout Europe and southern Africa, as well as to other continents.
Size 35cm (14in).
Habitat Originally cliffs, now on buildings in urban areas.
Nest Loose pile of twigs or similar material.
Eggs 2, white.
Food Mainly seeds.

WOOD PIGEON

Columba palumbus

Wood pigeons are one of the most common large birds seen in British gardens. They are often observed pecking on the lawn or drinking from birdbaths. In towns they frequent parks with stands of trees, descending into nearby gardens and allotments to raid growing crops. These pigeons can be significant agricultural pests in arable farming areas. However, they also occasionally eat potential crop pests such as snails. Pairs sometimes nest on buildings, although they usually prefer a suitable tree fork. Their calls are surprisingly loud and are often heard soon after dawn. Outside the breeding season these birds will often congregate in large numbers. If danger threatens, they can appear quite clumsy when taking off thanks to their relatively large size.

Identification
This pigeon has a grey head, with a reflective metallic-green area at the nape of the neck and characteristic white patches on the sides. The bill is reddish at the base, becoming yellow toward the top. The purplish breast becomes paler on the underparts. The tip of the tail is black. The white edging to the wings is most clearly seen in flight, when it forms a distinct band. The sexes are alike.

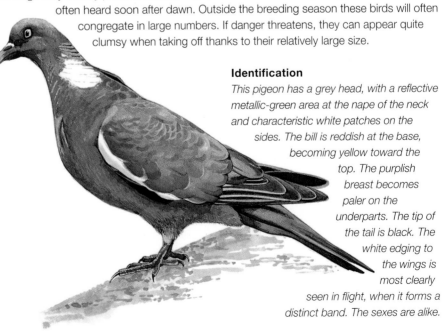

Distribution Throughout most of Europe except for northern Scandinavia and Iceland, ranging eastward into Asia. Also present in north-western Africa.
Size 43cm (17in).
Habitat Areas with tall trees.
Nest Flimsy platform of twigs in a tree or on a building.
Eggs 2, white.
Food Seeds, plant matter and additionally invertebrates.

RARE VISITORS AND INTRODUCTIONS

Hoopoes and white storks are rare but welcome visitors to Britain during the summer months. The latter is one of Europe's largest birds. Red-legged partridges were introduced for sport, while ring-necked parakeets arrived as cage birds, but populations of both species now exist in the wild within our shores.

HOOPOE

Eurasian hoopoe *Upupa epops*

Hoopoes are occasional visitors to gardens near farmland in southern England, especially in spring and summer. The distinctive appearance of these birds helps to identify them with ease. When in flight, the broad shape of the wings is clearly visible and the tall crest is held flat over the back of the head. Hoopoes often raise their crest on landing. They use their long bills to probe for worms in the ground, or grab insects scurrying through the grass. They can also often be observed dust-bathing, which keeps their plumage in good condition. Hoopoes are not especially shy of people, and pairs will sometimes nest in buildings. Their common name is derived from the sound of their "hoo, hoo" call.

Identification
Mainly pale buff, although more orange on the crown and with black edging to the feathers. Alternate bands of black-and-white coloration on the wings. Long, narrow, downward-curving bill. Sexes are alike.

Far left: *The black-and-white barring is shown to best effect in flight.*

Distribution Range extends through most of Europe, sometimes appearing in Britain. Overwinters in Africa south of the equator. Also occurs in parts of Africa, and extends east to the Arabian Peninsula and across Asia.
Size 29cm (11in).
Habitat Open country.
Nest Secluded hole.
Eggs 5–8, whitish to yellowish-olive.
Food Mainly invertebrates, especially worms, also lizards.

RING-NECKED PARAKEET

Rose-ringed parakeet *Psittacula krameri*

The ring-necked parakeet is the most widely distributed member of the parrot family in the world. Found naturally across Asia and Africa, flocks of these birds first appeared in Britain in the 1960s, having bred from escaped captive birds. They are now regularly seen in gardens in south-east England. This adaptable species appears in parks and gardens in cities, although it is usually observed in farmland and woodland. Historically, the spread of agriculture in Africa and Asia led to an increased food supply which helped these birds to expand their distribution. Ring-necked parakeets fly quite high, often in small groups, and their distinctive, screeching calls carry over long distances. These are unmistakable parakeets, especially when silhouetted in flight, with their long, tapering tails streaming behind their bodies.

Identification
The African race (P. k. krameri) has black on the bill and is more yellowish-green than the Asiatic form (illustrated), which is now established in various locations including parts of England, well outside its natural range. Hens and young birds of both sexes lack the distinctive neck collar seen in cocks, which is a combination of black and pink.

Distribution Found across Africa in a band south of the Sahara. Range also extends eastward through the Arabian Peninsula and across Asia as far as China. Now also introduced to south-east England.
Size 40cm (16in).
Habitat Light woodland.
Nest Tree cavity high off the ground, sometimes on a rocky ledge.
Eggs 3–6, white.
Food Cereals, fruit, seeds.

WHITE STORK

Ciconia ciconia

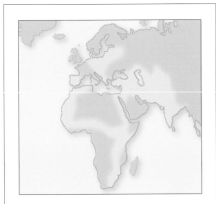

Distribution Summer visitor to much of mainland Europe, very occasionally seen in southern Britain. Winters in western and eastern parts of North Africa, depending on the flight path. Also occurs in Asia.
Size 110cm (43in).
Habitat Wetland areas.
Nest Large, bulky platform of sticks sited off the ground, including on rooftops and towers.
Eggs 3–5, chalky-white.
Food Amphibians, fish, small mammals and invertebrates.

White storks are very rare visitors to southern Britain, most often seen in warm spring weather. In Europe, where they are considered to bring good fortune, these birds often return each year to the same site, adding annually to their nest, which can become bulky. The return of the storks in April from their African wintering grounds helped to foster the myth of the link between storks and babies. Migrating birds are a spectacular sight, flying with necks extended and legs trailing behind. However, in many parts of Europe they are now declining due to changes in farmlands and also wetlands.

Identification
Large, tall, mainly white bird with prominent black areas on the back and wings. Long red bill and red legs. Sexes alike. Young birds are smaller with a dark tip to the bill.

RED-LEGGED PARTRIDGE

Alectoris rufa

Distribution Found naturally in Europe from the Iberian Peninsula to Italy. Introduced to the rest of Europe, including Britain.
Size 38cm (15in).
Habitat Open countryside, farmland.
Nest Scrape on the ground.
Eggs 9–12, pale yellowish-brown with dark spotting.
Food Mainly plant matter, also insects.

The red-legged partridge was brought to England as long ago as the late 1600s for shooting, and its adaptable nature ensured that its range steadily expanded. It is now widely seen in arable farmland and nearby gardens. However, during the 20th century the chukar partridge, which hybridizes with the red-legged variety, was also introduced to Britain. Today it can be difficult to determine whether partridges are pure or cross-bred red-legged individuals, thanks to their similarity in appearance to chukars. Red-legged partidges form individual pairs when breeding. The cock bird chooses and then prepares the nest site.

Identification
This partridge has a prominent black collar with distinctive black streaks extending around the sides of the neck to the eye. Black stripe continues through the eye to the bill, with a white stripe above and white below around the throat. Bluish-grey above the bill, and on the breast and barred flanks. Brownish abdomen. Hens are smaller and lack the tarsal spurs on the legs.

WOODPECKERS

Few groups of birds are more closely associated with woodlands than woodpeckers. They are well-equipped to thrive there, using their powerful bills as tools to obtain food and also create nesting chambers. However, not all are exclusively arboreal, since some species forage for food on the ground.

GREAT SPOTTED WOODPECKER

Dendrocopus major

Great spotted woodpeckers can be found in both coniferous and deciduous woodland, and in gardens where the trees are mature enough for the birds to excavate nesting chambers. Their powerful bills enable them to extract grubs hidden under bark and to wrest the seeds from pine cones – the birds use tree holes as vices to hold the cones fast. They also visit gardens to peck nuts from feeders and to forage at bird tables, especially in winter.

Identification
Black top to the head. Black areas also from the sides of the bill around the neck, linking with a red area at the back of the head. Wings and upperside of the tail are predominantly black, although there is a white area on the wings and white barring on the flight feathers. Underside of the tail mostly white. Deep red around the vent. Hens are similar but lack the red on the hindcrown.

Distribution Most of Europe except for Ireland, northern Scandinavia and much of south-eastern Europe. Also in North Africa. Ranges east into Asia.
Size 25cm (10in).
Habitat Woodland.
Nest Tree hollow.
Eggs 5–7, white.
Food Invertebrates, eggs and seeds.

LESSER SPOTTED WOODPECKER

Dendrocopus minor

The smallest of the three woodpeckers seen in Britain, the lesser spotted is not much larger than a robin. Its small size and shy, secretive habits mean that its presence often goes unnoticed. A bird of woodlands and large gardens with mature trees, it lives higher in trees than other woodpeckers. There it hides among the foliage of the crown and circles the bark in the manner of a treecreeper, searching for insect food. Two-thirds the size of the great spotted, it shares its cousin's pied plumage, with even more extensive barring on the wings and back. However, the barring is somewhat blurred. Unlike other woodpeckers it is very seldom seen on lawns, bird feeders or in the open generally. It produces a weaker drumming sound than the great spotted, and its high-pitched, peevish-sounding call is also weaker. The flight pattern is undulating. Lesser spotted woodpeckers breed between March and June, having excavated a nest hole high in a tree, where the female lays a single clutch of eggs.

Identification
Largish head is predominantly white with black stripes on the sides of the face, and buff around the bill. Males have an extensive red area on the crown, while hens have a black cap. Black wings have white barring, tail black. The predominantly white underparts have black streaking, with a reddish area around the vent.

Distribution Range extends throughout most of Europe except for Iceland, Ireland, northern Britain and much of Spain and Portugal. Also present south into Algeria and Tunisia, and eastward into Asia.
Size 16cm (6in).
Habitat Woodland.
Nest Tree hole.
Eggs 4–6, white.
Food Invertebrates, especially insects and grubs.

EURASIAN GREEN WOODPECKER

Picus viridis

Distribution Green woodpecker's range extends across most of Europe, although absent from much of Scandinavia, Ireland, Scotland and various islands in the Mediterranean. This species is also present in parts of north-western Africa.
Size 33cm (13in).
Habitat Open woodland.
Nest Tree hole.
Eggs 5–8, white.
Food Mainly invertebrates, especially ants and ant eggs.

Unlike many of its kind, green woodpeckers hunt for food mainly on the ground, using their powerful bills and long tongues to break open ants' nests. They are equally equipped to prey on earthworms, which are drawn to the surface of garden lawns after rain, and may catch small creatures such as lizards. In the autumn, fruit forms a more significant part of their diet, but they avoid seeds, and so are not drawn to bird feeders. Pairing begins during the winter, with excavation of the nesting chamber taking two weeks to a month to complete. Unlike many woodpeckers they do not drum loudly with their bills to advertise their presence, but pairs can be quite vocal. Incubation is shared, with the hen sitting during the day. Hatching takes just over a fortnight, with the young fledging when a month old.

Identification

Red crown, with red below the eyes and blackish in between. Regional variations. Underparts greyish to green. Back and wings darker green, with yellow spotting. Yellowish rump. Hens often have black rather than red stripes below the eyes. Young are heavily spotted and barred, with a greyer crown.

EURASIAN WRYNECK

Jynx torquilla

Distribution Breeds through most of mainland Europe, extending eastward into northern Asia. Absent from Ireland, and the only British breeding population is in Scotland. Overwinters in Africa in a broad band south of the Sahara, with a resident population also in the north-west.
Size 16.5cm (6½in).
Habitat Open country.
Nest Suitable hole.
Eggs 7–10, white.
Food Invertebrates, particularly ants and ant eggs.

Once found throughout Britain, the wryneck has declined dramatically, and now breeds only in Scotland. A woodland bird, it is a hole-nester which will take to using nest boxes. It appears in gardens in other parts of Britain only when blown off course on its way to or from its African wintering grounds. Wrynecks return to their breeding grounds by April, when pairs are very territorial. They seek a suitable hollow, which may be in a tree, on the ground or in a bank. When displaying, pairs face each other and shake their heads, opening their bills to reveal pink gapes. The two-week incubation is shared, and both adults care for their young, who fledge after three weeks. They are independent in a further two weeks. Two broods may be reared. If disturbed on the nest, a sitting adult will stretch out its head and neck, before suddenly withdrawing it, hissing like a snake. Wrynecks use their long, sticky tongues to rapidly pick up ants and other invertebrates, such as spiders.

Identification

Mottled grey on the upperparts, browner over the wings. Broad, tapering tail. Dark stripe through each eye, narrower adjacent white stripe above. Throat and chest are buff with streaking. Abdomen barred, mainly white with buff near the vent. Young birds are duller. Sexes are alike.

SWIFTS, SWALLOWS AND MARTINS

These birds spend most of their lives in flight. They undertake long journeys, migrating south to Africa in autumn, and returning to breed the following spring. Pairs frequently return to the same nest site they occupied previously – a remarkable feat of navigation after a journey covering thousands of kilometres.

SWIFT

Common swift *Apus apus*

Common summer visitors, swifts nest on buildings and sometimes in specialized nest boxes. They are most noticeable when uttering their distinctive, screaming calls, flying low overhead in search of winged insects. At other times they may appear as little more than distant specks in the sky, wheeling around at heights of 1,000m (3,300ft) or more. Their flight pattern is quite distinctive, consisting of a series of rapid wingbeats followed by gliding into the wind. Their tiny feet do not allow them to perch, although they can cling to vertical surfaces. Except when breeding, swifts spend their entire lives in the air, and are apparently able to sleep and mate in flight too. If hunting conditions are unfavourable, such as during a cool summer, nestling swifts respond by growing more slowly.

Identification

Dark overall, with relatively long, pointed wings and a forked tail. Pale whitish throat. Sexes are alike.

Distribution Found across virtually the whole of Europe, extending to northern Africa and Asia. Overwinters in southern Africa.
Size 16.5cm (6½in).
Habitat In the air.
Nest Cup-shaped, built under cover.
Eggs 2–3, white.
Food Flying invertebrates, such as midges and moths.

SWALLOW

Barn swallow *Hirundo rustica*

The swallows' return to their European breeding grounds is one of the most welcome signs of spring. They are seen mainly in the countryside and rural gardens. Although pairs return to the same nest site every year, they do not migrate together. Cock birds arrive back before their partners and jealously guard the site from would-be rivals. Cocks fight with surprising ferocity if one of the birds does not back down. Although swallows may use nesting sites such as caves, they more commonly nest inside buildings such as barns, choosing a site close to the eaves. It can take up to a thousand trips to collect enough damp mud, carried back in the bill, to complete a new nest.

Identification

Chestnut forehead and throat, dark blue head and back, and a narrow dark blue band across the chest. The wings are blackish and the underparts are white. Long tail streamers. Sexes are alike.

Distribution Throughout virtually the entire Northern Hemisphere. European populations overwinter in Africa south of the Sahara.
Size 19cm (7½in).
Habitat Open country, close to water.
Nest Made of mud, built off the ground.
Eggs 4–5, white with reddish-and-grey spotting.
Food Flying invertebrates.

HOUSE MARTIN

Delichon urbica

Distribution This species' range extends through the whole of Europe, and eastward across much of Asia. Overwinters in Africa south of the Sahara.
Size 13cm (5in).
Habitat Open country, close to water.
Nest Cup made of mud.
Eggs 4–5, white.
Food Flying invertebrates.

House martins are a familiar sight in gardens both in the town and the countryside in summer. The breeding habits of this species have changed significantly due to an increase in the number of buildings in rural areas. They traditionally nested on cliff-faces, but over the past century began to prefer the walls of houses and farm structures as sites, as well as beneath bridges and even on street lamps, where a ready supply of nocturnal insects are attracted to the light. The nest is usually spherical and normally made of mud. The base is built first, followed by the sides. On average, the whole process can take up to two weeks to complete. House martins are highly social by nature, nesting in huge colonies made up of thousands of pairs where conditions are suitable. Even outside the breeding period, they sometimes associate in large flocks comprising of hundreds of individuals.

Identification
This species has a dark bluish head and back. Black wings with white underwing coverts. The underparts and rump are also white. Forked tail is dark blue. Sexes are alike.

SAND MARTIN

African sand martin, bank swallow *Riparia riparia*

Distribution Sand martins' range extends across virtually the whole of Europe and south into parts of northern Africa. Also eastward into Asia. Overwinters in sub-Saharan Africa.
Size 11cm (4in).
Habitat Open country, close to water.
Nest Hole in an earthen bank or in soft sandstone.
Eggs 3–4, white.
Food Flying insects caught on the wing, usually over water.

Sand martins are migrants, and the first members of their group to arrive in Britain in spring. They are most often to be observed in gardens in the vicinity of lakes and other stretches of water, where they forage for food, frequently swooping down over the surface to catch flying insects. They are most likely to be nesting in colonies nearby, in tunnels excavated in suitable sandy banks or into soft rock. These burrows can extend up to 1m (3ft) into the bank, with the nesting chamber at the end being lined with grass, seaweed and similar material. The eggs are laid on a soft bed of feathers. Once the young martins leave the nest, they stay in groups with other chicks, waiting for their parents to return and feed them. The adults typically bring around 60 invertebrates back from each hunting expedition. Parents recognize their own offspring by their distinctive calls. If danger threatens, the repetitive alarm calls of the adult sand martins cause the young to rush back into their nesting tunnels for protection. This species can be identified by its weak-seeming, fluttery flight pattern and by its low, rasping or chattering call.

Identification
This species is brown on the head, back, wings and tail, with a brown band extending across the breast. The throat area and underparts are white, while the flight feathers are long. The bill is small and black. The sexes are alike. Young sand martins have shorter flight feathers, and are browner overall.

PIPITS AND WAGTAILS

Small and relatively slender birds with long tails, most pipits and wagtails are mainly insect-hunters, while pied wagtails also take molluscs and some seeds. Pied wagtails and tree pipits are birds of open countryside. Grey wagtails and particularly water pipits are notable for living and breeding close to water.

GREY WAGTAIL

Motacilla cinerea

Grey wagtails are most likely to be observed in gardens near fast-flowing streams and rivers, where they dart fearlessly across rocks in search of invertebrates. They live in pairs and construct their cup-shaped nest in a well-concealed locality, usually close to water and sometimes in among the roots of a tree or an ivy-clad wall. These wagtails have benefited from some changes in their environment, taking advantage of millstreams and adjacent buildings to expand their area of distribution, but they can still be forced to leave their territory in search of food during severe winters, especially if the water freezes.

Identification
Grey head and wings, with a narrow white band with black beneath running across the eyes. White border to the black bib on the throat. Underparts are yellow, which is brightest on the chest and at the base of the tail. Sexes similar but hens have a grey or even greyish-white bib and much whiter underparts. Darker feathering disappears from the throat in winter.

Distribution Resident throughout most of western Europe, except Scandinavia. Also present in North Africa and Asia, where the population tends to be more migratory.
Size 20cm (8in).
Habitat Near flowing water.
Nest In rock crevices and similar sites.
Eggs 4–6, buff with greyish, marbled markings.
Food Invertebrates, and occasionally small fish and amphibians.

PIED WAGTAIL

Motacilla alba

These lively birds are commonly seen in both rural and urban gardens, having adapted well to changes in their environment. Once birds of coastal areas and marshlands, they are now seen in farmland, and even hunting on and beside roads. Pied wagtails are not especially shy birds, and the movements of their tail feathers, which give them their common name, strike an unmistakable jaunty pose. The race that breeds in the British Isles is different from that observed elsewhere in Europe as cocks have black plumage on their backs during the summer. This area turns to grey for the rest of the year. The mainland European form is often described as the white wagtail as these birds have a greyish back for the whole year.

Identification
Variable through range. Prominent white area on the head with a black crown and nape. A black area extends from the throat down on to the chest. The remainder of the underparts are white. The back is grey or black depending on where the wagtail is from. Hens have more ashy-grey backs, which form a smudged border with the black feathering above.

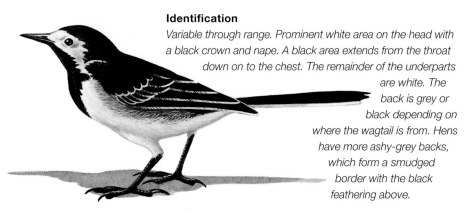

Distribution Throughout Europe and in western North Africa, with the winter distribution there more widespread. Scandinavia, Iceland and Asia in summer.
Size 19cm (7½in).
Habitat Open areas.
Nest Concealed, sometimes in walls.
Eggs 5–6, whitish with grey markings.
Food Invertebrates.

Distribution Occurs widely through
much of Europe up into Scandinavia
and eastward into Asia. Overwinters
across Africa south of the Sahara,
continuing down the eastern side of
the continent, with isolated populations
in Namibia and South Africa.
Size 15cm (6in).
Habitat Woodland.
Nest Made of grass.
Eggs 4–6, greyish with variable
markings.
Food Mainly invertebrates.

TREE PIPIT

Anthus trivialis

Tree pipits sing with increasing frequency at the start of the breeding period. These summer
visitors are most likely to be seen in rural gardens. Their nest is built close to the ground
in open countryside, hidden from predators. This need for camouflage may explain the
variable coloration of the eggs. Long-distance migrants, they overwinter in Africa, reaching
the south toward the end of October. Tree pipits feed on the ground, moving jauntily and
pausing to flick their tails up and down, flying to the safety of a nearby branch at any hint of
danger. As well as invertebrates they also eat seeds.
These solitary, quiet birds are not easily observed
away from their breeding grounds. They
begin returning to Europe in April.

Identification

*Brownish upperparts with dark
streaking. White edging to the
wing feathers. Buff stripe
above each eye, darker
brown stripes through and
below them. Throat whitish.
Underparts pale yellowish with
brownish streaking. Bill dark,
especially at the tip. Legs
and feet pinkish. Young
birds are more buff
overall. Sexes are alike.*

WATER PIPIT

Anthus spinoletta

Distribution Southern England and
much of western Europe, extending
to the northern African coast and into
South-east Asia.
Size 17cm (7in).
Habitat Overwinters by marshes and
still-water areas. Nests by streams in
mountainous areas.
Nest Made of vegetation.
Eggs 3–5, greenish with darker
markings.
Food Largely insectivorous.

These aquatic pipits are lively birds, and are sometimes encountered in small flocks. They
undertake regular seasonal movements, nesting at higher altitudes in the spring, where they
often frequent fast-flowing streams. Pairs nest nearby, choosing a well-concealed location.
Subsequently they retreat to lower altitudes for the winter months, sometimes moving into
areas of cultivation, such as watercress beds in southern Britain. At this time they are most
likely to be seen in gardens near coasts and wetlands, where they search the lawn for
invertebrates, but quickly retreat to cover should there be any hint of danger. Their song
is attractive, and rather similar to that of the closely related rock pipit (*A. petrosus*), with
studies of their song pattern revealing
regional variations between different
populations. Water pipits, like others
of their kind, often utter their song in
flight, and this is most likely to be heard
at the start of the nesting period.

Identification

*In breeding plumage, the water pipit has a
white stripe above the eye, a white throat
with a distinctly pinkish tone to the breast,
and a white abdomen. Slight streaking
evident on the flanks. The head is greyish and
the back and wings are brownish. During
winter, the breast becomes whitish
with very obvious streaking. Wings
are lighter brown overall. Regional
variations apply. Sexes are alike.*

CORVIDS

Studies suggest that corvids rank among the most intelligent of birds. Many display an instinctive desire to hoard food, such as acorns, to help sustain them through the winter. Their plumage is often mainly black, sometimes with grey and white areas. Corvids are generally noisy and quite aggressive by nature.

MAGPIE

Common magpie *Pica pica*

Bold and garrulous, magpies are a common sight in gardens, and are regular visitors to bird tables. They are often blamed for the decline of songbirds because of their habit of raiding the nests of other birds to steal eggs and nestlings. They are usually seen in small groups, although pairs will nest on their own. If a predator such as a cat ventures close to the nest, there will be a considerable commotion, resulting in the nesting magpies being joined by others in the neighbourhood to harry the unfortunate feline. Magpies sometimes take an equally direct approach when seeking food, chasing other birds, gulls in particular, to make them drop their food. These corvids are quite agile when walking, holding their long tails up as they move.

Identification

Black head, upper breast, back, rump and tail, with a broad white patch around the abdomen. Broad white wing stripe and dark blue areas evident below on folded wings. Depending on the light, there may be a green gloss apparent on the black plumage. Sexes alike, but the cock may have a longer tail.

Distribution Much of Europe and south to North Africa. Represented in parts of Asia and North America.
Size 51cm (20in).
Habitat Trees with surrounding open areas.
Nest Dome-shaped stick pile.
Eggs 2–8, bluish-green with darker markings.
Food Omnivorous.

JAY

Eurasian jay *Garrulus glandarius*

Jays are shy by nature and rarely allow a close approach. They store acorns and other seeds in autumn, and such caches help to sustain them through the winter when the ground may be covered in snow, restricting their opportunities to find food. This is the time when they are most likely to visit gardens in search of nourishment. During summer, jays may raid the nests of other birds, taking both eggs and chicks. Throughout their wide range, there is some local variation in their appearance, both in the depth of colour and the amount of black on the top of the head. However, their harsh call, which resembles a hoarse scream, coupled with a flash of colour, helps to identify them.

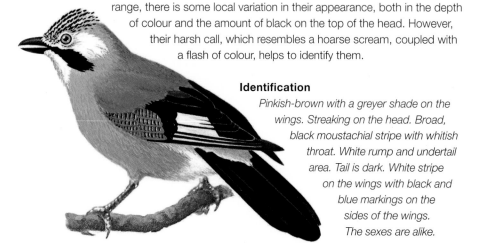

Identification

Pinkish-brown with a greyer shade on the wings. Streaking on the head. Broad, black moustachial stripe with whitish throat. White rump and undertail area. Tail is dark. White stripe on the wings with black and blue markings on the sides of the wings. The sexes are alike.

Distribution Range extends throughout most of Europe (except Scotland and the extreme north of Scandinavia). Also present in North Africa and Asia.
Size 35cm (14in).
Habitat Woodland.
Nest Platform of twigs.
Eggs 3–7, bluish green with dense speckling.
Food Omnivorous.

ROOK

Corvus frugilegus

Distribution Range extends throughout Europe and eastward into Asia. Some populations move south in the winter to the north Mediterranean.
Size 49cm (19in).
Habitat Close to farmland.
Nest Made of sticks, built in trees.
Eggs 2–7, bluish-green with dark markings.
Food Omnivorous, mainly invertebrates, but also grain, acorns and earthworms.

Rooks are most likely to be seen in gardens near farmland. They nest in colonies, partly because they inhabit areas of open countryside where there are few trees. These are highly social corvids, in which a strong bond also exists between breeding pairs. The rookery serves as the group's centre, which can make them vulnerable to human persecution, but although they eat corn, they are valued for consuming invertebrates as well. The rook's bill is adapted to digging in the ground to extract invertebrates, especially cranefly larvae. Outside the breeding season, it is not uncommon for rooks to associate with jackdaws, crows or ravens as an alternative to the rookery, which may be used as a roosting site at this time.

Identification
Entirely black plumage, with a pointed bill that has bare, pinkish skin at its base. The nostrils of adult rooks are unfeathered, distinguishing them from carrion crows. Rooks also have a flatter forehead and a peak to the crown. The sexes are alike.

RAVEN

Common raven *Corvus corax*

Distribution This species occurs in mainly south-western Europe and North Africa, north to Scandinavia. Range extends eastward throughout most of northern Asia. Also present in the British Isles, Greenland, Iceland and North America.
Size 67cm (26in).
Habitat Relatively open country.
Nest Bulky, made of sticks.
Eggs 3–7, bluish with darker spots.
Food Carrion.

Ravens are most likely to appear in gardens in upland areas. They may be recognized by their croaking calls and also their large size. They are the largest members of the crow family occurring in the Northern Hemisphere. The impression of bulk conveyed by these birds is reinforced by their shaggy throat feathers, which do not lie sleekly. There is a recognized decline in size across their range, with ravens in the far north being larger than those occurring farther south. Pairs occupy relatively large territories, and even outside the breeding season they tend not to associate in large flocks. When searching for food, ravens are able to fly easily over long distances, flapping their wings slowly.

Identification
Very large in size with a powerful, curved bill. Entirely black plumage. Wedge-shaped tail in flight, when the flight feathers stand out, creating a fingered appearance at the tips. Males often larger than females.

JACKDAWS, STARLINGS AND THRUSHES

Gregarious birds, jackdaws and starlings are often seen in groups. Both may be seen in British gardens at any time of year. Fieldfares and nightingales are seasonal visitors. Fieldfares visit British gardens in winter. Nightingales arrive in late spring. They are rarely seen but are known for their melodious songs.

JACKDAW

Eurasian jackdaw *Corvus monedula*

These corvids are very adaptable birds, just as likely to be seen foraging on rubbish dumps as visiting garden bird tables. When ants swarm on warm summer days, they are sufficiently agile to catch these flying insects on the wing. In agricultural areas, jackdaws learn to pull ticks off the backs of grazing animals such as sheep, as well as stealing their wool, which they use to line their nests. Pairs rarely nest in the open, preferring instead the relative security of an enclosed area, often utilizing buildings or even chimneys or church steeples. The hen incubates the eggs alone, with the young hatching after about 19 days. The chicks leave the nest after a further five weeks. Relatively social birds, jackdaws often associate in large groups in winter, sometimes being seen in the company of rooks (*Corvus frugilegus*) in agricultural areas.

Identification

Glossy blackish overall, darker on the crown, around the eyes and down on to the throat. Back of the head and neck are lighter, almost silvery, depending on the race. Black bill, legs and feet. Pale bluish irides. Young birds have blackish irides and darker, less glossy feathering.

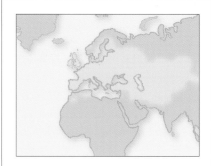

Distribution Resident throughout virtually the whole of Europe, although absent from large parts of Scandinavia. Range extends eastward into Asia. Also occurs in various parts of north-western Africa.
Size 39cm (15¼in).
Habitat Prefers relatively open country.
Nest Made from sticks, sited in a hole.
Eggs 3–8, pale bluish-green with darker markings.
Food Omnivorous.

COMMON STARLING

European starling *Sturnus vulgaris*

Small groups of starlings regularly visit bird tables, and may drive away other visitors. They are equally adept at seeking food on the ground, picking up seeds and probing for invertebrates. These familiar garden birds are resident in a vast range of areas. However, some populations, especially in the more northerly part of their range, migrate. This prompts the sudden arrival of hundreds of birds in urban areas, especially where there are groups of trees suitable for roosting. They often prove noisy in these surroundings, even singing after dusk if the area is well lit. In flight, large flocks are adept at avoiding pursuing predators, such as hawks, by weaving back and forth in a tight formation. When breeding, a pair will often adopt the nest of a woodpecker, or use a nest box.

Identification

Glossy. Purplish-black head, greenish hue on body, overlaid with spots. Dark brown wings and tail. Hens similar, but spots larger and base of tail is pinkish. Young birds duller, brownish and lack iridescence.

Distribution Throughout Europe and North Africa, with Scandinavian and eastern European populations migrating farther south for winter. Also east into Asia. Has been introduced to North America and Australia.
Size 22cm (8½in).
Habitat By houses and buildings.
Nest In a tree hole or birdhouse.
Eggs 2–9, white to pale blue or green.
Food Invertebrates, berries and bird table fare.

FIELDFARE

Turdus pilaris

Distribution This species occurs in central and northern Europe, and overwinters in the British Isles and south to the Mediterranean. A few pairs are now known to nest in northern and eastern Britain.

Size 27cm (10½in).

Habitat Breeds in deciduous woodlands and gardens, overwinters in more open areas.

Nest Cup-shaped.

Eggs 4–6, pale-blue with red speckles.

Food Invertebrates, fruit and berries.

This large member of the thrush family is a winter visitor to British gardens. It arrives from northern Europe and Scandinavia in late autumn, often in large flocks, which may also contain its smaller cousin, the redwing. Fieldfares generally feed on earthworms, snails and insects, but in harsh winter weather these birds enter gardens in search of fruit and berries. They can be attracted to your garden by fruit left on the ground. Normally quite shy by nature, greedy individuals will aggressively defend fruit or berry-bearing shrubs and trees against other birds. A flock of fieldfares can strip a cotoneaster, hawthorn or holly bush of berries in just a few hours before moving on in search of fresh food. After returning to their breeding grounds, these birds nest in isolated pairs or loose colonies of up to 50 birds. Breeding birds will vigorously defend their nest in a shrub or tree against cats, people or avian predators such as magpies. They swoop low to dive-bomb intruders while uttering loud cries and even splattering the enemy with droppings until they force a retreat. The call is a harsh, scolding "chack-chack", most often heard while in flight.

Identification

Large, strikingly marked thrush, with grey head, white eye stripe and small black mask. Bright yellow bill. A brown band joins the wings across the back. Grey rump. The buff-yellow band across the breast is speckled with bold dark markings, including on the flanks. Underparts are otherwise white. The flight pattern is undulating. The sexes are alike.

COMMON NIGHTINGALE

Luscinia megarhynchos

Distribution From southern England and mainland Europe on a similar latitude south to north-western Africa. Overwinters farther south in Africa.

Size 16cm (6in).

Habitat Woodlands, gardens.

Nest Cup-shaped.

Eggs 4–5, greyish-green to reddish-buff.

Food Mainly invertebrates.

Common nightingales are known for their beautiful singing, and in Europe their arrival is seen as heralding the spring. However, these birds are often difficult to spot, since they utter their musical calls toward dusk and even after dark on moonlit nights. Their relatively large eyes indicate that these members of the thrush family are crepuscular, becoming active around dusk. Their drab, subdued coloration enables them to blend easily into the dense shrubbery or woodland vegetation that they favour. They are only present in Europe from April to September, when they breed, before heading back to Africa for the winter.

Identification

Brown plumage extends from above the bill down over the back of the head and wings, becoming reddish-brown on the rump and tail. A sandy-buff area extends across the breast, while the lower underparts are whitish. The large eyes are dark and highlighted by a light eye ring. Sexes are alike.

GARDEN THRUSHES AND ORIOLES

The attractive song of some thrushes and orioles forms part of the dawn chorus in woodland areas, being especially conspicuous in spring when they are breeding. Robins, blackbirds and song thrushes may be seen in British gardens at any time of year. Golden orioles may visit eastern Britain in summer.

ROBIN

Erithacus rubecula

One of the best-loved garden birds, the robin's colourful appearance belies its strong aggressive streak, for these birds are highly territorial. In the garden, they can become very tame, regularly hopping down alongside the gardener's fork or spade to snatch invertebrates such as earthworms that come to the surface. Young, recently fledged robins look very different from mature individuals – they are almost entirely brown, with dense spotting on the head and chest. Robins sing quite melodiously all year round to defend their territories, also producing a tick-like call which is drawn-out and repeated, particularly when they are alarmed by the presence of a predator such as a cat. Since robins usually feed on the ground, they can be vulnerable to these predators.

Identification
Bright orange extends from just above the bill, around the eyes and down over virtually the entire breast. The lower underparts are whitish-grey, becoming browner on the flanks. The top of the head and the wings are brown, with a pale wing bar. The sexes are alike.

Distribution Resident in the British Isles, western Europe and parts of northern Africa. Scandinavian populations winter farther south.
Size 14cm (5½in).
Habitat Gardens, parks and woodland.
Nest Under cover, often near the ground, also in nest boxes.
Eggs 5–7, bluish-white with red markings.
Food Invertebrates, fruit and seeds.

SONG THRUSH

Turdus philomelos

The song of these thrushes is both powerful and musical. It can be heard particularly in the spring at the start of the breeding season, and is usually uttered from a relatively high branch. Song thrushes are welcomed by gardeners as they readily hunt and eat snails and other pests on the ground. Having grabbed a snail, the birds choose a special site known as an anvil where they smash it against a rock to break the shell and expose the mollusc within. These thrushes are excellent runners, and this allows them to pursue quarry such as leatherjackets (the larvae of certain species of cranefly, *Tipula* species). When breeding, song thrushes build a typical cup-shaped nest, which the hen is mainly or even solely responsible for constructing.

Identification
Brown back and wings, with some black evident, and a yellow-buff area across the chest. Dark markings that extend over the chest and abdomen are shaped like arrows. Sexes are alike. Young birds have smaller spots, usually less numerous on the underparts.

Distribution Ranges widely throughout the whole of Europe. Eastern populations head to the Mediterranean region for the winter. Also present in northern Africa, even as far south as the Sudan.
Size 22cm (8½in).
Habitat Woodland areas, parks and gardens.
Nest Cup-shaped.
Eggs 5–6, greenish-blue with reddish-brown markings.
Food Invertebrates, berries.

COMMON BLACKBIRD

Turdus merula

Distribution Resident throughout virtually the whole of Europe, except the far north of Scandinavia. Also present in northern Africa. The majority of Scandinavian and eastern European populations are migratory.
Size 29cm (11½in).
Habitat Woodland, gardens and parkland.
Nest Cup-shaped, hidden in a bush or tree.
Eggs 3–5, greenish-blue with reddish-brown markings.
Food Invertebrates, fruit and berries.

One of the most familiar garden birds, blackbirds frequently descend on lawns to search for invertebrates. Earthworms, which feature prominently in their diet, are most likely to be drawn to the surface after rain, and slugs and snails also emerge in wet conditions. In the 19th century, blackbirds were rarely seen in gardens, but today they have become commonplace. They are vocal and produce a range of fluty notes. Cocks are talented songsters, and both sexes will utter an urgent, harsh alarm call. Although blackbirds do not associate in flocks, pairs can be seen foraging together. As with other thrushes, their tails are surprisingly flexible and can be raised or lowered at will. It is not unusual to see pied blackbirds, with variable amounts of white among the black plumage. The majority of these birds, especially those with the most extensive white, are cocks.

Identification
Jet-black plumage contrasts with the bright yellow bill, which becomes a deeper yellow during the winter. Hens are drab in comparison, brownish overall with some streaking, notably on the breast, and have a darker bill.

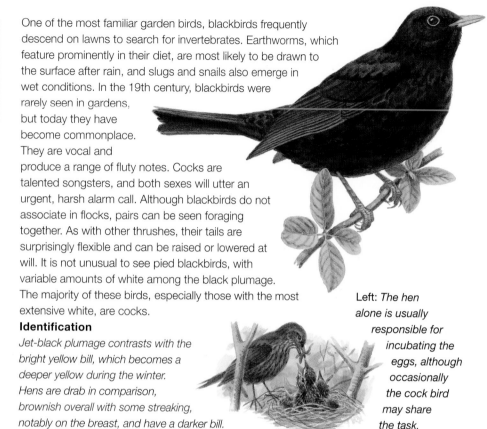

Left: *The hen alone is usually responsible for incubating the eggs, although occasionally the cock bird may share the task.*

EURASIAN GOLDEN ORIOLE

Oriolus oriolus

Distribution Golden oriole breeds right across mainland Europe, to the southernmost parts of Scandinavia, and extending eastward into Asia. In the British Isles, restricted to southern and eastern England. Also present in north-west Africa, overwintering throughout the continent.
Size 25cm (10in).
Habitat Prefers areas with deciduous woodlands.
Nest Cup-shaped.
Eggs 3–4, creamy-buff with dark spotting.
Food Invertebrates, berries and fruits.

These summer visitors to gardens in southern and eastern Britain are spectacular birds. However, despite their bright coloration, they are quite inconspicuous, preferring to hide away in the upper reaches of the woodland, although they will sometimes descend to the ground in search of food and water. Their diet varies, consisting mainly of invertebrates from spring onward, with fruits and berries more significant later in the year. Migrants arrive at the southern tip of Africa by November, and by March will have set off on the long journey back to Europe. The small north-west African population heads south also, returning by the middle of April. Males establish territories on arrival at their breeding grounds. There is no lasting pair bond.

Identification
Yellow. Black wings with a yellow patch. Red bill. Hens have greenish-yellow upperparts, streaked underparts mainly white, yellow flanks and blackish wings. Young are more greyish-green, with yellow on underparts.

THRUSHES AND WARBLERS

In some thrushes, the males at any rate are quite brightly coloured, but their shy habits make them fairly inconspicuous. Like thrushes, many warblers are talented singers. Warblers are smaller than thrushes, and their subdued colours make them hard to notice, but they can be recognized by their songs.

COMMON REDSTART

Phoenicurus phoenicurus

This member of the thrush family is most likely to be seen in gardens with mature trees or near woodlands. A summer visitor, it seeks cover when constructing its nest. This is often built inside a tree hole, but sometimes an abandoned building or even an underground tunnel is chosen. The hen incubates alone for two weeks until the eggs hatch, with both parents subsequently providing food for their growing brood. Fledging takes place around two weeks later. The pair may sometimes nest again, particularly if food is plentiful. When migrating south, birds from much of Europe take a westerly route through the Iberian Peninsula. The return journey back north begins in late March. Males generally leave first, enabling them to establish their breeding territories by the time they are joined by the hens.

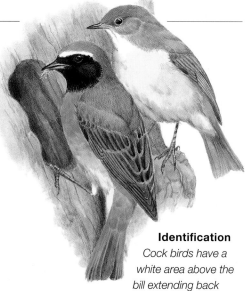

Identification
Cock birds have a white area above the bill extending back above the eyes. Remainder of the face is black, the head and back are grey. Chest is rufous, becoming paler on the underparts. Hens are duller, with a greyish-brown head and buff-white underparts. Young birds have brown heads and rufous tails.

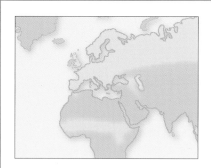

Distribution Breeding range extends across virtually the whole of Europe, including Scandinavia, and eastwards into Asia. Absent from Ireland. Also occurs in parts of north-west Africa, and overwinters south of the Sahara.
Size 15cm (6in).
Habitat Woodland.
Nest Built in a suitable hole.
Eggs 5–7, bluish with slight red spotting.
Food Mainly invertebrates and berries.

REDWING

Turdus iliacus

The smallest member of the thrush family, the redwing is a winter visitor to Britain from northern Europe. This neat bird with its boldly marked head is named for its russet-coloured underwings and flanks. Redwings arrive from Scandinavia and Iceland in late October or November, often forming mixed flocks with their larger cousins, fieldfares. These thrushes are not normally garden birds, but harsh or snowy weather will drive them to seek food in gardens in the form of fruit and berries. They feast on windfall apples and on the berries of shrubs such as hawthorn. In a matter of hours, a flock of redwings can strip a bush of all its berries. In March or April, the birds depart for their breeding grounds in northern Europe. In recent years some pairs have remained to breed in Scotland. Redwing pairs often nest in loose groups, building nests in trees, shrubs or on the ground.

Identification
A small, neat, dark thrush with a well-marked head. The rusty-red patches on the sides of the breast and underwings give the bird its name. Upperparts are dark brown; the throat and breast pale, streaked with dark-brown markings. Belly greyish. The sexes are alike.

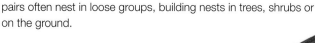

Distribution Breeds in northern and eastern Europe, eastward into Asia, overwinters in northern and southern Europe, including the British Isles. In the last 70 years redwing pairs have begun to breed in Scotland.
Size 21cm (8in).
Habitat Woods, conifer forests, heaths, agricultural land.
Nest Cup-shape of twigs and grass.
Eggs 4–6, pale-blue with red markings.
Food Invertebrates, seeds, berries.

DARTFORD WARBLER

Sylvia undata

These small warblers are resident in western Europe, but their most northerly breeding outpost is in southern Britain, where they maintain a tenuous foothold, with numbers becoming severely depleted in harsh winters. They roost in groups, which helps to conserve body heat. These warblers are most often seen in gardens near heathland. They forage low down in shrubbery, sometimes venturing to the ground, where they can run surprisingly quickly. Berries feature significantly in their diet during winter in northern areas. Males establish breeding territories in autumn. They sing more loudly and frequently during spring, raising the grey feathers on the sides of their faces as part of the courtship ritual. The nest is built by both adults, hidden in a shrub. The hen incubates mainly on her own, for two weeks, and the chicks fledge after a similar interval.

Identification

The cock bird has a greyish head, back and wings. White spots on the throat, reddish chest and a grey central area to the underparts. A red area of skin encircles each eye. The bill is yellowish with a dark tip, and the legs and feet are yellowish-brown. Hens are paler with white throats. The young birds have grey-buff underparts, with no orbital skin and dark irides.

Distribution This warbler's range extends through western parts of Europe, including the Iberian Peninsula, the western Mediterranean region and western parts of North Africa. Also present in localized southern parts of England.
Size 14cm (5½in).
Habitat Heathland.
Nest Cup-shaped, made from vegetation.
Eggs 3–5, whitish with darker markings.
Food Mostly invertebrates, but also some berries.

GRASSHOPPER WARBLER

Locustella naevia

Difficult to observe, these summer visitors may be spotted in gardens close to marshland, heaths and pastures with thorny scrub. They are very adept at clambering through grass and low vegetation. They may be spotted running across open ground, flying low if disturbed and seeking vegetation as cover. Their song, which is usually heard at dusk, may also betray their presence. They sing in bursts of up to a minute in duration, and their calls incorporate ringing notes that have been likened to the sound of a muffled alarm clock. Grasshopper warblers migrate largely without stopping, and have been observed in West Africa from August onward. They undertake the return journey to their breeding grounds in Europe and Asia between March and May, flying in a more easterly direction, often crossing the Mediterranean from Algeria. The breeding period extends from May until July, with the bulky nest built close to the ground. The chicks hatch after two weeks, and are reared by both adults before leaving the nest as early as 10 days old.

Identification

This warbler has olive-brown upperparts. Streaked head, back and undertail coverts. Faint eye stripe. Underparts whitish, more yellowish-green on the breast. Variable chest markings. Narrow, pointed bill. Pink legs and feet. Sexes are alike. The young birds have yellowish underparts.

Distribution Breeds through central and northern parts of Europe as far as southern Scandinavia. Present in much of the British Isles. Absent from the Mediterranean region. Overwinters in parts of Africa, especially on the western side.
Size 12.5cm (5in).
Habitat Marshland and grassland areas.
Nest Made of vegetation.
Eggs 6, creamy with brownish-red spotting.
Food Invertebrates.

WOODLAND WARBLERS

Spotting these birds in the garden is not always easy because of their small size. In many cases, the neutral coloration also blends in well with the foliage, and the more brightly coloured goldcrest is particularly tiny. Warblers generally favour overgrown areas that contain a good supply of invertebrates.

WILLOW WARBLER

Phylloscopus trochilus

The subdued coloration of these small birds is so effective that, despite being one of Europe's most common species, willow warblers are very inconspicuous. Difficult to observe in their wooded habitat, it is their song, which heralds their arrival in woodlands in early spring, that usually betrays their presence. In the British Isles, the willow species is the most numerous of all warblers, with a population estimated at around three million pairs. These warblers are most often spotted in rural gardens near woodlands and reside in Europe between April and September. They closely resemble chiffchaffs but can be distinguished by their songs. Their nest is hidden among the vegetation and features a low entry point. In late summer, willow warblers can often be seen in loose association with various tits, before they head off to their African wintering grounds.

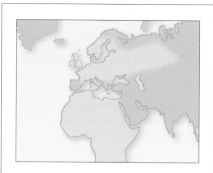

Distribution Occurs in the summer from the British Isles right across most of Europe. Overwinters in Africa.
Size 12cm (5in).
Habitat Wooded areas.
Nest Dome-shaped, constructed on the ground.
Eggs 6–7, pale pink with reddish spotting.
Food Insects and other small invertebrates.

Identification

Greyish-green upperparts, with a pale yellowish streak running across each eye. Pale yellow throat and chest, with whitish underparts. The yellow plumage is much whiter in birds from more northern areas.

GARDEN WARBLER

Sylvia borin

These warblers visit rural gardens with trees in summer, but their dull colours and small size mean they are fairly inconspicuous, particularly when darting among foliage. However, their attractive song and call notes may help identify them in the undergrowth. Garden warblers arrive in Britain to breed from middle of April onward, and construct a fairly large nest using a variety of plant matter, usually including stems of grass, and lining it with softer material. The hen sits alone through the incubation period, which lasts approximately 12 days, but subsequently both parents will seek food for their rapidly-growing brood. The young quickly leave the nest, sometimes when just 9 days old, and may be forced to scrabble among the vegetation to escape would-be predators until they are able to fly from danger. In more southern parts of their breeding range, pairs of garden warblers may produce two successive broods of chicks. They return to Africa in September.

Distribution Summer range extends from Scandinavia southwards across virtually all of Europe. Migrates south for the winter, ranging over much of Africa except the Horn and the south-west.
Size 14cm (5½in).
Habitat Gardens with trees, also parks.
Nest Made of vegetation.
Eggs 4–5, buff with brown spots.
Food Mainly invertebrates.

Identification

This species has an olive-brown head and upperparts, with a greyish area present at each side of the neck. The underparts are greyish-white, buffer along the flanks. Bill and legs are dark greyish. The young birds are similar to adults. The sexes are alike.

CHIFFCHAFF

Phylloscopus collybita

The chiffchaff is a lively warbler, generally common through its range and often seen in gardens, particularly those with trees nearby. Its arrival is a sign of spring. There are regional differences in appearance, with individuals found in western and central areas having brighter yellow coloration than birds occurring farther north and east. Its unusual name reflects its common two-note song pattern. Pairs are likely to start nesting from April onward, with the female building the nest on her own. This is positioned relatively close to the ground in a suitable bush or shrub that provides good cover, such as rhododendron, or sometimes in among brambles, offering protection against predators. The chiffchaffs slip in and out of the nest using a side entrance. The hen undertakes the incubation on her own, and this lasts for about 13 days, with the young chicks subsequently fledging after a similar interval. Chiffchaffs may rear two broods during the summer.

Identification

Yellowish stripe above each eye, with a black stripe passing through the centre. Underparts whitish, with variable yellow on the sides of the face and flanks. Rest of the upperparts are dark brownish-green. Pointed bill is dark. Legs and feet are black. The sexes are alike.

Distribution Occurs through most of Europe during the summer but absent from parts of northern Scandinavia and Scotland. Resident in parts of southern Britain and Ireland and farther south, near the Mediterranean. Overwinters in northern Africa and south of the Sahara. Also found in Asia.

Size 12cm (4in).

Habitat Wooded areas.

Nest Dome-shaped, made from vegetation.

Eggs 4–7, white with brownish spotting.

Food Invertebrates.

GOLDCREST

Regulus regulus

These warblers are the smallest birds in Europe and are surprisingly bold, drawing attention to themselves with their high-pitched calls and the way they jerkily flit from branch to branch. They can be easily distinguished from the slightly larger firecrest (*R. ignicapillus*) by the absence of a white streak above the eyes. Goldcrests may visit gardens especially with conifer trees in both urban and rural settings, but their small size makes them quite hard to detect. They associate in groups both of their own kind and also with other small birds such as tits, seeking food in the branches rather than at ground level. Pairs split off to breed in the early spring, with both sexes collecting moss and other material to construct their nest. This may be hung off a conifer branch, up to 12m (40ft) off the ground, although it may also be concealed among ivy or similar vegetation. Cobwebs act as thread to anchor the nest together, and the interior is lined with feathers. The young will have fledged by three weeks old, and the adults may nest again soon afterward and rear a second brood.

Identification

Dumpy appearance, with cock birds having an orange streak (yellow in hens) running down the centre of the head, bordered by black stripes on each side. Prominent area of white encircling the eyes, with much of the rest of the head pale grey. White wing bars. Back is greyish-green, underparts paler. Bill is black, legs and feet greyish. Young birds have greyish heads and pale bills.

Distribution Resident through much of Europe, except for northern Scotland and northern Scandinavia, where pairs spend the summer. Often moves south to the Mediterranean for the winter. Goldcrest's range also extends eastward into Asia.

Size 8.5cm (3¼ in).

Habitat Wooded areas, especially conifer woodlands.

Nest Suspended basket made of moss.

Eggs 7–8, buffy-white with brown markings.

Food Mainly invertebrates.

SPARROWS AND SMALL GARDEN BIRDS

Although sparrows, dunnocks and wrens commonly reside in gardens, these birds are not easily noticed because of their small stature. The dull-coloured plumage provides camouflage, blending in with vegetation. The presence of house sparrows is more obvious because they consort in twittering flocks.

HOUSE SPARROW

Passer domesticus

A common sight on garden bird tables and in city parks, house sparrows have adapted well to living closely alongside people, even to the extent of nesting under roofs of buildings. Highly social birds, these sparrows form loose flocks, with larger numbers congregating where food is readily available. They spend much of their time on the ground, hopping along but ever watchful for passing predators such as cats. It is not uncommon for them to construct nests during the winter, which serve as communal roosts rather than being used for breeding. The bills of cock birds turn black in the spring, at the start of the nesting period. During this time, several males will often court a single female in what has become known as a 'sparrows' wedding'. In more rural areas, house sparrows sometimes nest in tree holes, and occasionally construct domed nests. They also use nest boxes.

Distribution Very common, occurring throughout virtually the whole of Europe, and eastward across Asia. Also present in northern and south-east Africa.
Size 6in (15cm).
Habitat Urban and rural gardens.
Nest Tree holes, under roofs of buildings and in birdhouses.
Eggs 3–6, whitish with darker markings.
Food Includes invertebrates, seeds.

Identification

Rufous-brown head with a grey area on top. A black stripe runs across the eyes and a broad black bib runs down over the chest. The ear coverts and the entire underparts are greyish, and there is a whitish area under the tail. Hens are a duller shade of brown, with a pale stripe behind each eye and a fawn bar on each wing.

WREN

Troglodytes troglodytes

Although often difficult to spot due to their size and drab coloration, these tiny birds have a remarkably loud song which usually betrays their presence. Wrens can be found in gardens where there is plenty of cover, such as ivy-clad walls, scurrying under the vegetation in search of spiders and similar prey. During the winter, when their small size could make them vulnerable to hypothermia, they huddle together in roosts overnight to keep warm. However, populations are often badly affected by prolonged spells of severe weather. In the spring, the hen chooses one of several nests that the male has constructed, lining it with feathers to form a soft base for her eggs. Wrens are surprisingly common, although not always conspicuous, with the British population alone made up of an estimated ten million birds.

Distribution Resident throughout Europe, except in Scandinavia and neighbouring parts of Russia during the winter. European wrens move south in the winter. Present in northern Africa.
Size 10cm (4in).
Habitat Gardens and woodland.
Nest Ball-shaped, sometimes inside nest boxes.
Eggs 5–6, white with reddish-brown markings.
Food Mainly invertebrates.

Identification

Reddish-brown back and wings with visible barring. Lighter brown underparts and a narrow eye stripe. Short tail, often held vertically, which is greyish on its underside. Bill is long and relatively narrow. Sexes alike.

DUNNOCK

Prunella modularis

Distribution Resident in Britain all year round. Throughout Europe except for Iceland; seen in northern and eastern Europe only in summer, and in parts of southern Europe only in winter.
Size 14.5cm (6in).
Habitat Scrubland, woodlands, parks and gardens.
Nest Cup-shaped nest of twigs and grasses, lined with hair and feathers.
Eggs 4–6, sky-blue.
Food Invertebrates, seeds.

Once known as the hedge sparrow, the dunnock is actually a member of the accentor family – a group of small, streaked birds. It can be distinguished from the house sparrow, which it superficially resembles in size and in its dull colouring, by its pinkish-orange legs and slender bill. Dunnocks are frequent garden visitors, but their secretive ways and skulking, mouse-like habits make them difficult to notice. Generally keeping to the cover of hedges and shrubs they sometimes alight on bird tables, but more often peck crumbs and seeds from the ground. Research has revealed that the unassuming-looking dunnock has a complex sex life. During the breeding season males and females establish separate but overlapping territories, and both sexes often have several mates. For the male, the aim is to sire as many young as possible, while the advantage to the female is that any male with which she has mated will help to raise the chicks. Hens build their nests low in dense vegetation and may raise two to three broods in a season. The rapid, warbling song is similar to a wren's but quieter, with breeding birds keeping in touch with shrill, cheeping calls. Superficially falling into the category of 'little brown jobs', closer inspection reveals a delicately marked bird.

Identification

Dunnocks broadly resemble sparrows in size and appearance, but with a purplish-grey head, throat and breast, and sometimes a brownish mask around the eyes. The back and wings are chestnut-brown with darker streaks and black feather-centres. The rump is also grey, with a chestnut-brown tail. The warbler-like bill is slender and pointed, the legs pinkish-orange. Sexes are alike. Juveniles are browner and more streaked than the adults.

TREE SPARROW

Passer montanus

Distribution Breeds throughout much of Europe except for northern Scandinavia, eastern England, northern Scotland and central Ireland.
Size 14cm (5½in).
Habitat Woodland, farmland.
Nest Loose cup shape made of straw or grass.
Eggs 4–6, buff-coloured with dark spots.
Food Seeds, grain, buds, invertebrates.

This woodland bird is a relative of the house sparrow, which it quite closely resembles in size and markings. A distinctive black patch on each white cheek distinguishes these small birds from their cousins. Tree sparrows suffered a disastrous decline in western Europe during the 20th century. Once widespread, these birds are now absent from many parts of their former range. A sociable species, tree sparrows often form flocks, including mixed flocks with house sparrows outside the breeding season. Their natural habitat is woodland with scattered clearings, and farmland with clumps of trees. However, these birds are also seen in gardens in urban areas, where they visit bird tables to take seeds and nuts. They are shyer than house sparrows, but have a similar repertoire of calls, including chirruping and cheeping notes and a ticking sound in flight. In April they nest colonially in trees, buildings, cliffs or in nest boxes, producing two or even three clutches of eggs which hatch after 11–14 days. The young fledge 12–14 days after hatching.

Identification

In this species the top of the head is reddish-brown, with a black bib beneath the bill, which is also black. A white area on the cheeks below the eyes is broken by central black patches, and extends back around the neck. The chest is grey. The wings are light brown and black, broken by a white wing bar edged by black. The underparts are buffish, the tail is plain brown. The sexes are alike.

FLYCATCHERS AND INSECT-EATERS

Invertebrates provide nuthatches, creepers and flycatchers with much of their diet, while some also eat other foods – for example, nuts in the case of nuthatches. These insect-hunters use various techniques to capture prey, some combing the bark of trees, while others hunt in the air or on the ground.

EURASIAN NUTHATCH

Sitta europaea

With relatively large, strong feet and very powerful claws, Eurasian nuthatches are adept at scampering up and down tree trunks. They hunt for invertebrates, which they extract from the bark with their narrow bills, but their powerful beaks also enable them to feed on nuts. The nuthatches first wedge the nut into a suitable crevice in the bark, then hammer at the shell, breaking it open so they can extract the kernel. They will also store nuts, which they will eat when other food is in short supply. These birds are hole-nesters, including in birdhouses. The bill is also used to plaster over the entrance of their nest in spring, until the opening is just large enough to allow the adult birds to squeeze in and out. This helps to protect the young from predators. Eurasian nuthatches are most likely to be encountered in areas with broad-leaved trees, as these provide food such as acorns and hazelnuts.

Identification
Bluish-grey upperparts from head to tail. Distinctive black stripes running from the base of the bill down the sides of the head, encompassing the eyes. Underparts vary in colour from white through to a rusty shade of buff, depending on the race. Dark reddish-brown vent area, more brightly coloured in cocks.

Distribution Found throughout most of Europe, except for Ireland, northern England, Scotland and northern Scandinavia. Occurs in northern Africa opposite the Strait of Gibraltar.
Size 14cm (5½in).
Habitat Gardens and parks with mature trees.
Nest In a secluded spot or nest box.
Eggs 6–9, white with heavy reddish-brown speckling.
Food Invertebrates, nuts and seeds.

EURASIAN TREECREEPER

Brown creeper *Certhia familiaris*

These treecreepers can be distinguished from the southerly short-toed species (*C. brachydactyla*) by their longer hind toes, which assist them in climbing vertically up tree trunks when hunting insects. Having reached the top of the trunk, the treecreeper flies down to the base of a neighbouring tree and begins again, circling the bark, probing likely nooks and crannies with its bill. The pointed tips of the tail feathers provide extra support. Pairs start nesting in the spring, with the cock bird chasing his intended mate. They seek out a small, hidden cavity where a cup-shaped nest can be constructed. The hen incubates mainly on her own for two weeks, and the young fledge after a similar interval. It is not uncommon, especially in the south, for pairs to breed twice in succession.

Identification
Mottled brownish upperparts, variable white stripe above eyes. Underparts whitish. Narrow, curved bill. Young similar to adults. Sexes alike.

Right: *A small crevice in a tree trunk may be used by a treecreeper as a nesting site.*

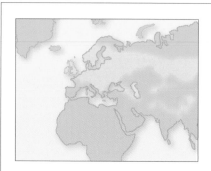

Distribution Much of northern Europe, except for the far north of Scandinavia. Sporadic distribution through France and northern Spain. Not present in northern Africa, but range extends eastward into Asia.
Size 14cm (5½in).
Habitat Dense woodland.
Nest Small hollow.
Eggs 5–7, white with reddish-brown markings.
Food Assorted invertebrates.

PIED FLYCATCHER

Ficedula hypoleuca

Pied flycatchers are summer visitors to British gardens with mature trees. These flycatchers hawk insects in flight, and will also catch slower-moving prey such as caterpillars by plucking them off vegetation. They can be seen in oak woodlands and nearby gardens during the summer. In Europe these birds may range north to the taiga, where mosquitoes hatching in pools of water during the brief Arctic summer provide an almost constant supply of food. They nest in tree holes and will also use nest boxes. Pied flycatchers are closely related to collared flycatchers (*F. albicollis*), and the two species may sometimes hybridize.

Distribution Summer visitor to Europe. Breeding range extends throughout virtually the whole of Europe including Scandinavia, although not the far north. Overwinters in Africa north of a line from coastal Nigeria to Djibouti.
Size 13cm (5in).
Habitat Most areas where insects are common.
Nest Hole in a tree or nest box.
Eggs 5–9, pale blue.
Food Invertebrates.

Identification

The cock's summer plumage is a combination of black and white. White patches are present above the bill and on the wings. The underparts are white, with the remainder of the plumage being black. The hens also have whitish underparts and white areas on the wings, while their upperparts are brownish. Cocks in their non-breeding plumage resemble adult hens, but retain the blackish wings and uppertail coverts.

SPOTTED FLYCATCHER

Muscicapa striata

As its name suggests, this species feeds itself and its young on insects – not only flies, but also aphids, butterflies, and even bees and wasps, whose stings must be first removed. It catches insects in mid-air, swooping from a perch in a tree to chase its prey with an erratic flight. Hovering briefly on long, slender wings to seize victims, it returns to the perch. It moves to a different perch when most of the insects in one area have been taken, only to return later to try its luck again. This is one of the last migrants to arrive from Africa, appearing in late May, when it builds its nest of grass, twigs and moss bound with cobwebs in a tree crevice, old nest, open-fronted nest box or on a creeper-covered wall. Its breeding is timed to coincide with the hottest time of year when there will be most insects to feed the young. In recent years the spotted flycatcher has suffered a notable decline, probably due to drought in its African wintering grounds. With its cryptic coloration, this bird is easiest recognized by its relatively large head, upright position on the perch, and insect-catching behaviour. Its quiet song, a series of thin squeaks, is rarely noticed.

Distribution Breeds throughout most of Europe, including Britain from May to September. Breeding grounds extend eastward into Asia and south to North Africa. Overwinters in Africa south of the Sahara.
Size 15cm (6in).
Habitat Open woodland and woodland edges, parks, large gardens.
Nest Cup-shaped nest of twigs, moss and grass.
Eggs 4–5, buff to greenish with red-brown markings.
Food Flying insects.

Identification

Greyish-brown upperparts, with darker streaking on the largish head extending to whitish underparts. The area above the bill is also white. Relatively long wings and a long, distinctive, square-tipped tail that can be spread to aid hovering. The bill, legs and feet are blackish. Sexes are alike. Young birds have dull yellowish markings extending from the head over the wings, rump and tail.

TITS, BUNTINGS AND SONGSTERS

Small and compact birds, tits and buntings, including the yellowhammer, are often talented singers. Cuckoos are considerably larger, but with their distinctive, repetitive call, they are more often heard rather than seen. Cuckoos have unusual breeding habits, relying on other birds to raise their chicks.

CRESTED TIT

Parus cristatus

The crest of this tit is always visible, although the crest feathers can be lowered slightly. This makes it easy to distinguish, even when foraging with other groups of tits, which happens especially during winter. These attractive tits may be seen in gardens near pinewoods in Scotland. They rarely venture high up, preferring to seek food on or near the ground. Invertebrates such as spiders are preferred, although they often resort to eating conifer seeds during winter. Crested tits frequently create food stores, particularly during autumn, to help them survive the harsh winter months when snow may blanket the ground. Seeds are gathered and secreted in holes in the bark, and among lichens, while invertebrates are decapitated and stored on a shorter-term basis. Nesting begins in March, with a pair choosing a hole, usually in rotten wood, which they enlarge before constructing a cup-shaped lining for their eggs. In more southerly areas, two broods of chicks may be reared in succession.

Identification
Triangular-shaped, blackish-white crest. Sides of the face are also blackish-white, with a blackish line running through each eye and curling round the hind cheeks. Black collar joins to a bib under the bill. Upperparts brownish. The underparts are paler buff, more rufous on the flanks. Young look similar to the adults but have brown rather than reddish irides. Sexes are alike.

Distribution Resident from Spain across to Scandinavia (although not the far north) and Russia. Present in the British Isles only in northern Scotland. Absent from Italy.
Size 12cm (4¾ in).
Habitat Conifer woodland.
Nest In a rotten tree stump.
Eggs 5–8, white with reddish markings.
Food Invertebrates; seeds in winter.

SNOW BUNTING

Plectrophenax nivalis

These buntings breed closer to the North Pole than any other passerine (perching bird). They arrive in Britain in autumn to escape the harsh northern winter, when they may visit gardens on coasts. Some pairs also breed in the highlands of northern Scotland. The cock has an attractive display flight, rising to about 10m (30ft) before starting to sing, then slowly fluttering down again. The nest is often sited among rocks, which provide shelter from cold winds. Outside the breeding season, snow buntings are social and can be seen in flocks, searching for food on the ground. They are usually quite wary, flying away to prevent a close approach. These buntings have a varied diet comprised of seeds and berries when invertebrates are scarce in winter.

Identification
Breeding males mainly white, with black on the back, wings, tail and flight feathers. Bill and legs black. Hens have dark brown streaking on the head, buff ear coverts and brown on the wings. Non-breeding males resemble hens but with a white rump and whiter wings. Young birds are greyish and streaked.

Distribution Breeds in Iceland, northern Scandinavia and the far north of Europe eastward into Asia. Overwinters farther south in Europe and Asia. Also present in North America. Populations from Greenland often overwinter in the British Isles.
Size 17cm (6¾ in).
Habitat Tundra, grassland.
Nest Scrape on the ground.
Eggs 4–6, white with reddish spots.
Food Seeds, invertebrates.

YELLOWHAMMER

Emberiza citrinella

This colourful, distinctive bunting is best known for its song – a rapid, rhythmic series of notes ending with a flourish, often likened to the phrase 'a little bit of bread and no cheese'. The males sing their song in summer near the nest, which is built low along a hedge. As seed- and grain-eaters, yellowhammers are birds of arable farmland that traditionally fed and nested far from gardens. Like many farmland birds however, their populations have declined in recent years. Formerly found throughout much of rural Britain except the far north and west, they no longer frequent much of their old range, but they are now more often seen in gardens, especially in winter, when they form feeding flocks with other buntings, finches or sparrows. Yellowhammers pair up in spring and raise two or three broods in a season. The eggs are incubated for 12–14 days with chicks fledging 11–13 days after hatching. The male helps the female to feed the young on insects, and takes over feeding altogether when his mate lays a new clutch.

Identification

A long, slender bunting with a long tail. The adult male in breeding plumage has a bright-yellow head and underparts, streaked with light-brown markings. The chest is light brown. Upperparts and rump are chestnut-brown with dark streaks on the back. Males are less brightly coloured in winter. Hens generally duller, having brownish-yellow plumage with darker streaks. Juveniles even browner.

Distribution Resident in Britain and breeds through much of Europe except for Iceland and parts of Portugal and Spain. Widespread in southern and western Europe in winter. Range also extends eastward into central Asia.
Size 16cm (6½in).
Habitat Farmland with hedges, grasslands, heaths, also coasts.
Nest Cup-shape of grass and moss.
Eggs 3–5, white to purplish with reddish markings.
Food Seeds, berries, invertebrates.

CUCKOO

Common cuckoo *Cuculus canorus*

The distinctive call of the cuckoo, heard when these birds return from their African wintering grounds, is traditionally regarded as one of the first signs of spring. Typically, they are only resident in Britain between April and September, when they are more often heard than seen in gardens. Adult cuckoos have an unusual ability to feed on hairy caterpillars, which are plentiful in wooded areas in summer. Common cuckoos are parasitic breeders – the hens lay single eggs in the nests of smaller birds such as hedge sparrows (*Prunella modularis*), meadow pipits (*Anthus pratensis*) and wagtails (*Motacilla* species). The unsuspecting hosts hatch a monster, with the cuckoo chick ejecting other eggs or potential rivals from the nest in order to monopolize the food supply.

Distribution Throughout the whole of Europe, ranging eastward into Asia. Also present in northern Africa. Populations in Northern Europe overwinter in eastern and southern parts of Africa, while Asiatic birds migrate as far as the Philippines.
Size 36cm (14in).
Habitat Various.
Nest None – lays directly in other birds' nests.
Eggs 1 per nest, resembling those of its host.
Food Mainly invertebrates, including caterpillars.

Identification

Grey head, upper chest, wings and tail, and black edging to the white feathers of the underparts. In hens this barring extends almost to the throat, offset against a more yellowish background. Some hens belong to a brown colour morph, with rufous feathering replacing the grey, and black barring apparent on the upperparts.

Left: *The young cuckoo lifts an egg on to its back to heave it from the nest. If the host's eggs survive long enough to hatch, the cuckoo will eject the chicks.*

GARDEN TITS

Given their small size, tits are most likely to be spotted in gardens during winter, when the absence of leaves makes them more conspicuous, and they more frequently visit feeders and tables. Tits are very resourceful when seeking food, displaying acrobatic skills as they dart about, even feeding upside down.

COAL TIT

Parus ater

These tits are often seen in gardens feeding on bird tables, sometimes taking foods such as nuts which they then store in a variety of locations, ranging from caches on the ground to suitable holes in trees. The urge to store food in this way becomes strongest in late summer and during autumn, and helps the birds to maintain a food supply through the coldest months of the year. This hoarding strategy appears to be very successful, since coal tit populations rarely crash like many other small birds following a particularly harsh winter. In fact, these tits have increased their breeding range significantly over recent years, with their distribution now extending to various islands off the British coast, including the Isles of Scilly. During winter, in their natural habitat of coniferous forest, they may form flocks comprised of many thousands of individuals, yet in gardens they are only usually seen in quite small numbers.

Identification

Jet-black head, with white patches on the sides of the face and a similar area on the nape. Greyish-olive upperparts, with white wing bars, and brownish-white underparts, although some marked regional variations. Young birds have pale yellowish cheek patches. Sexes very similar, but the female's head markings may be duller. The bill is black. Legs are greyish.

Distribution Resident throughout the whole of Europe except for northern Scandinavia. Range extends south to north-western parts of Africa, and spreads right across Asia to Japan.
Size 11cm (4½in).
Habitat Wooded areas.
Nest Cup-shaped, made from vegetation.
Eggs 8–11, white with reddish markings.
Food Mostly invertebrates and seeds.

GREAT TIT

Parus major

Great tits form groups after the breeding season, often associating with other small birds, foraging for food in woodlands as well as visiting bird tables, where their bold, jaunty nature makes them conspicuous. Although they do not hoard food like some tits, they are able to lower their body temperature significantly overnight when roosting, effectively lessening the amount of energy they need. Great tits become much more territorial at the start of the breeding season, which in Europe typically starts during March. They build their nest in a tree hole, but readily use garden nest boxes where provided. Studies have shown that the male seeks out potential nesting sites within the pair's territory, but it is the female who has the final choice. Pairs may nest twice during the breeding period, which lasts until July.

Identification

Cock has a black head with white cheek patches. Broad band of black extends down the centre of chest, with yellow on either side. Wings olive-green at the top, becoming bluish on the sides, flight feathers and tail. Hens similar but with a narrower black band. Young paler, with yellowish cheeks and less of the black band.

Distribution Found through all of Europe except in parts of northern Scandinavia, and ranges south as far as northern Africa. Also extends widely across much of Asia.
Size 14cm (5½in).
Habitat Woodland.
Nest Cup-shaped, made from vegetation; will use nest boxes.
Eggs 5–12, white with reddish spotting.
Food Invertebrates, seeds.

BLUE TIT

Parus caeruleus

Distribution Throughout Europe except the far north of Scandinavia. Also present in north-western Africa.
Size 12cm (5in).
Habitat Wooded areas, parks and gardens.
Nest Tree holes and nest boxes.
Eggs 7–16, white with reddish-brown markings.
Food Invertebrates, seeds and nuts.

A common visitor to bird tables, blue tits are lively, active birds by nature, and are welcomed by gardeners because they eat aphids. Their small size allows them to hop up the stems of thin plants and, hanging upside down, seek pests under the leaves. Blue tits are well-adapted to garden life and readily adopt nest boxes supplied for them. Their young leave the nest before they are able to fly properly, and are therefore vulnerable to predators such as cats. Those that do survive the critical early weeks can be easily distinguished by the presence of yellow rather than white cheek patches.

Identification

Has a distinctive blue crown edged with white, and a narrow black stripe running back through each eye. The cheeks are white. Underparts are yellowish, and the back is greyish-green. There is a whitish bar across the top of the blue wings. The tail is also blue. Sexes are similar but hens duller.

LONG-TAILED TIT

Aegithalos caudatus

Distribution Resident throughout virtually the whole of Europe, but absent from central and northern parts of Scandinavia. Extends into Asia, but not found in Africa.
Size 15cm (6in).
Habitat Deciduous and mixed woodlands.
Nest Ball-shaped, usually incorporating moss.
Eggs 7–12, white with reddish speckling.
Food Invertebrates, seeds.

The tail feathers of these tits can account for nearly half their total length. Those birds occurring in northern Europe have a completely white head and underparts. Long-tailed tits are lively birds, usually seen in small parties, and frequently in the company of other tits. They are often most conspicuous during winter, when small groups of these birds are seen flitting among the leafless branches. In cold weather they roost together, which helps to conserve their body heat – sometimes as many as 50 birds may be clustered together. Groups of these birds can be quite noisy when foraging by day. In harsh winter weather they visit bird tables and feeders to take scraps of fat and peanuts. Their breeding period starts early, in late February, and may extend right through until June.

Identification

This species is distinguished by its dumpy shape and long tail. Black stripe above each eye extends back to form a collar. Head and upper breast otherwise whitish. Underparts rose-pink. Reddish-brown shoulders, white edges to the flight feathers. Young birds duller, with brown on their heads. Sexes alike.

Left: *Long-tailed tits build a large nest with a side entrance, made of moss and twigs bound with cobwebs.*

GARDEN FINCHES

Finches feed mainly on seeds but, by adopting different feeding strategies, they can exploit a variety of food sources without competing with each other. Goldfinches, for example, eat small seeds such as teasel, whereas the hawfinch can crack very tough seeds such as cherry with its strong, stout bill.

CHAFFINCH

Fringilla coelebs

The behaviour of chaffinches changes significantly during the year. These birds can be seen in groups during the winter, but at the onset of spring and the breeding season, cock birds become very territorial, driving away any rivals. While resident chaffinches remain in gardens through the year, mainly feeding on the lawn, large groups of migrants seek refuge from harsh winter weather in farmland areas, associating in large flocks. Chaffinches usually prefer to feed on the ground, hopping and walking along in search of seeds. They seek invertebrates almost exclusively for rearing their chicks.

Identification
Cock in summer plumage has a black band above the bill, with grey over the head and neck. Cheeks and underparts pinkish. The back is brown, and there are two distinctive white wing bars. Cocks less brightly coloured in winter. Hens have dull grey cheek patches and dark greyish-green upperparts, while their underparts are buff to greyish-white. Young similar to hens.

Distribution Resident in the British Isles and western Europe, and a summer visitor to Scandinavia and eastern Europe. Also resident in the west of northern Africa and at the south-western tip.
Size 16cm (6in).
Habitat Woodland, parks and gardens.
Nest Cup-shaped, usually in a tree fork.
Eggs 4–5, light brown or blue with dark, very often smudgy, markings.
Food Seeds, also invertebrates.

EUROPEAN GOLDFINCH

Carduelis carduelis

The long, narrow bill of the goldfinch enables it to prise kernels from seeds. These birds often congregate in winter to feed on stands of thistle heads and teasel in wild corners of the garden. Alder cones are also a favoured food at this time, and they will also take peanuts and seed from bird tables. Goldfinches are very agile, able to cling on to narrow stems when feeding. They are social by nature, usually mixing in small flocks in areas where food is plentiful, although they are shy when feeding on the ground. They have a relatively loud, attractive, twittering song. Pairs usually prefer to build their nest in a tree fork rather than hiding it in a hedge.

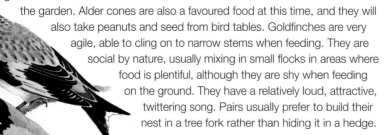

Identification
Bright red face with black lores. Black area across the top of the crown that broadens to a collar on the neck. White extends around the throat, and a brown necklace separates the white on the throat from the paler underparts. Brown back and flanks, underparts otherwise white. The bill is narrow and pointed. Wings are black with white spotting and yellow barring. Tail is black with white markings. Hens display duller coloration with yellow less apparent.

Distribution Occurs throughout much of the British Isles and mainland Europe, including Denmark but confined to the extreme south of Scandinavia. Also present in northern Africa.
Size 13cm (5in).
Habitat Woodland and more open areas.
Nest Cup-shaped, made from vegetation.
Eggs 5–6, bluish-white with darker markings.
Food Seeds, also invertebrates.

EUROPEAN GREENFINCH

Carduelis chloris

Distribution Range extends throughout Europe and much of northern Africa, but absent from more northern parts of Scandinavia.
Size 16cm (6in).
Habitat Woodland edges and more open areas, gardens, farmland.
Nest Bulky, cup-shaped.
Eggs 4–6, whitish to pale blue with darker markings.
Food Largely seeds and some invertebrates.

Greenfinches have quite stout bills that enable them to crack open tough seed casings to reach the edible kernels inside. These birds are most likely to be seen in gardens where there are trees and bushes to provide nesting cover. In winter, European greenfinches visit bird tables, readily taking seeds and peanuts as well as foraging in gardens. Groups of these birds are also sighted in more open areas of countryside, such as farmland, searching for weed seeds and grains that may have been dropped during harvesting. However, as farming has become more intensive in recent decades, so these birds have gradually moved to urban areas to seek food. They begin breeding in April, usually choosing evergreens as nest sites. Pairs will often nest two or three times in succession during summer, and when there are chicks in the nest the birds consume invertebrates in much larger quantities.

Identification
Cock bird has a greenish head, with greyer areas on the sides of the face and wings. Yellowish-green breast, with yellow also evident on the flight feathers. Relatively large, conical bill suitable for cracking seeds. Hen is duller, with greyer tone overall, brownish mantle and less yellow on the wings. The young birds are also dull, with dark streaking on their upperparts and a little yellow on the wings.

EUROPEAN SERIN

Serinus serinus

Distribution Resident in coastal areas of France south through the Iberian Peninsula to northern Africa and around the northern Mediterranean area. A summer visitor elsewhere in mainland Europe.
Size 12cm (5in).
Habitat Parks and gardens.
Nest Cup-shaped, in a tree.
Eggs 3–5, pale blue with darker markings.
Food Seeds and some invertebrates.

Although mainly confined to relatively southerly latitudes, these tiny colourful finches are occasionally seen in the British Isles and have even bred successfully in southern England. It appears that European serins are slowly extending their northerly distribution, with records revealing that they had spread to central Europe by 1875 and had started to colonize France within another 50 years. These finches forage for seeds in gardens, parks, orchards, and along the sides of roads. They often seek out stands of conifers as nest sites, although they also frequent citrus groves in the south of their range. Serins construct a tiny, hair-lined nest where up to four eggs are laid. Two to three broods may be raised between May and July. In autumn, northern populations move south to winter mainly around the Mediterranean.

Identification
Cock has a bright yellow forehead which extends to a stripe above each eye, encircling the cheeks and joining with the yellow breast. Back is yellow and streaked with brown, as are the white flanks. Hens duller in coloration overall, with streaked, greenish-grey upperparts, paler underparts and a pale yellow rump. Young differ from adults in being mainly brown and lacking yellow in the plumage.

WOODLAND FINCHES

Many seed-eaters live in open country, but some types of finches prefer woodlands – broad-leaved woodlands in the case of bramblings and bullfinches, while crossbills frequent conifer forests. Here trees offer shelter and food especially in winter. Crossbills have evolved specialized beaks to extract seeds.

COMMON BULLFINCH

Pyrrhula pyrrhula

These birds are unmistakable thanks to their stocky appearance and the bright pink coloration of the males. They are often seen in gardens but may also be encountered in woodland. Bullfinches are regarded as a potential pest by fruit farmers since they eat buds in the early spring. The seeds of trees such as ash and beech form part of their diet in winter, and they also benefit farmers by eating a range of invertebrates, particularly when rearing their young. Breeding starts from mid-April onward, with a pair constructing their nest using twigs and a softer lining. The hen sits alone, with incubation lasting 14 days, after which both adults feed their growing brood. The chicks fledge at about two and a half weeks old.

Identification

The cock bird has a black face and top to the head, with deep rosy-pink underparts, lighter around the vent. Grey back, black wings and tail with a white area on the rump. The bill, legs and feet are all black. Hen is similar to cock but with brownish rather than pink underparts. The young birds lack the black cap seen in hens, and show brownish coloration on their wing coverts.

Distribution Ranges widely across Europe, except northern Scandinavia and the southern Iberian Peninsula. Extends eastwards through Asia. Also present on the Azores.
Size 16cm (6¼in).
Habitat Woodland areas.
Nest Cup-shaped, constructed from vegetation.
Eggs 4–6, greenish-blue with dark brownish markings.
Food Seeds, invertebrates.

BRAMBLING

Fringilla montifringilla

Bramblings are winter visitors to British gardens. After breeding in northern Europe, the harsh winter weather forces them to migrate south in search of food. Here they are seen in fields and other areas of open countryside. These finches feed largely on beech nuts, relying on forests to sustain them over winter. In cold weather they will take seeds scattered on the ground. Although normally occurring in small flocks, millions of individuals occasionally congregate in forests. Bramblings have a rather jerky walk, sometimes hopping along the ground when searching for food. Their diet is more varied during the summer months, when they are nesting. Caterpillars of moths in particular are eagerly devoured at this time and used to rear the young. Bramblings have a relatively rapid breeding cycle. The hen incubates the eggs on her own, with the young hatching after about a fortnight. The young leave the nest after a similar interval.

Identification

Black head and bill. Orange underparts, white rump and white wing bars. Underparts whitish, blackish markings on the orange flanks. Duller in winter, with pale head markings and yellowish bill. Hens like winter males, but have greyer sides to the face. Young birds like hens but brown, with a yellowish rump.

Distribution Breeds in the far north of Europe, through most of Scandinavia into Russia, extending eastward into Asia. Overwinters farther south throughout Europe, extending to parts of north-western Africa.
Size 18cm (7in).
Habitat Woodland.
Nest Cup-shaped, made from vegetation.
Eggs 5–7, a dark greenish-blue colour.
Food Seeds and nuts.

Distribution Resident in most of Europe, although absent from Ireland. Breeds in the south of Scandinavia and farther east into Asia, where these populations are only summer visitors. Some reported sightings on various Mediterranean islands and parts of north-western Africa.
Size 16.5cm (6½in).
Habitat Mixed woodland.
Nest Cup-shaped, made of plant matter.
Eggs 3–6, bluish-white to green, with dark markings.
Food Seeds, invertebrates.

HAWFINCH

Coccothraustes coccothraustes

With their stocky, powerful bills, hawfinches are able to crack open cherry stones and the hard kernels of similar fruits and feed on the seeds within. They usually feed off the ground, and may sometimes descend to pick up fallen fruits. These finches are most likely to be observed in small flocks over the winter, with populations breeding in northerly areas moving southward. It is at this time, particularly in harsh weather, that they are most likely to appear in rural gardens, searching for seeds and berries. In spring they eat buds and also feed on invertebrates, with their stout bills enabling them to prey on even hard-bodied beetles without difficulty. In spring they form pairs, with the cock bird harrying the female for a period beforehand. She will then start to build the nest, which can be located in the fork of a tree more than 22m (75ft) above the ground. The incubation period lasts approximately 12 days, and the young leave the nest after a similar interval.

Identification
Adult male in breeding plumage has a black area around the bill and eyes, with a brown crown and grey around the neck. Whitish area on the wings and black flight feathers. Underparts brownish. Bill is black, but paler outside the breeding season, as is the head. Hens have paler and greyer heads, and greyer secondary flight feathers. Young birds have distinct streaking on their underparts.

COMMON CROSSBILL

Loxia curvirostra

Distribution Resident throughout much of Scandinavia and northern Europe, extending into Asia. Found elsewhere in Europe, usually in areas of coniferous forest, extending as far as northern Africa.
Size 15cm (6in).
Habitat Coniferous forests.
Nest Cup-shaped, made from vegetation.
Eggs 3–4, whitish-blue with reddish-brown markings.
Food Mainly the seeds of pine cones.

The crossbill's highly distinctive bill can crack the hard casing of conifer seeds, enabling it to extract the inner kernel with its tongue. These finches also eat the pips of various fruits, and prey on invertebrates, particularly when they have young to feed. Common crossbills rarely descend to the ground except to drink, unless the pine crop is very poor. When faced with a food shortage, they move to areas far outside their normal range, sometimes seeking food in gardens. This phenomenon, known as an irruption, occurs once a decade in Europe. Living on seeds, they also need to drink, and sometimes use birdbaths. The breeding season varies through their range, starting later in the north. Both birds build the nest, which is constructed in a conifer, sometimes more than 18m (60ft) high.

Identification
The cock birds are reddish with darker, blackish feathering on the top of the head and also evident on the wings. The underparts are reddish, paler toward the vent. The upper and lower parts of the distinctive blackish bill are conspicuously curved at the tip, and suitable for extracting seeds from cones on twigs. Hens are olive-green, with darker areas over the back and wings, and have a paler rump. The young birds resemble hens, but have evident streaking on their bodies.

TEMPLATES

The templates provided here will enable you to complete some of the more complex projects illustrated in this book. They should be used in conjunction with the instructions and cutting lists for timber given earlier. Each template provides specific dimensions for the project. All the dimensions are listed in both metric and imperial measurements. You should decide which system you are going to use and then follow it, not mixing the two. You might like to make paper templates from these plans and arrange them on your timber before cutting. It's always a good idea to double-check your measurements before cutting.

Left: *This hanging nest box with a small, round entrance hole will suit acrobatic species such as tits and wrens. It is best hung from a branch.*

Above: *A nest box with a small entrance hole will suit tits, wrens and sparrows. A taller box would suit woodpeckers.*

Above: *Open-fronted nest boxes will attract robins, wrens, flycatchers and wagtails. Other species may use the box as a roost.*

Above: *Birdhouses such as this one look highly ornamental in the garden and can be finished according to personal taste.*

PALLADIAN BIRD TABLE, page 118

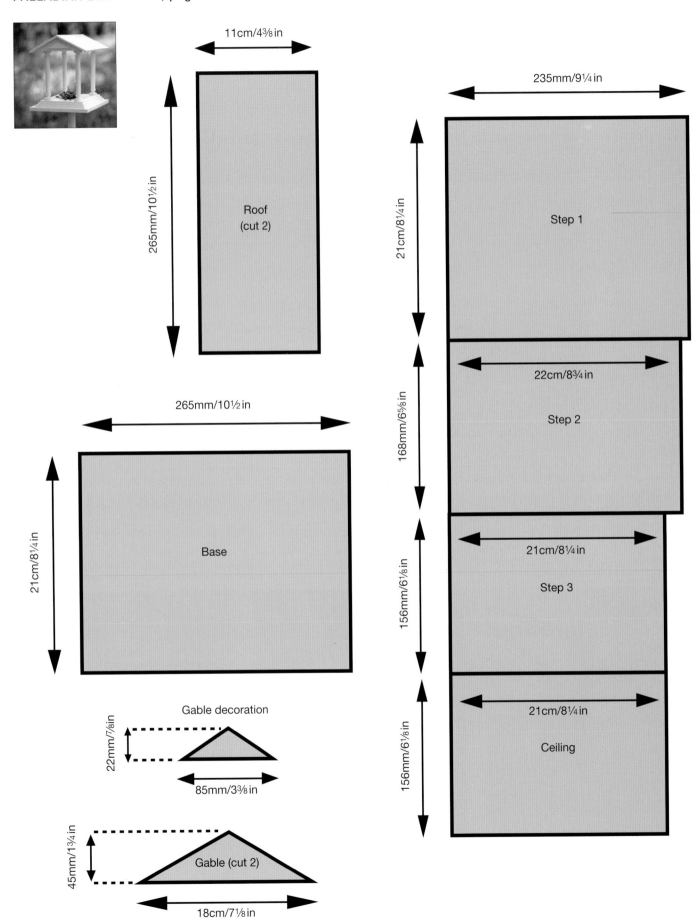

11cm/4⅜in

265mm/10½in

Roof
(cut 2)

235mm/9¼in

21cm/8¼in

Step 1

22cm/8¾in

168mm/6⅝in

Step 2

265mm/10½in

Base

21cm/8¼in

21cm/8¼in

156mm/6⅛in

Step 3

Gable decoration

22mm/⅞in

85mm/3⅜in

21cm/8¼in

156mm/6⅛in

Ceiling

45mm/1¾in

Gable (cut 2)

18cm/7⅛in

SEASIDE BIRD TABLE, page 120

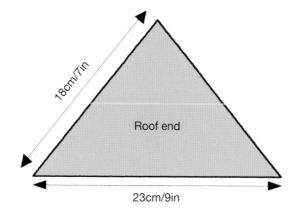

Roof end

18cm/7in

23cm/9in

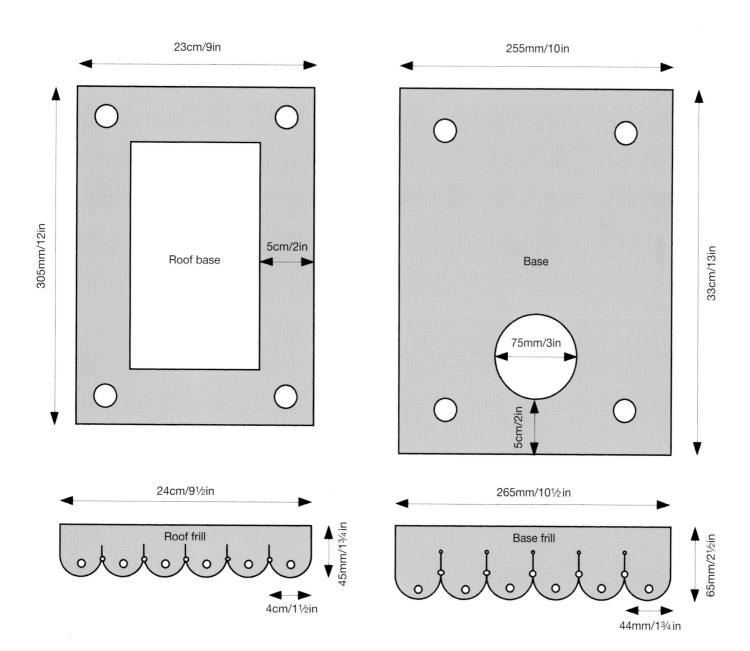

23cm/9in

Roof base

305mm/12in

5cm/2in

255mm/10in

Base

75mm/3in

5cm/2in

33cm/13in

24cm/9½in

Roof frill

45mm/1¾in

4cm/1½in

265mm/10½in

Base frill

65mm/2½in

44mm/1¾in

BAMBOO BIRD TABLE, page 122

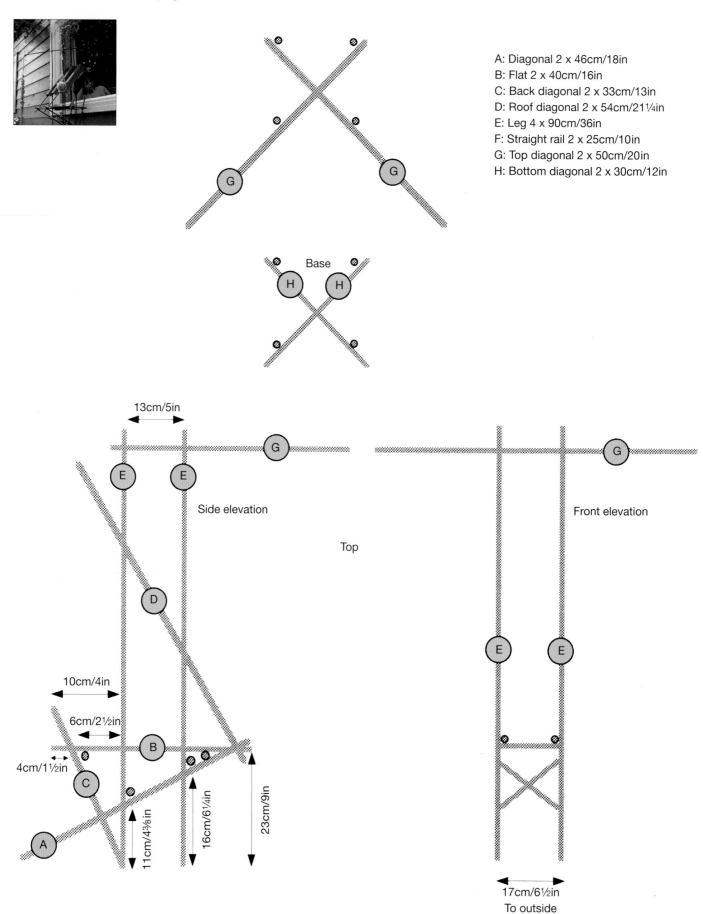

A: Diagonal 2 x 46cm/18in
B: Flat 2 x 40cm/16in
C: Back diagonal 2 x 33cm/13in
D: Roof diagonal 2 x 54cm/21¼in
E: Leg 4 x 90cm/36in
F: Straight rail 2 x 25cm/10in
G: Top diagonal 2 x 50cm/20in
H: Bottom diagonal 2 x 30cm/12in

Base

13cm/5in

G

E E

Side elevation

Top

G

Front elevation

E E

D

10cm/4in

6cm/2½in

B

4cm/1½in

C

A

11cm/4⅜in

16cm/6¼in

23cm/9in

17cm/6½in

To outside

ENCLOSED NEST BOX, page 138

OPEN-FRONTED NEST BOX, page 140

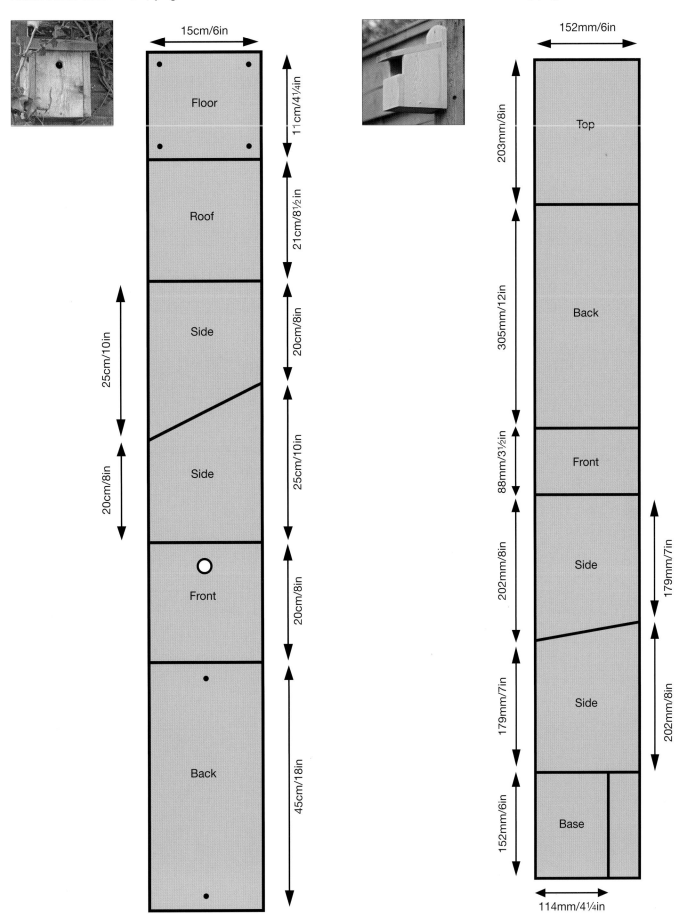

ENCLOSED NEST BOX

15cm/6in

Floor

Roof

Side

Side

Front

Back

11cm/4¼in

21cm/8½in

20cm/8in

25cm/10in

20cm/8in

45cm/18in

25cm/10in

20cm/8in

OPEN-FRONTED NEST BOX

152mm/6in

Top

Back

Front

Side

Side

Base

203mm/8in

305mm/12in

88mm/3½in

202mm/8in

179mm/7in

152mm/6in

179mm/7in

202mm/8in

114mm/4¼in

LAVENDER HIDEAWAY, page 146

POST BOX, page 158

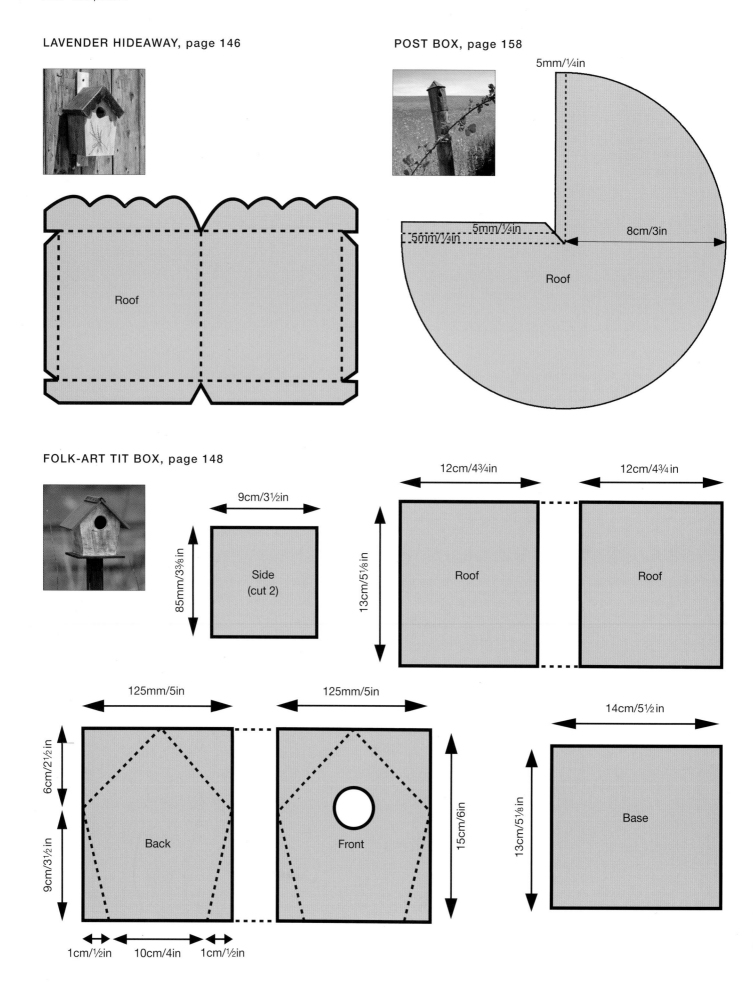

Roof

5mm/¼in

5mm/¼in

5mm/¼in

8cm/3in

Roof

FOLK-ART TIT BOX, page 148

9cm/3½in

85mm/3⅜in

Side
(cut 2)

12cm/4¾in

12cm/4¾in

13cm/5⅛in

Roof

Roof

125mm/5in

125mm/5in

6cm/2½in

9cm/3½in

Back

15cm/6in

Front

14cm/5½in

13cm/5⅛in

Base

1cm/½in 10cm/4in 1cm/½in

ROCK-A-BYE BIRDIE BOX, page 150

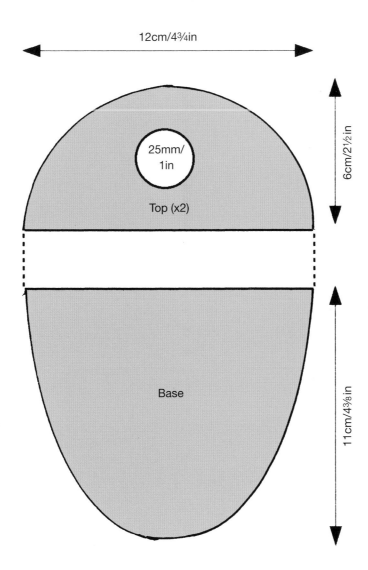

12cm/4¾in

6cm/2½in

25mm/
1in

Top (x2)

Base

11cm/4⅜in

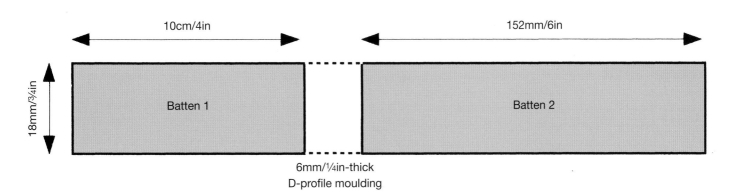

10cm/4in

152mm/6in

18mm/¾in

Batten 1

Batten 2

6mm/¼in-thick
D-profile moulding

SLATE-ROOFED COTTAGE, page 152

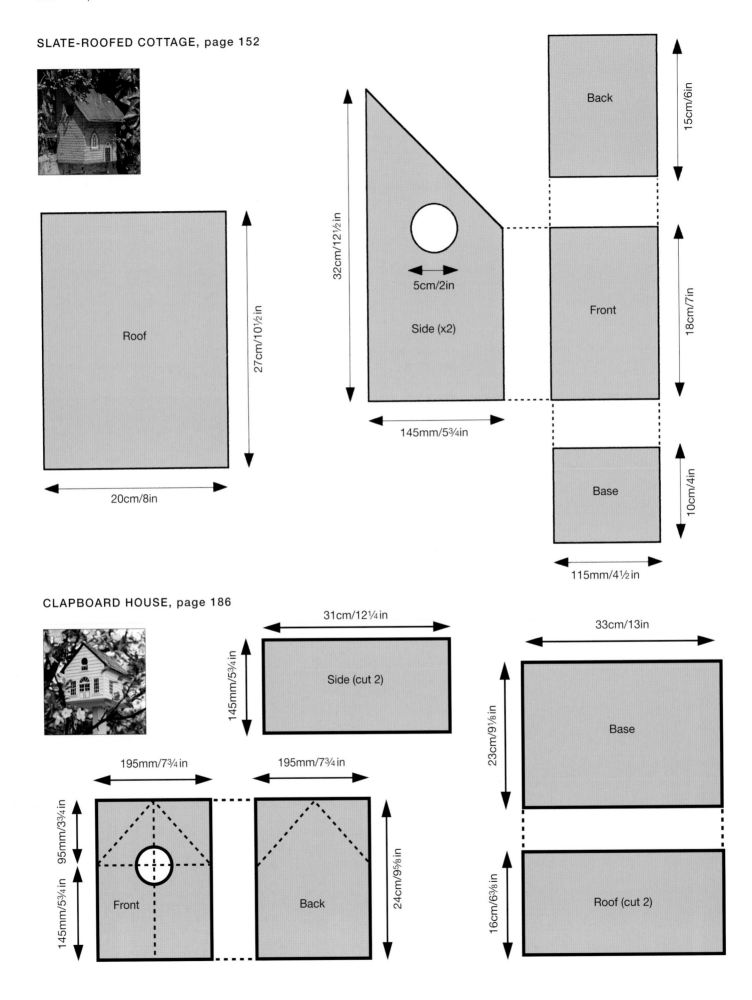

Roof

27cm/10½in

20cm/8in

32cm/12½in

5cm/2in

Side (x2)

145mm/5¾in

Back

15cm/6in

Front

18cm/7in

Base

10cm/4in

115mm/4½in

CLAPBOARD HOUSE, page 186

31cm/12¼in

Side (cut 2)

145mm/5¾in

33cm/13in

Base

23cm/9⅛in

195mm/7¾in

95mm/3¾in

Front

145mm/5¾in

195mm/7¾in

Back

24cm/9⅝in

Roof (cut 2)

16cm/6⅜in

RIDGE TILE RETREAT, page 154

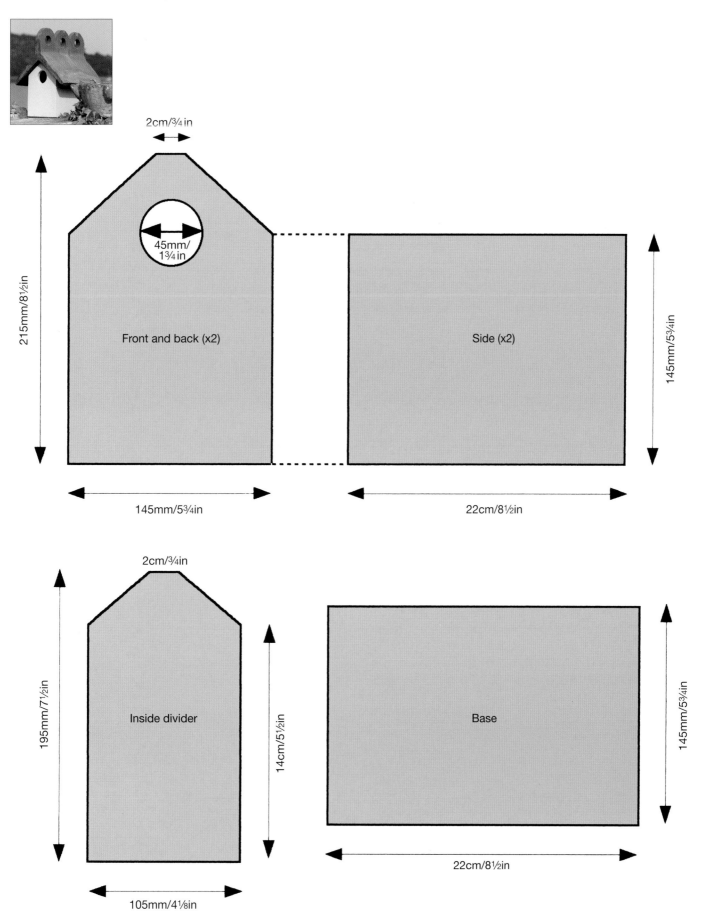

2cm/¾in

45mm/
1¾in

215mm/8½in

Front and back (x2)

145mm/5¾in

Side (x2)

145mm/5¾in

22cm/8½in

2cm/¾in

195mm/7½in

Inside divider

105mm/4⅛in

14cm/5½in

Base

145mm/5¾in

22cm/8½in

SWIFT NURSERY, page 156

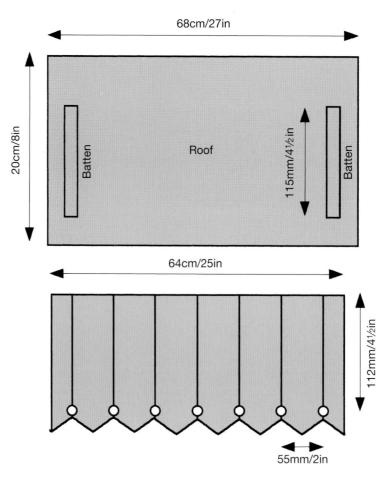

68cm/27in

20cm/8in

Batten

Roof

115mm/4½in

Batten

64cm/25in

112mm/4½in

55mm/2in

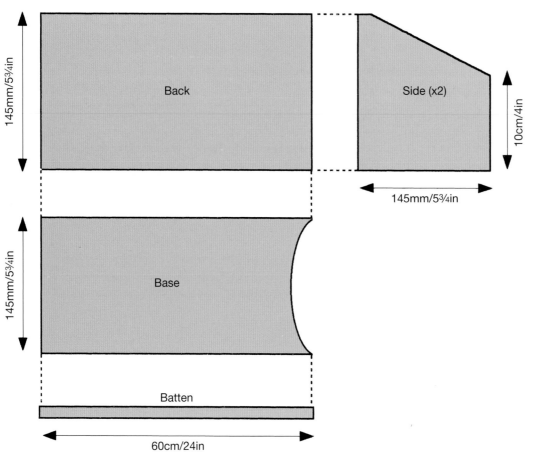

145mm/5¾in

Back

Side (x2)

10cm/4in

145mm/5¾in

145mm/5¾in

Base

Batten

60cm/24in

EDWARDIAN NEST BOX, page 162

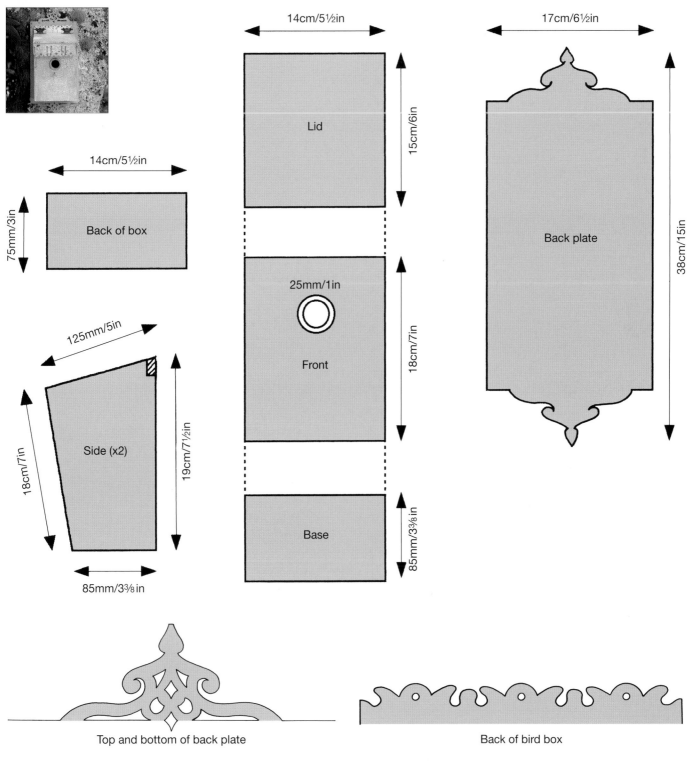

14cm/5½in

Back of box

75mm/3in

125mm/5in

Side (x2)

18cm/7in

19cm/7½in

85mm/3⅜in

14cm/5½in

Lid

15cm/6in

25mm/1in

Front

18cm/7in

Base

85mm/3⅜in

17cm/6½in

Back plate

38cm/15in

Top and bottom of back plate

Back of bird box

Front frill of lid

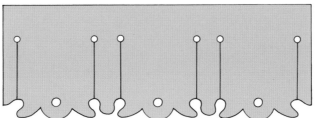

DUCK HOUSE, page 164

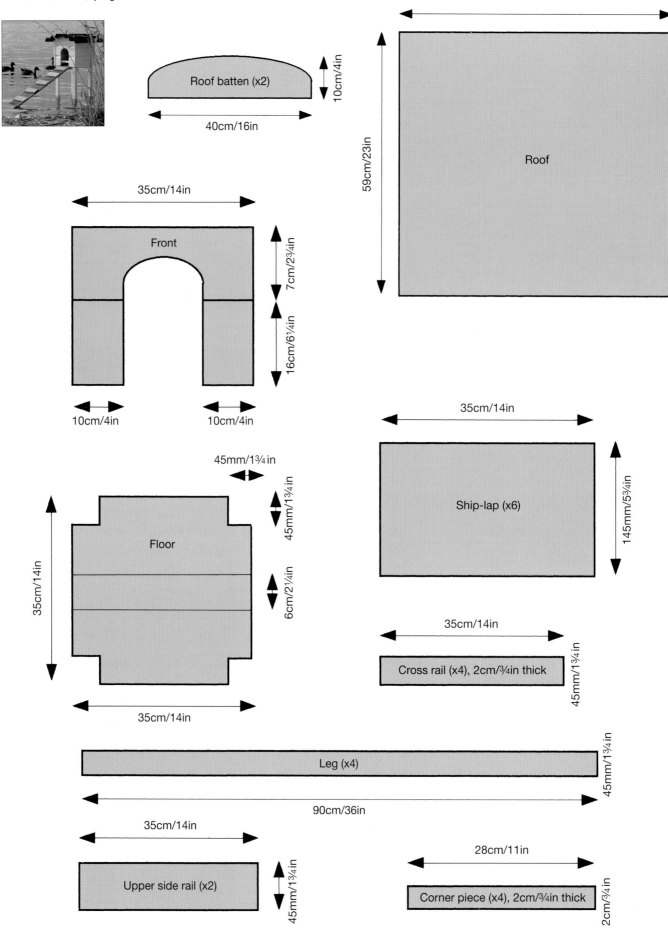

Roof batten (x2)

10cm/4in

40cm/16in

Roof

59cm/23in

35cm/14in

Front

7cm/2¾in

16cm/6¼in

10cm/4in

10cm/4in

35cm/14in

Ship-lap (x6)

145mm/5¾in

45mm/1¾in

45mm/1¾in

Floor

6cm/2¼in

35cm/14in

35cm/14in

Cross rail (x4), 2cm/¾in thick

45mm/1¾in

35cm/14in

Leg (x4)

45mm/1¾in

90cm/36in

35cm/14in

28cm/11in

Upper side rail (x2)

45mm/1¾in

Corner piece (x4), 2cm/¾in thick

2cm/¾in

RUSTIC CABIN, page 168

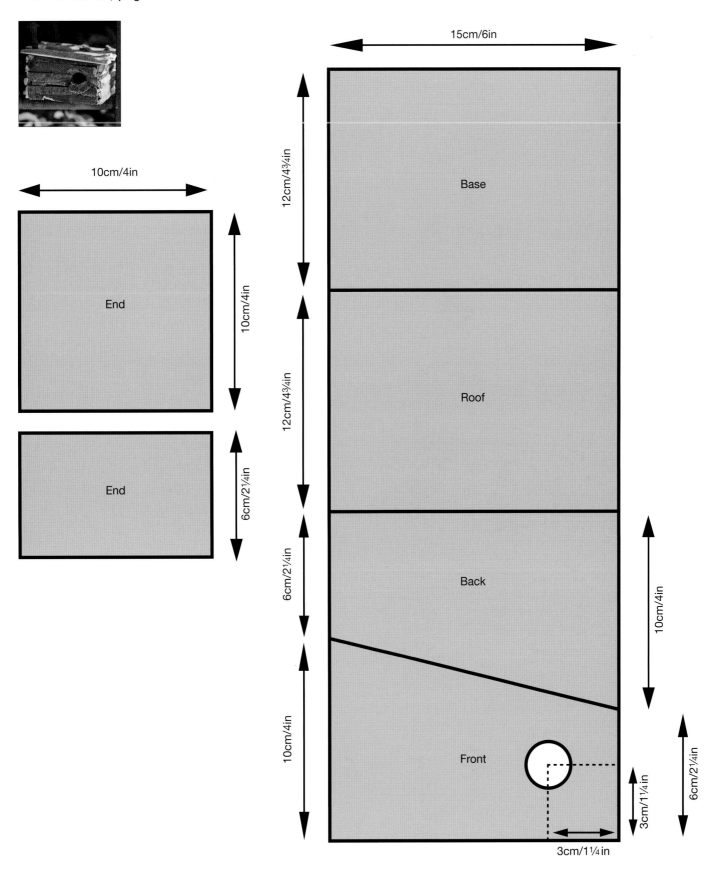

10cm/4in

End

End

15cm/6in

12cm/4¾in

Base

12cm/4¾in

Roof

6cm/2¼in

Back

10cm/4in

Front

10cm/4in

10cm/4in

6cm/2¼in

6cm/2¼in

3cm/1¼in

3cm/1¼in

THATCHED BIRDHOUSE, page 172

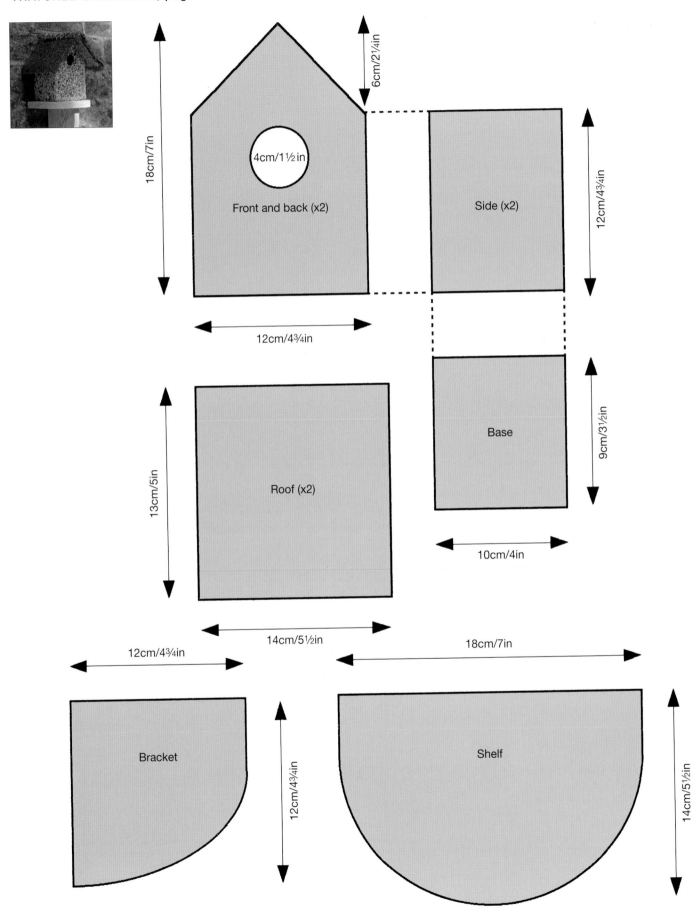

18cm/7in

6cm/2¼in

4cm/1½in

Front and back (x2)

12cm/4¾in

Side (x2)

12cm/4¾in

13cm/5in

Roof (x2)

Base

9cm/3½in

10cm/4in

14cm/5½in

12cm/4¾in

18cm/7in

Bracket

12cm/4¾in

Shelf

14cm/5½in

DOVECOTE, page 184

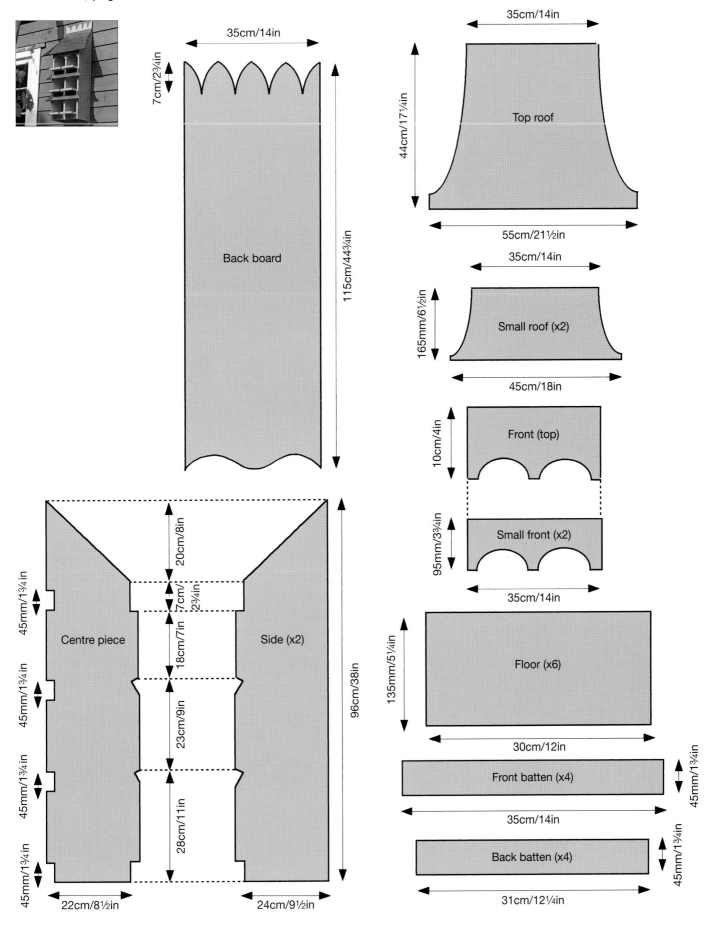

35cm/14in

7cm/2¾in

Back board

115cm/44¾in

35cm/14in

44cm/17¼in

Top roof

55cm/21½in

35cm/14in

165mm/6½in

Small roof (x2)

45cm/18in

10cm/4in

Front (top)

95mm/3¾in

Small front (x2)

35cm/14in

135mm/5¼in

Floor (x6)

30cm/12in

Front batten (x4)

45mm/1¾in

35cm/14in

Back batten (x4)

45mm/1¾in

31cm/12¼in

20cm/8in

7cm/2¾in

45mm/1¾in

Centre piece

Side (x2)

18cm/7in

96cm/38in

45mm/1¾in

23cm/9in

45mm/1¾in

28cm/11in

45mm/1¾in

22cm/8½in

24cm/9½in

NEST BOX SIZES

The dimensions given here will enable you to modify basic nest box designs to suit a wide range of bird species. You may need to alter the dimensions slightly according to the thickness of your timber. Inner surfaces can be left rough, but you should drill a few small holes in the floor of the box for drainage.

ENCLOSED NEST BOXES

These have a small, round entrance hole high on the front face. They are suitable for birds that usually nest in tree holes, such as wrens, tits, sparrows and nuthatches. Starlings, woodpeckers, jackdaws and pigeons will nest in a larger box of this type.

	Floor size	Depth of box	Height of entrance	Diameter of entrance	Positioning/comments
Wren	10 x 10cm/4 x 4in	15–20cm/6–8in	12cm/4½in	3cm/1¼in	Low in dense vegetation
Tits	15 x 12cm/6 x 4½in	20–25cm/8–10in	12cm/4½in	3cm/1¼in	2m/7ft above ground
Sparrows	15 x 15cm/6 x 6in	20–25cm/8–10in	15cm/6in	3cm/1¼in	Secluded position
Nuthatch	15 x 15cm/6 x 6in	20–25m//8–10in	12cm/4½in	3cm/1¼in	High in a tree
Starling	15 x 15cm/6 x 6in	40–45cm/16–18in	30cm/12in	5cm/2in	5m/16ft above ground
Woodpeckers	15 x 15cm/6 x 6in	30–38cm/12–15in	40cm/16in	6cm/2½in	High in a tree
Jackdaw	20 x 20cm/8 x 8in	30–38cm/12–15in	40cm/16in	15cm/6in	High, secluded location
Street pigeon	20 x 20cm/8 x 8in	30–38cm/12–15in	10cm/4in	10cm/4in	Add a perch below entrance

OPEN-FRONTED NEST BOXES

Not all birds like nest boxes with small entrance holes. The open-fronted types have a larger, rectangular entrance area at the front. This style of box is suitable for wrens and robins. A kestrel will nest in a larger box of this type.

	Floor size	Depth of box	Height to top of front	Positioning/comments
Wren	10 x 10cm/4 x 4in	15cm/6in	10cm/4in	Low in dense vegetation
Robin	10 x 10cm/4 x 4in	15cm/6in	5cm/2in	1.5–5.5m/5–18ft above ground
Kestrel	30 x 50cm/12 x 20in	30cm/12in	15cm/6in	5m/16ft above ground

BIRD SHELVES

Some birds do not like using enclosed nest boxes with entrance holes or open faces, instead preferring shelves that are completely open. Bird shelves are suitable for pied wagtails, spotted flycatchers and blackbirds.

	Floor size	Depth of box	Height to top of front	Positioning/comments
Pied wagtail	10 x 10cm/4 x 4in	10cm/4in	2.5cm/1in	1.5–5.5m/5–18ft above ground
Spotted flycatcher	15 x 15cm/6 x 6in	10cm/4in	2.5cm/1in	1.5–5.5m/5–18ft above ground
Blackbird	20 x 20cm/8 x 8in	20cm/8in	2.5cm/1in	In dense vegetation

UNUSUAL NEST BOXES

Species such as members of the swift family, owls and ducks require special types of nest boxes. Most are constructed of timber, but cup nests for swallows and house martins can be made of papier mâché or a wood-chip mix.

	Description	Positioning/comments
Swallow	Cup-shaped nest	On shed or stable
House martin	Cup-shaped nest	Fix under eaves of house or shed
Swift	Oblong box, 60 x 15 x 15cm/24 x 6 x 6in, with an entrance underneath	Place horizontally under eaves of house
Barn owl	Oblong box, 25 x 46 x 40cm/10 x 18 x 16in	4.5m/15ft above ground
Tawny owl	Oblong box, 76 x 26 x 22cm/30 x10½ x 9in	In a tree under a branch
Little owl	120 x 20cm/4ft x 8in, with a 10cm/4in hole 30cm/12in from the floor	In a tree
Mallard	35 x 35cm x 33cm/14 x 14 x 13in	On a raft or island

USEFUL CONTACTS

UNITED KINGDOM
Organizations
British Birds Rarities Committee
http://www.bbrc.org.uk/

British Garden Birds
http://www.garden-birds.co.uk/

British Ornithologists' Club
http://www.boc-online.org/

British Ornithologists' Union
http://www.bou.org.uk/

British Trust for Ornithology (BTO)
http://www.bto.org.uk

BTO Garden Birdwatch
http://www.bto.org/gbw/

Fat Birder
http://www.fatbirder.com

Hawk Conservancy
http://www.hawk-conservancy.org/

Hawk and Owl Trust
http://www.hawkandowl.org/

Rare Breeding Birds Panel
http://www.rbbp.org.uk/

Royal Society for the Protection of Birds
(RSPB)
http://www.rspb.org.uk

Wildfowl & Wetlands Trust
http://www.wwt.org.uk

Advice on gardening for birds
Field Studies Council
www.field-studies-council.org

Flora locale
http://www.floralocale.org/

RSPB advice on gardening
http://www.rspb.org.uk/advice/gardening/

The Wildlife Trusts
www.wildlifetrusts.org

Bird boxes and food suppliers
CJ WildBird Foods Ltd
www.birdfood.co.uk

Food for Wild Birds
http://www.food4wildbirds.co.uk/

Garden Bird Supplies
http://www.gardenbird.com/

RSPB Shop: bird food
http://shopping.rspb.org.uk/c/Birdfood.htm

The Specialist Bird Food Company
www.wild-bird-food.co.uk

Vine House Farm Bird Foods
http://vinehousefarm.co.uk/

WWF Wildlife Shop
http://shop.wwf.org.uk/wildlife

INTERNATIONAL ORGANIZATIONS
Africa
African Bird Club
http://www.africanbirdclub.org

African Bird Club: South Africa
http://www.africanbirdclub.org/countries/
SouthAfrica/conservation.html

Americas
American Birding Association
http://www.americanbirding.org/

American Bird Conservancy
http://www.abcbirds.org/

Birdnet.com
http://www.nmnh.si.edu/BIRDNET/

Bird Studies Canada
http://www.bsc-eoc.org/

National Bird-Feeding Society (US-based)
http://www.birdfeeding.org/

Neotropical Bird Club
http://www.neotropicalbirdclub.org/

Ornithological Societies of North America
http://www.osnabirds.org/

Pacific Seabird Group
http://www.pacificseabirdgroup.org/

Asia
Oriental Bird Club
http://www.orientalbirdclub.org

Australia and New Zealand
Birds Australia
http://www.birdsaustralia.com.au

Bird Observers Club of Australia
http://www.birdobservers.org.au

New Zealand Birds and Birding
http://www.nzbirds.com/

Ornithological Society of New Zealand
http://www.osnz.org.nz/

Royal Forest and Bird Protection Society
of New Zealand
www.forestandbird.org.nz

Europe/Middle East
European Ornithologists' Union
http://www.eou.at

Ornithological Society of the Middle East
http://www.osme.org/

International
BirdLife International
http://www.birdlife.org/

International Ornithological Committee
http://www.i-o-c.org/IOComm/

Working Group on International Waderbird
and Wetland Research
http://home.wanadoo.nl/rene.t.vos/wiwo/
wiwo1.htm

Rare Birds of the World
http://www.geocities.com/RainForest/Vines/
2408/critical.html

INDEX

ACKNOWLEDGEMENTS

The publisher would like to thank the following for allowing their photographs to be reproduced in the book (l = left, r = right, t = top, m = middle, b = bottom):
Ardea: 13b.
Lucy Doncaster: 31m.
Felicity Forster: 5r, 44b, 47tl, 97l, 97r, 103bl.
Dan Hurst: 170tl.
iStockphoto: 1, 2, 3l, 3m, 3r, 4l, 5l, 6, 8, 9r, 11 (photos), 13tl, 13tr, 14tl, 14tr, 17bl, 17br, 18l, 19t, 19bl, 19br, 20t, 20bl, 20br, 21t, 21b, 25b, 26tr, 26b, 27t, 27bl, 28t, 28b, 29b, 30t, 30b, 31b, 32t, 32m, 32b, 34r, 36l, 36r, 38tl, 38tr, 38b, 46, 47tr, 48t, 49tr, 50t, 50b, 51tr, 51b, 53tl, 56ml, 61tl, 61tr, 64bl, 66t, 68bl, 69t, 70t, 71bl, 72tr, 74t, 77tl, 78tl, 84t, 85tl, 86tr, 87bl, 88bl, 88br, 89bm, 89br, 91br, 92bl,

94br, 103t, 104tl, 104tr, 104b, 105b, 106b, 110tl, 112tl, 114t, 118tl, 122tl, 124tl, 128tl, 134bl, 140tl, 142tl, 146bl, 150tl, 152tl, 154br, 160tl, 162tl, 164t, 164m, 168b, 172tl, 174tl, 178bl, 180tl, 182tl, 184tl, 186l, 188, 189l, 189m, 189r, 249, 251t, 252b, 255b.
NHPA/Photoshot: 26tl (George Bernard), 27br (Manfred Danegger), 31t (Alan Williams), 136tl (Stephen Dalton), 156tl (Alan Barnes).
Nigel Partridge: 51tl.
Photolibrary Group: 12l, 23br.
Woodfall/Photoshot: 25m (John Robinson).

Illustrations were provided by the following:
Peter Barrett: 11 (finches), 29t, 33, 35, 37, 39, 190t, 190b, 191t, 191b, 192t, 192b, 193t, 193b, 194t, 194b, 195t, 195b, 196t, 196b, 197t, 197b,

198t, 198b, 199t, 199b, 200b, 202b, 203t, 203b, 204t, 205t, 205b, 206t, 206b, 207t, 207b, 209t, 209b, 212t, 212b, 213b, 214t, 214b, 215t, 215b, 216t, 217t, 217b, 218t, 218b, 219t, 219b, 220t, 220b, 222t, 222b, 223t, 224t, 224b, 225b, 226t, 226b, 227t, 227b, 228t, 228b, 229t, 229b, 230t, 230b, 231t, 231b.
Anthony Duke: 190–231 (distribution maps).
Studio Galante: 200t, 201t, 201b, 202t.
Lucinda Ganderton: 234–247 (templates).
Stuart Jackson-Carter: 204b, 213t, 216b, 221t, 221b, 223b, 225t.
Martin Knowelden: 10, 14–15b, 15tr, 16l, 17t, 18r, 23m, 24b, 40l.
Liz Pepperell: 61b, 63t, 79b.
Tim Thackeray: 208t, 208b, 210t, 210b, 211t, 211b.